UML™ for the IT Business Analyst: A Practical Guide to Object-Oriented Requirements Gathering

Howard Podeswa

THOMSON

COURSE TECHNOLOGY

Professional ■ Technical ■ Reference

ISBN- 13: 978-1-59200-912-1
ISBN- 10: 1-59200-912-3

Library of Congress Catalog Card Number: 2005924934

Printed in Canada

07 08 09 WC 10 9 8 7 6 5 4

Publisher and General Manager, Thomson Course Technology PTR:
Stacy L. Hiquet

Associate Director of Marketing:
Sarah O'Donnell

Manager of Editorial Services:
Heather Talbot

Marketing Manager:
Kristin Eisenzopf

Acquisitions Editor:
Mitzi Koontz

Senior Editor:
Mark Garvey

Marketing Coordinator:
Jordan Casey

Project Editor:
Kim Benbow

Technical Reviewer:
Brian Lyons

Thomson Course Technology PTR Editorial Services Coordinator:
Elizabeth Furbish

Copyeditor:
Andy Saff

Interior Layout Tech:
Bill Hartman

Cover Designer:
Mike Tanamachi

Indexer:
Sharon Shock

Proofreader:
Kezia Endsley

Cover paintings:
From the OOPS Series,
by Howard Podeswa

THOMSON

COURSE TECHNOLOGY
Professional ■ Technical ■ Reference

Thomson Course Technology PTR, a division of Thomson Course Technology
25 Thomson Place ■ Boston, MA 02210 ■ http://www.courseptr.com

This book is dedicated to Joy Walker.

PREFACE

From 1998-2000, I spent part of my winters on the Cape Town peninsula in South Africa. It was one those rare times when all aspects of life lined up. There were days when I prepared for an art exhibition, facilitated workshops in poor neighborhoods, and analyzed IT systems—all in the same day. This book is one of the products of that exciting and very productive time: Its case study is drawn from IT work my company did there for the CPP (Community Peace Program)—an organization that is trying to reduce violence in poverty-stricken neighborhoods through a process of dispute resolution, called restorative justice.

One of the communities I visited often due to my work was the township of Zweletemba. There is one point in the drive to Zweletemba where you enter a tunnel that goes right through the mountains. I always fell asleep at that time and awoke just as we were exiting the tunnel into what seemed like a magical world. There, inside the mountainous interior of the peninsula, lies Zweletemba—a place of contradictions: There is great poverty, where many people live in ramshackle homes built of materials salvaged from junk piles, but there is also great physical beauty, personal warmth, music, and humor.

When I began work on this book, I was looking for a case study that would be complex enough to include the intricacies of typical systems. The CPP's restorative justice system came to mind because it has stakeholders that play multiple roles (in the same manner as customers of an insurance firm that appear as beneficiaries, policy holders, etc.), a key business object that events, actions, and information items are tied to (similar to a Customer Call in a CRM system), as well as other complex characteristics that show up time and again in business systems. And, as an unfamiliar system, it puts the reader in the position of extreme Business Analysis—really not knowing anything about the system at the start of the project. This is the side of Business Analysis that I like most about the profession: The way it introduced me to a variety of systems and, through them, to the people behind those systems. Through Business Analysis I have met and worked with people from all walks of life—defense contractors, social workers, investment bankers, funeral directors—and they have, in turn, satisfied an endless curiosity about people and how they do things. This quality of endless curiosity is a trait I've seen in many of the Business Analysts I've met. If it describes you, you've found a great profession. I hope that this book will help you excel at it so that it gives you the enjoyment it has given to me over the years.

A portion of each book sale goes to support the work of the Peace Committees in South Africa. Every cent of this contribution will be spent in and on the poorest of the poor in South Africa to create work and enable them to decide how best to build and strengthen their communities. If you would like to support their work, please contact John Cartwright at john.cartwright@ideaswork.org.

—Howard Podeswa
  howardpodeswa@nobleinc.ca
  www.nobleinc.ca

ACKNOWLEDGMENTS

S pecial thanks go out to Charlie Orosz, Scott Williams, Tim Lloyd, Gerry de Koning, Fern Lawrence, Clifford Shearing, Ideaswork (formerly Community Peace Program), and the Zweletemba Peace Committee.

And a personal thank you to the technical editor, Brian Lyons, for an incredibly knowledgeable and thorough review. The experience of being put under the Lyons microscope is a challenging one—but one I wouldn't have missed for the world.

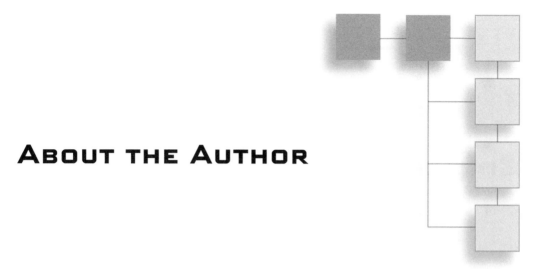

ABOUT THE AUTHOR

Howard Podeswa is the co-founder of Noble, Inc., a Business Analysis (BA) consulting and training company. He has 26 years of experience in many aspects of the software industry, beginning as a developer for Atomic Energy of Canada, Ltd., and continuing as Systems Analyst, Business Analyst, consultant, and author of courseware for IT professionals. He has provided consulting services to a diverse client base, including the Canadian Air Force (MASIS), the South African Community Peace Program, and major financial institutions (Deloitte and Touche, CIBC bank, CGU, etc.) and is a sought-after speaker at international BA conferences. In addition, Howard collaborates with CDI Education on object-oriented projects and training and has designed BA OO training programs for numerous institutions, including Boston University, Humber College, and Polar Bear. Most recently, he was brought on as a subject matter expert for NITAS—a BA apprenticeship program for CompTIA. Howard is also a recognized visual artist whose work has been exhibited and reviewed internationally and supported by the Canada Council for the Arts. His most recent exhibition—Object Oriented Painting Show (OOPS)—was the first to combine his two passions—OO technology and painting.

Contents

chapter 8 **Gathering Across-the-Board Rules with Class Diagrams 169**

Job Aids

INTRODUCTION

I began working on this book in the year 2000. As a former developer and current IT Business Analyst, I could see an approaching technological wave affecting my colleagues. Thanks in large part to client-server applications and the Internet, OO (Object-Oriented) languages like C++ and Java were taking over the development world. This had already changed the way the technical members of an IT team (Systems Analysts, coders, and so on) were working, but Business Analysts—the people who communicated requirements to the developers—were still working, by and large, as though OO didn't exist. The result was BA documentation that had to first be translated into OO by the developers—an inefficient and error-prone step. I knew it was only a matter of time until companies began to expect their BAs to work with OO conventions, so I began to put together B.O.O.M. (Business Object-Oriented Modeling)—a step-by-step program to mentor and train BAs to work efficiently on OO projects.

Since I developed B.O.O.M., I have used it to mentor BAs working on OO projects in wealth management, insurance, accounting, defense, government, credit card systems, telecommunications, hospitality, and other business areas. They have, in turn, helped me improve the process by sharing with me their best practices, templates, and other tools they use on the job. This knowledge has made its way back into B.O.O.M.

This year, I had an opportunity to publish B.O.O.M. as a book. I believe it fills a real need out there. Today, with most new development done in OO environments such as .NET, BAs often find themselves working on OO projects; yet they still have a long way to go to exploit the technology beyond the adoption of use cases (just one part of OO). When BAs look around for guidance in OO, however, they find a dearth of OO literature written for the BA. There are some BA books on narrow aspects of OO (such as use cases) and OO books with a technical perspective—but there is little that explains how a BA can pull together all of the OO tools and fully exploit them during an IT project. I wrote this book to fill that gap. This is not a "theory" book. I believe that you learn best by doing—and in keeping with that, you and I will, together, develop and validate the requirements for an IT system as we move through the steps. By the time you have completed the book—and the case study in it—you will have hands-on experience in using OO standards (UML 2) and techniques and in integrating these with other, non-OO techniques over the course of an OO IT project. If you are a Rational Rose user, you will also learn how to exploit this popular product for business analysis activities.

Who This Book Is For

This book is intended for the Information Technology Business Analyst (IT BA)—an integral part of a software development team responsible for documenting and verifying the business and user requirements for a software system. If you are a new IT BA, or are an experienced BA who is new to Object-Orientation, this book is for you. This book will also be of benefit to the developer who is interested in expanding his or her role to encompass IT BA activities. In this case, you may be wondering how you can exploit the UML tools and techniques you already know to include the gathering and documentation of business requirements. This book will guide you through that process.

How You and Your Organization Can Benefit from B.O.O.M.

Many organizations are good at developing good software products. Where they are often weak is in developing the right software product. The mismatch between what the user wants and what the developers deliver can often be traced to poor practices in business analysis and quality control. B.O.O.M. provides a step-by-step procedure that helps ensure the completeness, correctness, and clarity of the requirements documentation.

In addition, many IT projects are experiencing time and cost overruns due to the difficulty in responding to a rapidly changing business environment. A major contributing factor to this problem is the "ripple effect"—one change in the business that leads to many changes in project deliverables. B.O.O.M. helps by using OO techniques to minimize redundancies in the requirements. With "one fact in one place,"[1] the requirements are easier to revise.

Finally, many project failures are due to faulty communication between those who know the business and those who write the software. With B.O.O.M., the BA documents business rules and requirements using the same types of diagrams, concepts, and terminology used by OO developers, thus reducing the risk of miscommunication. Improvements in

---

[1]Thanks to Tony Alderson for this description of "non-redundancy."

communication are even more dramatic if the organization is using a software development tool like IBM Rational Rose. In this book, you'll learn how to use Rational Rose right from the start to model requirements. You can then pass the model (a Rose file) to the developers who can use it directly as the starting point for their design. It doesn't get much more efficient or direct than that. (Keep in mind, however, that you don't need to use software such as Rose to benefit from OO BA practices or from this book.)

Once You've Read This Book, You'll Be Able to. . .

- Create a Business Requirements Document (BRD) that conforms to the latest UML 2 standard and that incorporates use cases, class diagrams, and other OOA (Object-Oriented Analysis) techniques.
- Follow a step-by-step OOA process for interviewing, researching, and documenting requirements.
- Incorporate still-useful pre-OO techniques within OOA.
- Actively use the accompanying Job Aids while working on-the-job.
- Use the following artifacts:
  - Business use-case diagrams
  - System use-case diagrams and use-case templates
  - Package diagrams
  - Class diagrams
  - Composite structure diagrams
  - Static object diagrams
  - Activity diagrams with and without partitions
  - State machine diagrams
  - Decision table

The CPP Case Study

One case study runs throughout the book. It is based on a business analysis project my company performed for the Community Peace Program (CPP) in Cape Town, South Africa (with adjustments made for learning purposes). I encourage you to work through the case study yourself. Only by trying out the ideas as you learn them will you really be able to practically apply the techniques presented in this book.

The Job Aids

At the end of this book is a section called "Job Aids." Keep it by your desk, when you're back at work. The Job Aids contain the "condensed methodology," including examples of every diagram covered in the book, templates, lists of questions to ask at various stages of the interview, and a glossary of UML symbols and terms.

Remember—It's All Just a Game!

You will be spending a lot of time during this book analyzing complex relationships in a system. It's easy to get uptight about whether you've got the right solution. Well, here's the good news: there is no "right" solution because there is more than one way to model the real world. So the best approach is to just play with an idea and see where it leads you.

You'll know you've gone in a good direction if your model has these qualities:

Elegance: A simple solution to a complex problem.

Adaptability: Can easily be changed to reflect a change in the requirements.

Non-redundancy: Does not repeat itself—each fact is "in one place."

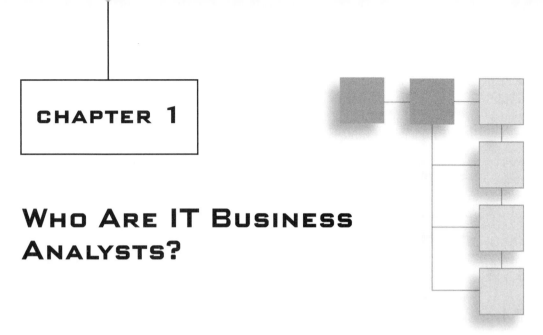

CHAPTER 1

WHO ARE IT BUSINESS ANALYSTS?

Chapter Objectives

At the end of this chapter, you will

1. Understand the role of the IT Business Analyst throughout a project's life cycle.
2. Understand what is meant by a business model, dynamic model and static model.

The IT and Non-IT BA

There are two types of Business Analysts. Just to clear up any possible confusion:

- A *Business Analyst* is someone who works within the context of the business. This person is involved in process improvement, cost-cutting, and so on.
- An *Information Technology Business Analyst* (IT BA) works within the context of IT projects—projects to buy, purchase, or modify some software.

This book is directed to the IT BA.

Perspective on the IT BA Role

The IT BA discipline is a work in progress right now. For example, the National IT Apprenticeship System (NITAS)—a BA program sponsored by the U.S. Dept. of Labor in conjunction with compTIA (Computing Technology Industry Association), has only recently been working on a definition of the knowledge areas and activities of a BA.[1]

---

[1]I acted as subject matter expert on this project. The project is currently on hold.

Similarly, another organization, the IIBA (International Institute of Business Analysis), is seeking to standardize the BA profession in much the same way as the PMI (Project Management Institute) has standardized project management. In practice, though, most organizations have a pretty similar idea of what the IT BA does.

An IT BA is a *liaison* between the stakeholders of a software system and the developers who create or modify it. A stakeholder is a person or organization impacted by a project: a user, customer not directly using the system, sponsor, and so on. The IT BA's primary function is to represent stakeholders' interests to designers, programmers, and other team members.

The IT BA is expected to discover, analyze, negotiate, represent, and validate the requirements of a new or modified software system. Basically, this means capturing the requirements and testing whether the software meets them.

Why Modeling Is a Good Thing

Listen up!

A *business model* is an abstract representation of a clearly delimited area of a business. It may take many forms, for example, pictures with supporting text or the underlying format used by a tool such as Rational Rose to produce diagrams and generate code.

In this book, you'll be asked to draw a lot of diagrams. What's the point? After all, most users can't read them, and they are reluctant to sign off on anything but text.

The fast answer is that the diagrams are for the developers: The diagrams are important because they get across the requirements in an unambiguous, standardized[2] way.

The slow answer is that the diagrams are more than that. Here's how to get the most out of them:

- **Use the diagrams to drive the interviews.** There is a logical step-by-step process to drawing a diagram. At each step, you have to ask the user certain questions to discover what to draw next. The act of drawing the diagram tells you what questions to ask and when, and even when the interview is complete (which is when all the diagram elements have been resolved).
- **Use diagrams whenever you need to reconcile differing viewpoints.** For example, on a consulting job for an accountancy firm, I was asked to help the team make changes to its CRM (Customer Relations Management) processes. The current system involved too much double entry. Here, a diagram[3] was useful to pool together the group's views on what was and should be happening in the system.

[2]That standard is UML 2.

[3]The diagram was called an activity diagram with partitions. It describes the sequence of activities and who (or what) is responsible for each activity.

In this book, you'll earn how to create two different types of diagrams, or models:

- Dynamic model (also known as the behavioral model)
- Static model (also known as the structural model)

The Dynamic (Behavioral) Model

Dynamic modeling asks—and tries to answer—the question, "What does the system *do*?" It's very verb-oriented: The dynamic model judges (analyzes) the system by its *actions*.

Listen up!

A *dynamic model* is an abstract representation of what the system *does*.

It is a collection of all useful *stimulus and response patterns* that together define the behavior of the system.[4]

In this book, the artifacts that fall into this category are

- Activity (workflow) diagrams
- State machine diagrams
- Timing diagrams (described briefly)
- System use-case diagrams
- Business use-case diagrams
- Sequence diagrams (described briefly)
- Communication diagrams (described briefly)
- Use-case specifications
- Decision tables
- Decision trees

The Static (Structural) Model

The motto of static modeling would be, "Ask not what you do, ask what you *are*." The static model answers the question, "What *is* this system?" As a static modeler, you want to know what every noun used within the business really means. For example, while working with a telecommunications team, I asked the members to define exactly what they meant by a "product group." I used static modeling diagrams to help me pin down its meaning and its relationship to other nouns, such as "line" and "feature." This process

---

[4]The diagrams covered under the "Dynamic Model" heading are sometimes referred to as *process models* (showing activities but not sequencing) and *workflow models* (which do show sequencing).

brought out the fact that there were two different definitions floating around among the team members. Using static modeling, I was able to discover these two definitions and help the team develop a common language.

Structure (Static) Diagram

"A *structure diagram* is form of diagram that depicts the elements in a specification that are irrespective of time. Class diagrams and component diagrams are examples of structure diagrams."[5]

In this book, the artifacts that fall into this category are

- Class diagrams (the standard type of diagram for static modeling)
- Static object diagrams
- Package diagrams
- Composite structure diagrams

For Those Trained in Structured Analysis

Warning: If you don't know Structured Analysis, this part may bore you!

The diagrams I have been discussing focus on an object-oriented (OO) view of a business or system. OO is an approach to breaking down a complex system into smaller components. (We'll look more deeply into OO in the next chapter.) The OO approach is often at odds with an older and still-used approach called Structured Analysis. This being the case, those with prior experience with Structured Analysis may be wondering at this point whether they have to throw away everything they already know because of OO. The good news is that despite the theoretical differences between the approaches, many of the OO diagrams are quite similar to the Structured Analysis ones—at least as they are used in a BA context. (Things are much more serious for programmers switching to OO.)

Table 1.1 lists diagrams used within Structured Analysis and matches them with their approximate counterparts in OO.

Table 1.2 matches terms used within Structured Analysis with their approximate counterparts in OO.

---

[5]The UML (Unified Modeling Language) is a standard used in object-oriented development. The current version of this standard is UML 2.

Table 1.1

Structured Analysis Diagram	OO Counterpart
Data Flow Diagram (DFD)	There is no exact counterpart because OO views a system as objects that pass messages to each other, while a DFD views it as processes that move data. However, some OO diagrams have similarities to the DFD: A use-case diagram is similar to a Level 1 DFD. An activity diagram (with object states) can be used similarly to a Level 2 or higher DFD.
System Flowchart	Activity diagram
Swimline Workflow Diagram	Activity diagram with partitions
Entity Relationship Diagram (ERD)	Class diagram

Table 1.2

Structured Analysis Term	OO Counterpart
Entity	Class, entity class
Occurrence	Instance; object
Attribute	Attribute
Process	Use case, operation, method, activity
Relationship	Association

Chapter Summary

In this chapter, you learned the following:

1. The role of the IT BA is to represent the user to the development community.
2. The main duties of the IT BA are to discover and communicate requirements to the developers and to supervise testing.
3. A business model is an abstract representation of a business area.
4. The dynamic model describes what the system does.
5. The static model describes what the system is.

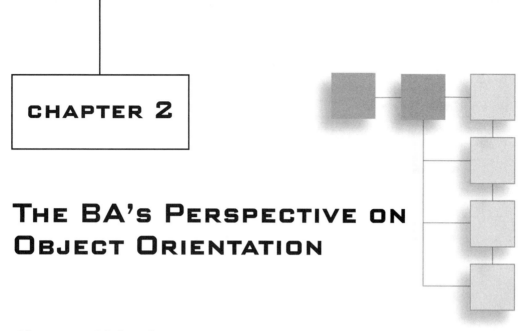

CHAPTER 2

THE BA'S PERSPECTIVE ON OBJECT ORIENTATION

Chapter Objectives

At the end of this chapter, you will

1. Understand how OO affects the BA role on IT projects.
2. Understand key OO concepts:
   - Objects
   - Operations and attributes
   - Encapsulation
   - Classes
   - Entity classes
   - Relationships
   - Generalization
   - Association
   - Aggregation
   - Composition
   - Polymorphism
   - System use cases
   - Business use cases
   - Unified Modeling Language (UML)

What Is OO?

OO is a complete conceptual framework that covers the entire life cycle of an IT project.

- OO affects the way the BA analyzes and models the requirements.
- OO affects the way the software engineer (technical systems analyst) designs the system.
- OO affects the way the code itself is structured: Object-Oriented languages such as JAVA and platforms such as .NET, support OO concepts and structures.

All of these are based on the same theoretical framework—one that we'll explore in this chapter.

The UML Standard

UML is an acronym for Unified Modeling Language, a widely accepted standard for OO first developed by the "Three Amigos"—Grady Booch, Jim Rumbaugh, and Ivar Jacobson—and now owned by the OMG (Object Management Group). The UML standards cover terminology and diagramming conventions. This book uses the latest version of that standard, UML 2.

I've seen many projects get bogged down over arguments about whether it's "legal" to do this or that according to the UML. If this happens with your team, ask what difference the outcome of the argument will have on the quality of the resulting software. In many cases, particularly during business analysis, there _are_ no ramifications. In such cases, discuss it, make a decision, and move on.

Cognitive Psychology and OO?

As a Business Analyst, your job is to get inside the heads of your stakeholders so that you can extract what they know about a piece of the real world—a _business system_—and pass it on to the developers, who will simulate that system on a computer. If you were choosing an approach for doing all this, you'd want something that goes as directly as possible from the stakeholders' heads to the IT solution. This approach would have to begin with an understanding of how people actually think about the world, and would have to be broad enough to take the project from requirements gathering right through to construction of the software. Object Orientation is one such approach. It begins by proposing that the object is the basic unit by which we organize knowledge. In the following discussion, we'll see how OO takes this simple idea and builds an entire edifice of powerful concepts that can be used to understand and build complex systems.

Objects

OO begins with the observation that when you perceive the world, you don't just take it in as a blur of sensations. You distinguish individual objects, and you have internal images of them that you can see in your mind's eye. Taken together, these internal objects model a segment of the real world.

The BA Perspective

You begin to analyze a business system by asking stakeholders to describe its business objects. A business object is something the business (and the IT system that automates it) must keep track of, or that participates in business processes. Examples of such an object might include an invoice, a customer service representative, and a call.

Attributes and Operations

OO theory continues by examining the kind of knowledge that is attached to each internal object. Because we are able to recognize an object again after having seen it once, the internal representation of the object must include a record of its properties. For example, we remember that a shirt object's color is *blue* and its size is *large*. In OO, *color* and *size* are referred to as *attributes*; *blue* and *large* are *attribute values*. Every object has its own set of attribute values.

Something else we remember about an object is its function. For example, the first time you saw a crayon, it took you some time to learn that it could be used to scribble on the walls. Unfortunately for your parents, the next time you saw that crayon, you knew *exactly* what to do with it. Why? Because you remembered that *scribble* was something you could do with that object. In OO, *scribble* is referred to as an *operation*.

To sum up what we've established so far: Two things we remember about objects are the *values of their attributes* and the *operations* that we can do with them.

The BA Perspective

The next step in analyzing a business system is to find out what attributes and business operations apply to each object. For example, two *attributes* that apply to an account object are *balance* and *date last accessed*; two *operations* that relate to the object are *deposit* and *withdraw*.

An object's operations usually change or query the values of its attributes. For example, the *withdraw* operation changes the value of the object's *balance* attribute. But this is not always the case. For example, *view transaction history*—another operation that applies to the account object—displays information about all the transaction objects tied to the account; however, it might not refer to any of the account's attributes.

Operations and Methods

Going one step further, you don't just remember *what* you can do with an object, you also remember *how* you do it. For example, you know that you can *place a call* with a particular mobile phone—but you also remember that to do so, you must follow a particular procedure: first you enter the phone number and then you press the *send* key. In OO terms, *place a call* is an *operation*; the *procedure* used to carry it out is called a *method*.

The BA Perspective

Next, you take each operation and ask stakeholders what procedure they use to carry it out. You document the procedure as a *method*. For example, you ask stakeholders what procedure they follow when withdrawing funds from an account. They tell you that they first check to see if there is a hold on the account and whether there are sufficient funds available for withdrawal. If everything is in order, they reduce the balance and create an audit trail of the transaction. You document this procedure as the *method* used to carry out the *withdraw* operation.

Encapsulation

Every day you use objects without knowing how they work or what their internal structure is. This is a useful aspect of the way we human objects interact with other objects. It keeps us from having to know too much. And it also means that we can easily switch to another object with a different internal structure as long as it behaves the same way externally.

This is the OO principle of *encapsulation*: Only an object's *operations* are visible to other objects. Attributes and methods remain hidden from view.

The BA Perspective

When you describe the method of an object, don't mention the attributes of another object, or presume to know how another object performs its operations. The benefit is that if the method or attributes related to a business object ever change, you'll have to make corrections to only one part of the model.

OO Concept: Classes

You have seen that our ability to internally model an object allows us to use it the next time we encounter it without relearning it. But this does not automatically mean that we can apply what we've learned to other objects of the same type. Yet we do this all the time. For example, once we've learned how use one *Samsung camera phone* object, we know how to use them all. We can do this because we recognize that all these objects belong to the same type: *Samsung camera phone*. In OO, the category that an object belongs to is called its *class*.

> If you weren't able to group objects into classes, you wouldn't realize that a blue metallic pot and a green ceramic pot belong to the same group but that a blue metallic pot and a blue metallic car do not. (Oliver Sacks has an interesting book on the subject, called *The Man Who Mistook His Wife for a Hat*. He speaks of one of his patients who, unable to classify objects, wrongly concluded that his wife was a hat and tried to put her on his head, as he was leaving the office.)

The minute you know that two objects belong to the class *Samsung camera phone*, you know a number of things about them:

- The *same attributes* apply to both objects. For example, you know that both objects will have a *serial number*, a *phone number*, and various *camera settings*.
- Each object will have its own values for these attributes.
- The *same operations* apply to both objects. For example, you can *place a call* and *take a picture* with each of these objects.
- The same *methods* apply. For example, the procedure for placing a call is the same for both phones.

See the Sidebar to find out how the Unified Modeling Language (the UML)—the predominant standard for Object Orientation—defines a class.

> What they say:
>
> "*Class*: A classifier that describes a set of objects that share the same specifications of features, constraints, and semantics." (UML 2)
>
> What they mean:
>
> A class is a *category*. All objects that belong to the same category have the same attributes and operations (but the values of the attributes may change from object to object).

Let's summarize what we've learned so far:

- Attributes and operations are defined at the class level and apply to all objects within that class.
- All objects in a class have the same attributes; the same properties are significant for all objects in a class; however, the value of the attributes may change from object to object within a class—the color of one pen is blue, the color of another is green.
- All objects in a class have the same operations and methods; all objects in a class can do the same things and they do them the same way.
- You'll learn later that relationships (such as that between a customer and an invoice) can also be stated at the class level.

The BA Perspective

Despite the name *object*-oriented analysis, you'll be spending most of your time defining *classes*, not objects. The classes you'll be interested in are those that relate to the business. These are termed *entity classes*. For example, in a banking system, you'd define the characteristics of an *Account* entity class and a *Customer* entity class.

OO Concept: Relationships

We often define one class in terms of another class. For example, a *Car* is a kind of a *Vehicle*. Both *Car* and *Vehicle* are classes. The phrase "a kind of" describes a *relationship* between the two classes.

The UML defines a number of types of relationships that are useful to the BA: generalization, association, aggregation, and composition.

OO Concept: Generalization

The concept of a class allows us to make statements about a set of objects that we treat *exactly* the same way. But sometimes we run into objects that are only *partially* alike. For example, we may own a store that has a number of *Samsung camera phone* objects and a number of *Motorola Razr phone* objects. The Samsung camera phones are not exactly like the Motorola Razr phones, but they do share some characteristics—for example, the ability to place a mobile call. We treat this situation by thinking of these objects not only as *Samsung camera phones* or *Motorola Razr phones*—but also as *mobile phones*. A particular phone object, for example, might be able to take a picture by virtue of being a *Samsung camera phone*—but it can also place a mobile call by virtue of being a mobile phone. In OO, *Mobile phone* is referred to as the generalized class; *Samsung camera phone* and *Motorola Razr phone* are referred to as its specialized classes. The *relationship* between the

Mobile phone class and either of its subtypes (*Samsung camera phone* or *Motorola Razr phone)* is called *generalization.*

Why do we generalize? It allows us to make statements that cover a broad range of objects. For example, when we say that a mobile phone can receive a text message, we are stating a rule that applies to all of its specializations.

> What they say:
>
> *"Generalization:* A taxonomic relationship between a more general classifier and a more specific classifier. Each instance of the specific classifier is also an indirect instance of the general classifier. Thus the specific classifier indirectly has features of the more general classifier." (UML 2)
>
> What they mean:
>
> When an object belongs to a specialized class (for example, *Samsung camera phone),* this automatically implies that it belongs to a generalization of that class (for example, *mobile phone.*) Furthermore, any attribute or operation that applies to the generalized class also applies to the specialized class.

Other terms in use:

Generalized Class	Specialized Class
Superclass	Subclass
Base class	Derived class
Parent	Child

The idea that a specialized class automatically adopts the attributes and operations of its generalized class is given a special name in OO—*inheritance.*

> What they say:
>
> *"Inheritance:* The mechanism by which more specific elements incorporate structure and behavior of more general elements." (UML 2)
>
> What they mean:
>
> *Inheritance* refers to the mechanism by which a specialized class adopts—that is, *inherits*—all the attributes and operations of a generalized class.[1]

---

[1]Attributes and operations are not the only things that are inherited. A specialized class also inherits any *relationships* the generalized class has to other classes as well as the *methods* of the generalized class (though the methods may be overridden due to polymorphism).

The BA Perspective

You look for classes of business objects that are subtypes of a more general type. For example, *Chequing Account* and *Savings Account* are two kinds (specialized classes) of *Accounts*. Then you document which attributes and operations apply to all *Accounts,* which apply only to *Chequing Accounts,* and which to *Savings Accounts.* By structuring your requirements this way, you only have to document rules common to all account types once. This makes it easier to revise the documentation if these business rules ever change. It also gives you the opportunity to state rules about *Accounts* that must apply to all future account types—even ones you don't know about yet.

OO Concept: Association

Another way that classes may be related to each other is through association. When you connect a mouse to a PC, you are associating *mouse* with *PC.*

What they say:

"*Association*: A relationship that may occur between instances of classifiers." (UML 2)

What they mean:

You state an association at the class level. An association between classes indicates that objects of one class may be related to objects of the other class.

The BA Perspective

You analyze how the business associates objects of one class with those of another (or, sometimes, with other objects of the same class). For example, the military needs to track which mechanics serviced each piece of equipment, what the maintenance schedule is for each one, and so on. As a BA, you document these types of rules as associations. This is a critical part of your job. Miss an association—or document it incorrectly—and you may end up with software that does not support an important business rule.

I once worked with a municipality that had just purchased a Human Resources (HR) system. Since they only intended to purchase ready-made software, they didn't think it necessary to do much analysis and, therefore, did not analyze associations. Had they done so, they would have included in their requirements the fact that the business needed to be able to associate each employee with one or more unions.[2] (The business context for this was that some employees held a number

---

[2]The "one or more" aspect of the association is known as *multiplicity.*

of positions, each covered by a different union.) As a result of the omission, not only did the municipality end up purchasing HR software that did not support this requirement, they also had to absorb the cost of customization. Had they included the requirement, they would have been unlikely to purchase this software in the first place and, even if they had, they would have been able to pass the modification cost on to the vendor.

OO Concept: Aggregation

Aggregation is the relationship between a whole and its parts. For example, the trade organization CompTIA is an aggregation of member organizations; an insurance policy is an aggregation of a basic policy and amendments to the policy and a stamp collection is an aggregation of stamps.

> *"Aggregation:* A special form of association that specifies a whole-part relationship between the aggregate (whole) and a component part." (UML 2)

With aggregation, a part may belong to more than one whole. For example, a *catalogue* object is a collection (aggregation) that consists of many product objects. However, any particular product may appear in more than one *catalogue.*

The BA Perspective

You look for business objects that are made of other business objects. You model these relationships as aggregations. Then you focus on which rules (attributes, operations, and relationships) apply to the whole and which apply to the parts. One thing that this process enables you to do is to reuse the requirements of a part object in a new context. For example, you model an ATM card as an aggregate, one of whose parts is a PIN. You define the attributes and operations of a PIN. Later you reuse the PIN requirements for a credit card system that also uses PINs.

Formally, aggregation is a specific kind of association, as it relates objects of one class to another.

OO Concept: Composition

Composition is a special form of aggregation wherein each part may belong to only one whole at a time. When the whole is destroyed, so are its parts.

What they say:

"*Composition*: A form of aggregation which requires that a part instance be included in at most one composite at a time, and that the composite object is responsible for the creation and destruction of the parts. Synonym: composite aggregation." (UML 2)

What they mean:

Formally, composition is a specific kind of aggregation. In aggregation, a part may belong to more than one whole at the same time; in composition, however, the object may belong to only one whole at a time. The parts are destroyed whenever the whole is destroyed.

Let's recap what OO says about association, aggregation, and composition:

The most general relationship is association, followed by aggregation, and, finally, composition.

Tip

Don't get too distraught if you are unable to decide whether a particular whole-part relationship is best described as an *aggregation* or *composition*. While the distinction (from a BA perspective) is helpful, it is not critical. If you have any problem deciding, specify the whole-part relationship as *aggregation*.

The BA Perspective

You model strong whole-part relationships between classes of business objects as composition. For example, in analyzing a CRO (Clinical Research Organization) system, I modeled a *Case Report Form* as a composition of *Modules*. The *Case Report Form* was a record of everything that was recorded about a subject on the drug; each *Module* was a record of one visit to the clinic by the subject. Developers would understood from this model that each *Module* could only belong to one *Case Report Form* at a time and that when a *Case Report Form* was removed from the system, all of its *Modules* needed to be removed as well.

OO Concept: Polymorphism

Polymorphism means the ability to take on many forms. The term is applied both to objects and to operations.

Polymorphic Objects

Suppose that a financial company handles different subtypes of *Funds*, such as an *Asia Fund*, *Domestic Fund*, and so on, each with its own idiosyncrasies. The BA models this situation using a generalized class, *Fund*, and a specialized class for each subtype of *Fund*.

Next, the BA moves on to capture investment rules in an *Investment* class. Checking with the stakeholders, the BA finds that one of its operations, *invest capital*, deals with all *Funds* the same way, regardless of subtype. The BA handles this by ensuring that the documentation for the *invest capital* operation refers exclusively to the generalized class *Fund*—not to any of its specializations. When the operation is actually executed, though, the *Fund* object will *take on one of many forms*—for example, an *Asia Fund* or a *Domestic Fund*. In other words, the *Fund* object is polymorphic.

Polymorphic Operations

Continuing with the same example, since all the *Fund* subtypes have to be able to accept deposits, the BA defines a *Fund* operation called *accept deposit*. This operation is inherited by all the specializations. The BA can also specify a method for this *Fund* operation that will be inherited by the specializations. But what if one or more of the specializations—for example, the *Asia Fund*—uses a different procedure for accepting deposits? In this case, the BA can add documentation to the *Asia Fund* class that describes a method that overrides the one inherited from the generalized class. (For example, the method described might involve supplementary charges.) In practice, when capital investment causes a *Fund* to *accept a deposit*, the method that is used to carry out the operation *will take on one of many forms*. This is what is meant by a *polymorphic operation*. With polymorphic operations, the selection of the method depends on which particular class (*Asia Fund*, *Domestic Fund*, and so on) is carrying it out.

> A *polymorphic operation* is one whose method may take on many forms based on the class of the object carrying it out.

The BA Perspective

When you define operations for a generalized class, you look for those that all specializations must be able to support. If you can, you define a method that describes how the operation is typically carried out. If any specialized classes have different ways of doing the operation, you define a new method for it at the specialized class level. This simplifies the documentation. You don't need to write, "If the type is *X*, then do one method; if it is *Y*, do another one." Instead, you get this across by *where* you document the method in the model.

> Polymorphism means "one interface, many possible implementations." Cars, for example, are designed with polymorphism in mind. They all use the same interface—an accelerator pedal—to change speed even though the internal method may differ from model to model. The auto industry designs cars this way so that the drivers do not have to learn a new interface for each new model of car.

Use Cases and Scenarios

A *use case* is a use to which the system will be put. It's an external perspective on the system from the point of view of the user. For example, some of the use cases that customers need in a Web-based banking system are *Make bill payment*, *Stop payment*, and *Order cheques*.

> What they say:
>
> "*Use case*: The specification of a sequence of actions, including variants, that a system (or other entity) can perform, interacting with actors [entities external to the system under design, such as users and other computer systems] of the system." (UML 2)
>
> What they mean:
>
> A use case is a *use to which the system will be put* as someone or something interacts with it. The description of the use case should describe the series of steps that take place during the interaction and include different ways that this interaction could play out.

> What they say:
>
> "*Scenario:* A specific sequence of actions that illustrates behaviors. A scenario may be used to illustrate an interaction or the execution of a use-case instance." (UML 2)
>
> What they mean:
>
> A *scenario* is one path through a use case—one way that it might play out.

For example, the *Make bill payment* use case may play out in one of the following ways:

Scenario 1: Attempt to make a payment and succeed in doing so.

Scenario 2: Attempt to make a payment from an account and fail because there is a hold on the account.

The BA Perspective

During dynamic analysis, you identify and document the use cases of the system—what the users want to do with it. You do this by identifying and describing its scenarios—all the ways it could play out. These use cases and scenarios are your user requirements.

Business and System Use Cases

Over time, practitioners began to distinguish between two kinds of use cases: business use cases and systems use cases. This distinction is not part of the core UML but is a UML extension.[3]

A *use case* (unqualified) refers to an interaction with any type of system. The question is, what *type* of system is being referring to?

A *business use case* is an interaction with a *business system*. For example, *Process Claim* is a business use case describing an interaction with an insurance company.

A *system use case* is an interaction with an *IT system*. For example, system use cases that support the above business use case are *Record Claim, Validate Coverage, Assign Adjuster*, and so on. Each of these describes an interaction between a user and the computer system.

A system use case typically involves one initiating (primary) user and takes place over a single session on the computer. At the end of the system use case, the user should feel that he or she has achieved a useful goal.

The BA Perspective

Early in a project, you identify and describe the business use cases that the IT project will impact. At this point, you focus on the business aspect of proposed changes—how they will affect workflow and the human roles within the business. Next, you analyze each business use case, looking for activities that the IT project will cover. You group these activities into system use cases, taking care to ensure that each system use case gives the user something of real benefit. These system use cases then drive the whole development process. For example, in each release, a planned set of system use cases is analyzed (unless this was done up front), designed, coded, and implemented. With this use case-centered approach, users get features that add real value to their jobs with each software release.

[3]The extensions are realized through the invention of new "stereotypes" for existing UML model elements. A stereotype extends the meaning of a model element. For example, in business modeling, a *business actor* is a stereotype of the UML "actor." For a more complete discussion of business modeling, see Pan-Wei Ng, "Effective Business Modeling with UML: Describing Business Use Cases and Realizations," *Rational Edge*. UML business modeling extensions are described in the jointly authored paper, Rational Software, Microsoft, Hewlett-Packard, Oracle, Sterling Software, MCI Systemhouse, Unisys, ICON Computing, IntelliCorp, i-Logix, IBM, ObjecTime, Platinum Technology, Ptech, Taskon, Reich Technologies, and Softeam "UML Extension for Business Modeling, Version 1.1," 1 September 1997.

Chapter Summary

In this chapter, you learned the following concepts:

1. *OO:* An acronym for object-oriented, an approach to analysis, design, and pro-gramming that is based upon dividing a system up into collaborating objects.

2. *Object:* A particular "thing" that plays a role in the system and/or that the system tracks—for example, the customer *Jane Dell Ray.* An object has *attributes* and *oper-ations* associated with it. The *object* is the basic unit of an OO system.

3. *Attribute:* A data element of an object.

4. *Operation:* A service that a class of objects can carry out.

5. *Method:* The process used to carry out an operation.

6. *Encapsulation:* An OO principle stating that an object's methods and properties are contained within the object. No other object may refer directly to another's attrib-utes or rely on a knowledge of how its operations are carried out.

7. *Class:* A category of object. Objects of the same class share the same attributes and methods.

8. *Entity class:* A subject the business keeps information about, for example, *Customer.*

9. *Relationship:* A connection between classes. A number of different types of rela-tionships were discussed in this chapter: generalization, association, aggregation, and composition.

10. *Generalization:* An OO property that models partial similarities among objects. A *generalized class* describes the commonalities. Each variation is called a *specialized class.* A specialized class *inherits* all the operations, attributes, and relationships of the generalized class.

11. *Association:* An association between classes indicates a link between its objects—for example, between an *Account* object and its *Customer* owner.

12. *Aggregation:* A relationship between a whole and its parts.

13. *Composition:* A specific form of aggregation wherein each part may belong to only one whole at a time. When the whole is destroyed, so are its parts.

14. *Polymorphic operations:* An OO concept allowing one operation name to stand for different procedures that achieve the same end. The class of the acting object deter-mines which action is selected.

15. *Use case:* A typical interaction between the user and system that achieves a useful result for the user.

16. *Business use case:* A business process.

17. *System use case:* A typical interaction with an IT system.

18. *UML:* Unified Modeling Language, a widely accepted standard for OO.

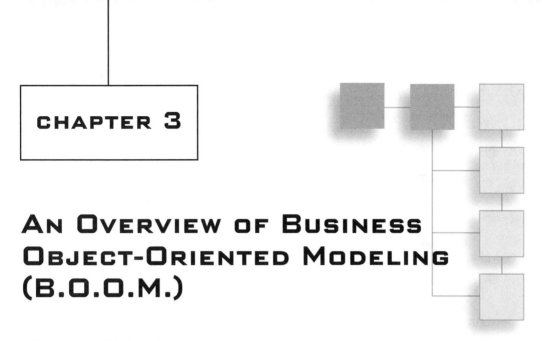

CHAPTER 3

AN OVERVIEW OF BUSINESS OBJECT-ORIENTED MODELING (B.O.O.M.)

Chapter Objectives

At the end of this chapter, you will know the steps of B.O.O.M. (Business Object-Oriented Modeling)—a procedure for eliciting, analyzing, documenting, and testing requirements using object-oriented and complementary techniques.

B.O.O.M. and SDLCs

Many large companies adopt a *Systems Development Life Cycle* or *SDLC* for managing their IT projects. The SDLC defines the specific phases and activities of a project. The names of the phases differ from SDLC to SDLC, but most SDLCs have something close to the following phases[1]:

- *Initiation*: Make the initial business case for the project.
- *Analysis*: Determine the business requirements.
- *Execution*: Design and code the software.
- *Test*: Assure quality of the product.
- *Close Out*: End project activities.

The B.O.O.M. steps take place during the Initiation and Analysis phases. The testing activities included in B.O.O.M., occur during the Analysis phase rather than in a separate Testing phase.

[1]For example, RUP has Inception, Elaboration, Construction, and Transition phases. These phases, as a whole, encompass those described above, but the correspondence is not straightforward, since RUP's iterative approach allows for certain activities (such as coding) to occur in a number of different phases.

The B.O.O.M. Steps

1: Initiation

The purpose of Initiation is to get a rough cut at the business case for a proposed IT project. The conundrum is that without knowing the requirements, it's impossible to estimate the cost of the project; on the other hand, without a business justification for the project, it is difficult to justify much requirement analysis. The trick is to do *just enough* research to be able to create a ballpark estimate. In this book, you'll learn how to do this using a number of UML techniques that keep you focused on high-level needs. These techniques are

- *Business use cases*: A tool for identifying and describing end-to-end business processes impacted by the project.
- *Activity diagrams*: Used to help you and stakeholders form a consensus regarding the workflow of each business use case.
- *Actors*: These describe the users and external systems that will interact with the proposed IT system.
- *System use cases*: Used to help stakeholders break out the end-to-end business processes into meaningful interactions with the IT system.

By the end of this phase, you will have a rough idea about the project as well as a fairly comprehensive list of system use cases, and you will know which users will be involved with each system use case. You won't know the *details* of each system use case yet, but you will know enough to be able to ballpark the project—for example, to say whether it will take days, weeks, or months.

The main deliverable of this phase is a Business Requirements Document (BRD). In this book, I'll take a "living document" approach to the BRD. You'll create it in this phase, and revise it as the project progresses. To help manage scope, you'll save a copy of the document at the end of each phase. This is what I mean below by *set baseline*. *Baselining* allows you to see what the requirements looked like at various checkpoints in order to see, for example, whether a feature requested later by a stakeholder was within the scope as defined at that time or not.

Below is a list of the steps you'll learn to carry out during this phase. (The main artifacts produced by the BA at each step are shown in parentheses.)

    1a) Model business use cases

        i) Identify business use cases (business use-case diagram)

       ii) Scope business use cases (activity diagram)

1b) Model system use cases

  i)   Identify actors (role map)

  ii) Identify system use-case packages (system use-case diagram)

  iii) Identify system use cases (system use-case diagram)

1c) Begin static model (class diagrams for key business classes)

1d) Set baseline for analysis (BRD/initiation)

2: Analysis

The purpose of the Analysis phase is to elicit the *detailed* requirements from stakeholders, then analyze and document them for verification by stakeholders and for use by the developers. You will exploit a number of UML and complementary techniques to assist in requirements elicitation, analysis, and documentation during this phase. Some of the main techniques you'll learn to use include

- System use-case descriptions, storyboarding the interaction between users, and the proposed IT system as each system use case is played out.
- State machine diagrams, describing the life cycle of key business objects.
- Class diagrams, describing key business concepts and business rules that apply to business objects, such as accounts, investments, complaints, claims, and so on.

Following accepted Quality Assurance practices, I introduce testing long before the code is written. Hence, you'll find testing activities also included in this phase. You'll learn to specify the *degree* of technical testing (white-box and system testing) required from the developers, as well as how to design *effective* requirements-based test cases (black-box tests). By doing this now, during analysis, not only are you giving the project enough lead-time to set up these tests, but you are also declaring *measurable* criteria for the project's success: If the tests you've described don't "work as advertised," the product will not be accepted.

Following are the steps you'll learn to carry out during this phase:

2a) Dynamic analysis

  i) Describe system use cases (use-case description)

  ii) Describe state behavior (state machine diagram)

    1. Identify states of critical objects

    2. Identify state transitions

    3. Identify state activities

    4. Identify superstates

    5. Identify concurrent states

2b) Static analysis (object/data model) (class diagram)

    i) Identify entity classes

    ii) Model generalizations

    iii) Model transient roles

    iv) Model whole/part relationships

    v) Analyze associations

    vi) Analyze multiplicity

    vii) Link system use cases to the static model

    viii) Add attributes

    ix) Add look-up tables

    x) Distribute operations

    xi) Revise class structure

2c) Specify testing (test plan/decision tables)

    i) Specify white-box testing quality level

    ii) Specify black-box test cases

    iii) Specify system tests

2d) Specify implementation plan (implementation plan)

2e) Set baseline for development (BRD/analysis)

Sequencing the Steps

Steps 2a), dynamic analysis, and 2b), static analysis, should be performed in parallel. In working through the case study in this book, I've separated these activities for pedagogical purposes; it's difficult, when learning this for the first time, to jump back and forth continually between the two types of modeling. Here's how you should intersperse these steps once you have some experience behind you:

1. You begin working on the static model during Initiation, describing key business classes and their relationships to each other.

2. During the Analysis phase, you describe a system use case (step 2ai), then verify it against the existing static model: Does the system use case comply with rules expressed in the static model? Has the system use case introduced new classes? You resolve any differences between the system use case and the static model and update the static model if necessary.

3. By the time you have described the last system use case, the static model should be complete and fully verified.

What Do You Define First—Attributes or Operations?

The OO principle of encapsulation suggests that in understanding how each object is used in a system, it's more important to know its operations than its attributes; operations are all that objects see of each other. However, within the context of business analysis, it's usually easy to identify the attributes of a class: The attributes show up as fields on screens and reports, and its often fairly obvious what class of objects they describe. Ascribing operations to classes is not quite as easy. I like to do the easy things first. (However, when I'm doing OOD, I start with the operations.)

Feel free to make changes to the order described for analyzing operations, attributes, or any other step. Consider B.O.O.M. your starting point. But you should, over time, customize the process as you see fit.

Chapter Summary

In this chapter, you learned the following concepts:

1. *OO:* An acronym for object-oriented, an approach to analysis, design, and programming that is based upon dividing a system up into collaborating objects.
2. The phases during which B.O.O.M. applies are
   - *Intitation*, during which a business case is made for the project.
   - *Analysis*, during which the detailed requirements are elicited, analyzed, and documented. Testing activities also occur during this phase.

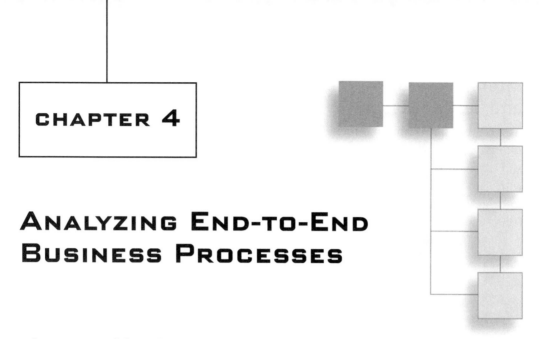

CHAPTER 4

ANALYZING END-TO-END BUSINESS PROCESSES

Chapter Objectives

By the end of this chapter, you will

1. Be able to gather requirements about end-to-end business processes using business use cases.
2. Know the layout of a Business Requirement Document (BRD).
3. Know how to fill the role of the IT Business Analyst during the Initiation phase of a project.
4. Identify business use cases.
5. Use business use-case diagrams effectively to gain consensus about which stake-holders interact with the business as each business use case is carried out.
6. Use activity diagrams to gain consensus about workflow.

B.O.O.M. Steps

In this chapter, we'll be walking through the following B.O.O.M. steps:

1. Initiation

1a) Model business use cases

       i) Identify business use cases (business use-case diagram)

       ii) Scope business use cases (activity diagram)

Interviews During the Initiation, Analysis, and Test Phases

As a BA, you'll carry out interviews with users at various phases of a project. During the *Initiation* phase, you'll interview stakeholders in order to establish the business rationale and scope for the project and to collect initial requirements. During *Analysis*, you'll meet with users to discover and document the business requirements for the new (or revised) software system. You'll hold quality assurance sessions with stakeholders to verify the correctness and completeness of the requirements.

As you go through this book, you'll learn what questions to ask during these interviews. Table 4.1 describes different options for structuring these interviews.

Table 4.1   Interview Formats

Format	What	When	Benefits	Disadvantages
One-on-one interviews		During Initiation and Analysis phases	Is easy to organize	Reconciling discrepancies is time consuming
Brainstorming	Group interview for enlisting new ideas	During Initiation phase and whenever the project is "stuck"	Breaks old ways of thinking	Does not yield detailed requirements

Joint Application Development (JAD)	Group interview to gather requirements	During Analysis phase	Simplifies reconciling of discrepancies, decreasing analysis time. Can be used to create various deliverables, including
			  BRD
			  Proof of concept
			  Strategy
			  Screens
			  Decision tables
				Difficult to get all interviewees in one room at same time
				Group-think

Structured Walkthrough	Group interview to verify requirements	During Analysis phase, after early draft of requirements is available	Moves QA (Quality Assurance) forward, reducing the impact of mistakes	

Step 1: Initiation

The first phase in a project is *Initiation*. Different approaches to IT project management each have their own terms for this phase and the precise activities that go on within it. *Approximate* counterparts for this phase are

- Envisioning (Microsoft Solutions Framework—MSF): This chapter addresses the following MSF objectives regarding the Envisioning phase: "High-level view of project goals," "Business requirements must be identified and analyzed."[1]
- Inception (RUP)
- Initiate (PMI)

What Happens During Initiation?

During Initiation, the project grows from an idea in someone's mind into a "bare-bones" proposal that outlines the main aspects of the project and describes the main reasons for pursuing it. During this phase, your job as a Business Analyst is to identify and analyze the business requirements for the project. You'll identify *high-level business* goals as *business use cases.* You'll be working with stakeholders to analyze *stakeholder participation* using *business use-case diagrams.* And you'll communicate to stakeholders an emerging consensus regarding workflow using *activity diagrams.*

How Long Does the Initiation Phase Take?

Basically, it "should be a few days' work to consider if it is worth doing a few months' work of deeper investigation."[2] For larger projects, it may take months.

Deliverables of the Initiation Step: BRD (Initiation Version)

As you work through the B.O.O.M. steps, you'll use a single document, the Business Requirement Document, or BRD, to describe business requirements throughout the project life cycle. You begin working on the BRD during Initiation. Different organizations handle this documentation in different ways. Some other names for documentation produced during Initiation include

- Opportunity Evaluation, which documents the proposed benefits of the project.
- Project Vision and Scope, which describes what the project hopes to achieve.
- Product Vision and Scope, which describes the objectives for the software product.

---

[1]These are described in the MSF White Paper *Process Model V3.1.*

[2]M. Fowler, *UML Distilled,* 1997, p. 16 (in his discussion of the "Initiation" phase of Objectory).

Key components of the BRD produced during Initiation are

- Business use-case specifications including business use-case diagrams
- Role map
- System use-case diagram
- Initial class diagram, describing key business classes

We'll walk through the creation of these components, but first, I'll introduce the BRD.

Business Requirements Document Template

In the following pages you'll find a template for a business requirements document (BRD). The document includes many best practices in use today. Don't be limited by the template, however—adapt it to your needs, adding or subtracting sections as required. Once your organization has settled on a template, adjust it regularly based on lessons learned from previous projects. After each project, ask, "What type of requirements documenation did we miss on this project?" "Where did we go into more detail than we needed to?" Based on the reponses to these questions, your organization may decide to add, contract, or remove entire sections of the BRD. Finally, the best way to use the template is to allow for some flexibility: Allow individual projects to deviate from the template, but define how and when deviations may occur, and require any project that uses an altered template to justify the deviation.

The BRD template that follows gives each technique covered in this book "a home" in the final requirements documentation. You may find it useful to return to this template (conveniently located in the Job Aids) whenever you want to get your bearings on how a UML diagram or other document fits in with the rest of the requirements documentation.

Business Requirements Document (BRD)

Project No. _____

Production Priority _____

Target date: _____

Approved by:

_____   _____

Name of user, department   Date

_____   _____

Name of user, department   Date

Prepared by: _____

Date: _____

Filename: _____

Version no.: _____

Table of Contents

- Version Control
    - ▲ Revision History
    - ▲ RACI Chart
- Executive Summary
    - ▲ Overview
    - ▲ Background
    - ▲ Objectives
    - ▲ Requirements
    - ▲ Proposed Strategy
    - ▲ Next Steps
- Scope
    - ▲ Included in Scope
    - ▲ Excluded from Scope
    - ▲ Constraints
    - ▲ Impact of Proposed Changes
- Risk Analysis
    - ▲ Technological Risks
    - ▲ Skills Risks
    - ▲ Political Risks
    - ▲ Business Risks
    - ▲ Requirements Risks
    - ▲ Other
- Business Case
    - ▲ Cost/Benefit Analysis, ROI, etc.
- Timetable
- Business Use Cases
    - ▲ Business Use-Case Diagrams
    - ▲ Business Use-Case Descriptions (text and/or activity diagram)
- Actors
    - ▲ Workers
    - ▲ Business Actors
    - ▲ Other Systems
    - ▲ Role Map

- User Requirements
    - ▲ System Use-Case Diagrams
    - ▲ System Use-Case Descriptions
- State Machine Diagrams
- Nonfunctional Requirements
    - ▲ Performance Requirements
        - ♦ Stress Requirements
        - ♦ Response-Time Requirements
        - ♦ Throughput Requirements
    - ▲ Usability Requirements
    - ▲ Security Requirements
    - ▲ Volume and Storage Requirements
    - ▲ Configuration Requirements
    - ▲ Compatibility Requirements
    - ▲ Reliability Requirements
    - ▲ Backup/Recovery Requirements
    - ▲ Training Requirements
- Business Rules
- State Requirements
    - ▲ Testing State
    - ▲ Disabled State
- Static Model
    - ▲ Class Diagrams: Entity Classes
    - ▲ Entity Class Documentation
- Test Plan
- Implementation Plan
    - ▲ Training
    - ▲ Conversion
    - ▲ Scheduling of Jobs
    - ▲ Rollout
- End User Procedures
- Post Implementation Follow-Up
- Other Issues
- Sign-Off

Version Control

Revision History

Version #	Date	Authorization	Responsibility (Author)	Description

RACI Chart for This Document

RACI stands for Responsible, Accountable, Consulted, and Informed. These are the main codes that appear in a RACI chart, used here to describe the roles played by team members and stakeholders in the production of the BRD. The following table describes the full list of codes used in the table:

*	Authorize	Has ultimate signing authority for any changes to the document.
R	Responsible	Responsible for creating this document.
A	Accountable	Accountable for accuracy of this document (for example, the project manager).
S	Supports	Provides supporting services in the production of this document.
C	Consulted	Provides input (such as an interviewee).
I	Informed	Must be informed of any changes.

Name	Position	*	R	A	S	C	I

Executive Summary

(This is a one-page summary of the document, divided into the following subsections.)

Overview

(This one-paragraph introduction explains the nature of the project.)

Background

(This subsection provides details leading up to the project that explain why the project is being considered. Discuss the following where appropriate: marketplace drivers, business drivers, and technology drivers.)

Objectives

(This subsection details the business objectives addressed by the project.)

Requirements

(This is a *brief* summary of the requirements addressed in this document.)

Proposed Strategy

(This subsection recommends a strategy for proceeding based on alternatives.)

Next Steps

Action: (Describe the specific action to be taken.)

Responsibility: (State who is responsible for taking this action.)

Expected Date: (State when the action is expected to be taken.)

Scope

Included in Scope

(This is a brief description of business areas covered by the project.)

Excluded from Scope

(This subsection briefly describes business areas *not* covered by the project.)

Constraints

(These are predefined requirements and conditions.)

Impact of Proposed Changes

Business Use Case	New?	Desired Functionality	Current Functionality (If a Change)	Stakeholders/ Systems	Priority

Risk Analysis

(A risk is something that could impact the success or failure of a project. Good project management involves a constant reassessment of risk.)

For each risk, document:

- Likelihood
- Cost
- Strategy: Strategies include
    - *Avoid:* Do something to eliminate the risk.
    - *Mitigate:* Do something to reduce damage if risk materializes.
    - *Transfer:* Pass the risk up or out to another entity.
    - *Accept:* Do nothing about the risk. Accept the consequences.

Technological Risks

(This subsection specifies new technology issues that could affect the project.)

Skills Risks

(This subsection specifies the risk of not getting staff with the required expertise for the project.)

Political Risks

(This subsection identifies political forces that could derail or affect the project.)

Business Risks

(This subsection describes the business implications if the project is canceled.)

Requirements Risks

(This subsection describes the risk of erroneous requirements. List areas whose requirements are most likely to be incorrectly captured.)

Other Risks

Business Case

(Describe the business rationale for this project. This section may contain estimates on cost/benefit, return on investment (ROI), payback [length of time for the project to pay for itself], market share benefits, and so on. Quantify each cost or benefit so that business objectives may be measured after implementation.)

Timetable

Business Use Cases

(Complete this section if the project involves changes to the workflow of end-to-end business processes. Document each end-to-end business process affected by the project as a business use case. If necessary, describe existing workflow for the business use case as well as the new, proposed workflow.)

Business Use-Case Diagrams

(Business use-case diagrams describe stakeholder involvement in each business use case.)

Business Use-Case Descriptions

(Describe the work flow of each business use case with text and/or an activity diagram. If you are documenting with text, use an informal style or the use-case template described in the "User Requirements" section below.)

Actors

Workers

(List and describe stakeholders who act within the business in carrying out business use cases.)

Department/ Position	General Impact of Project

Business Actors

(List and describe external parties, such as customers and partners, who interact with the business.)

Actor	General Impact of Project

Other Systems

(List computer systems potentially impacted by this project. Include any system that will be linked to the proposed system.)

System	General Impact of Project

Role Map

(The role map describes the roles played by actors [users and external systems] that interact with the IT system.)

User Requirements

(Describe requirements for automated processes from a user perspective.)

System Use-Case Diagrams

(System use-case diagrams describe which users use which features and the dependencies between use cases.)

System Use-Case Descriptions

(During Initiation, only short descriptions of the use cases are provided. During Analysis, the following template is filled out for each medium to high-risk use case. Low-risk use cases may be described informally. This template may also be used to document the business use cases included earlier in the BRD.)

Use-Case Description Template

1. Use Case: (the use-case name as it appears on system use-case diagrams)

   Perspective: Business use case/system use case

   Type: Base use case/extension/generalized/specialized/inclusion

   1.1 Brief Description
       (Briefly describe the use case in approximately one paragraph.)

   1.2 Business Goals and Benefits
       (Briefly describe the business rationale for the use case.)

   1.3 Actors

       1.3.1 Primary Actors
             (Identify the users or systems that initiate the use case.)

       1.3.2 Secondary Actors
             (List the users or systems that receive messages from the use case.
             Include users who receive reports or on-line messages.)

       1.3.3 Off-Stage Stakeholders
             (Identify non-participating stakeholders who have interests in this
             use case.)

   1.4 Rules of Precedence

       1.4.1 Triggers
             (Describe the event or condition that "kick-starts" the use case:
             such as *User calls Call Center*; *Inventory low*. If the trigger is time-
             driven, describe the temporal condition, such as *end-of-month*.)

       1.4.2 Preconditions
             (List conditions that must be true before the use case begins. If a
             condition *forces* the use case to occur whenever it becomes true, do
             not list it here; list it as a trigger.)

   1.5 Postconditions

       1.5.1 Postconditions on Success
             (Describe the status of the system after the use case ends success-
             fully. Any condition listed here is guaranteed to be true on success-
             ful completion.)

       1.5.2 Postconditions on Failure
             (Describe the status of the system after the use case ends in failure.
             Any condition listed here is guaranteed to be true when the use case
             fails as described in the exception flows.)

   1.6 Extension Points
       (Name and describe points at which extension use cases may extend this use
       case.)

Example of extension point declaration

1.6.1 Preferred Customer: 2.5-2.9

1.7 Priority

1.8 Status
Your status report might resemble the following example:
Use-case brief complete: 2005/06/01
Basic flow + risky alternatives complete: 2005/06/15
All flows complete: 2005/07/15
Coded: 2005/07/20
Tested: 2005/08/10
Internally released: 2005/09/15
Deployed: 2005/09/30

1.9 Expected Implementation Date

1.10 Actual Implementation Date

1.11 Context Diagram
(Include a system use-case diagram showing this use case, all its relation-ships [includes, extends, and generalizes] with other use cases and its associ-ations with actors.)

2. Flow of Events

Basic Flow

2.1 (Insert basic flow steps.)

Alternate Flows

2.Xa (Insert the alternate flow name):
(The alternate flow name should describe the condition that triggers the alter-nate flow. "2.X" is step number in basic flow where interruption occurs. Describe the steps in paragraph or point form.)

Exception Flows

2.Xa (Insert the exception flow name):
(The flow name should describe the condition that triggers the exception flow. An exception flow is one that causes the use case to end in failure and for which "postconditions on failure" apply. "2.X" is step number in basic flow where interruption occurs. Describe the steps in paragraph or point form.)

3. Special Requirements
(List any special requirements or constraints that apply specifically to this use case.)

3.1 Nonfunctional requirements:
(List requirements not visible to the user during the use case—security, per-formance, reliability, and so on.)

    3.2 Constraints
        (List technological, architectural, and other constraints on the use case.)

4. Activity Diagram
(If it is helpful, include an activity diagram showing workflow for this system use case, or for select parts of the use case.)

5. User Interface
(Initially, include description/storyboard/prototype only to help the reader visualize the interface, not to constrain the design. Later, provide links to screen design artifacts.)

6. Class Diagram
(Include a class diagram depicting business classes, relationships, and multiplicities of all objects participating in this use case.)

7. Assumptions
(List any assumptions you made when writing the use case. Verify all assumptions with stakeholders before sign-off.)

8. Information Items
(Include a link or reference to documentation describing rules for data items that relate to this use case. Documentation of this sort is often found in a data dictionary. The purpose of this section and the following sections is to keep the details out of the use case proper, so that you do not need to amend it every time you change a rule.)

9. Prompts and Messages
(Any prompts and messages that appear in the use case proper should be identified by name only, as in *Invalid Card Message*. The *Prompts and Messages* section should contain the actual text of the messages or direct the reader to the documentation that contains text.)

10. Business Rules
(The "Business Rules" section of the use-case documentation should provide links or references to the specific business rules that are active during the use case. An example of a business rule for an airline package is "Airplane weight must never exceed the maximum allowed for its aircraft type." Organizations often keep such rules in an automated business rules engine or manually in a binder.)

11. External Interfaces
(List interfaces to external systems.)

12. Related Artifacts
(The purpose of this section is to provide a point of reference for other details that relate to this use case, but would distract from the overall flow. Include references to artifacts such as decision tables, complex algorithms, and so on.)

State Machine Diagrams

(Insert state machine diagrams describing the events that trigger changes of state of significant business objects.)

Nonfunctional Requirements

(Describe across-the-board requirements not covered in the use-case documentation. Details follow.)

Performance Requirements

(Describe requirements relating to the system's speed.)

Stress Requirements

(This subsection of performance requirements describes the degree of simultaneous activity that the system must be able to support. For example, "The system must be able to support 2,000 users accessing financial records simultaneously.")

Response-Time Requirements

(This subsection of performance requirements describes the maximum allowable wait time from the moment the user submits a request until the system comes back with a response.)

Throughput Requirements

(This subsection of performance requirements describes the number of transactions per unit of time that the system must be able to process.)

Usability Requirements

(Describe quantitatively the level of usability required. For example, "A novice operator, given two hours of training, must be able to complete the following functions without assistance…." Also, refer to any usability standards and guidelines that must be adhered to.)

Security Requirements

(Describe security requirements relating to virus protection, firewalls, the functions and data accessible by each user group, and so on.)

Volume and Storage Requirements

(Describe the maximum volume [for example, the number of accounts] that the system must be able to support, as well as random access memory [RAM] and disk restrictions.)

Configuration Requirements

(Describe the hardware and operating systems that must be supported.)

Compatibility Requirements

(Describe compatibility requirements with respect to the existing system and external systems with which the system under design must interact.)

Reliability Requirements

(Describe the level of fault-tolerance required by the system.)

Backup/Recovery Requirements

(Describe the backup and recovery facilities required.)

Training Requirements

(Describe the level of training required and clearly state which organizations will be required to develop and deliver training programs.)

Business Rules

(List business rules that must be complied with throughout the system. For example, a flight reservation system might have a rule that the baggage weight on an aircraft must never exceed a given maximum. If an external rules engine is being used, this section should refer the reader to the location of these rules.)

State Requirements

(Describe how the system's behavior changes when in different states. Describe the features that will be available and those that will be disabled in each state.)

Testing State

(Describe what the user may and may not do while the system is in the test state.)

Disabled State

(Describe what is to happen as the system goes down [that is, how it "dies gracefully"]. Clearly define what the user will and will not be able to do.)

Static Model

Class Diagrams: Entity Classes

(Insert class diagrams representing classes of business objects and relationships among the classes. This section centralizes rules that govern business objects, such as the numerical relationships among objects, the operations associated with each object, and so on.)

Entity Class Documentation

(Insert documentation to support each of the classes that appear in the class diagrams. Not every class needs to be fully documented. First do a risk analysis to determine where full documentation would most benefit the project.)

Class Name:

Alias: (List any other names by which the class is known within the business domain.)

Description:

Example: (Provide an example of an object of this class.)

Attributes: (These may be documented in a table, as follows.)

Attribute	Derived?	Derivation	Type	Format	Length	Range	Dependency

(When your requirements are complete up to this point and approved by the appropriate people, submit them to developers. You can then work on the test plan, implementation plan, and end user procedures.)

Test Plan[3]

(To standardize the testing, you should develop a test plan document for analysts to follow when constructing project test plans. Although every project is different, the following may be used as a guideline. Each project should consider the following stages during testing):

1. Submit the requirements to the technical team. The technical team completes development. Concurrently, the BA builds numbered test scenarios for requirements-based testing. Consider using decision tables to identify scenarios and boundary value analysis to select test data. The technical team conducts white-box testing, to verify whether programs, fields, and calculations function as specified. The BA or technical team specifies the required quality level for white-box testing, such as multiple-condition coverage.

2. Perform requirements-based testing. The BA or dedicated QA (Quality Assurance) staff administers or supervises tests to prove or disprove compliance with requirements. Ensure that all formulae are calculated properly. Describe principles and techniques to be used in black-box testing, such as structured testing guidelines and boundary value analysis.

3. Conduct system testing. Ensure that the integrity of the system and data remain intact. For example:

   - *Regression test*: Retest all features (using a regression test bed).
   - *Stress test*: Test multiple users at the same time.
   - *Integration tests*: Make sure that the changes do not negatively affect the overall workflow across IT and manual systems.
   - *Volume test*: Test the system with high volume.

4. Perform user acceptance testing. Involve the end users at this stage. Choose key users to review the changes in the test environment.

[3]These requirements are often described in a separate test plan. If they are not addressed elsewhere, describe them here in the BRD.

Implementation Plan

Training

(Specify who is responsible for training.)

(Specify who is to be trained.)

(Specify how training will be done.)

Conversion

(Specify existing data that must be converted.)

(Promote programs to new release.)

(Grant privileges to the users.)

Scheduling of Jobs

(Advise Information Systems [IS] operations which jobs to add to the production run. Specify the frequency of the run: daily, weekly, monthly, quarterly, semi-annually, or annually.)

(Ensure that the job is placed in the correct sequence.)

(Advise IS operations of the reports to be printed and the distribution list for reports and files.)

Rollout

(Advise all affected users when the project is promoted.)

End User Procedures

(Write up the procedures for the affected departments. Distribute this document to them in addition to providing any hands-on training.)

Post Implementation Follow-Up

(Follow up within a reasonable time frame after implementation to ensure that the project is running successfully. Determine whether any further enhancements or changes are needed to ensure success of the project.)

Other Issues

Sign-Off

Step 1a: Model Business Use Cases

In your first meetings with stakeholders, you want to identify the end-to-end business processes that the IT project will affect. These processes are *business use cases*.

> *Business use case:*
>
> A business process, representing a specific workflow in the business; an interaction that a stakeholder has with the business that achieves a business goal. It may involve both manual and automated processes and may take place over an extended period of time.
>
> "A business use case defines what should happen in the business when it is performed; it describes the performance of a sequence of actions that produces a valuable result to a particular business actor [someone external to the business]." (*Source: Rational Rose*)

Any IT project has the potential to change the business environment: how steps—both manual and automated—within a business are performed and the roles and responsibilities of employees. By focusing on business use cases at the outset of the project, you ensure that this business perspective is not forgotten.

How Do You Document Business Use Cases?

Use business use-case diagrams to describe the players who take part in each business use case. Use text or a workflow diagram (such as an activity diagram) to describe the interaction between the players and the business as the use case is played out. Let's start with the business use-case diagram.

Step 1a i: Identify Business Use Cases (Business Use-Case Diagram)

> *Business use-case diagrams:*
>
> "The business use-case model is a diagram illustrating the scope of the business being modeled. The diagram contains business actors [roles played by organizations, people, or systems external to the business] and the services or functions they request from the business." (*Source: IconProcess*)

Recall that the business use-case diagram is not a part of the core UML standard, but rather an extension to it. Because of this, the terms and symbols related to business use cases are not as standardized as those that are part of the UML proper.

Figure 4.1 shows some of the symbols used in business use-case diagrams.

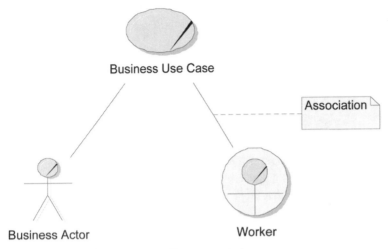

Figure 4.1 Business use-case diagram symbols

(Note the "stroke" in each of the above symbols differentiates them from symbols used in system use-case diagrams.)

Business actor: Someone external to the business, such as a customer or supplier.

Worker: Someone who works within the business, such as an employee or customer service representative.

Association: The line that connects an actor (business actor or worker) to a business use case. An association between an actor and a business use case indicates that the actor interacts with the business over the course of the business use case—for example, by initiating the use case or by carrying it out.

Other Model Elements

Other types of actors are also sometimes used in business modeling. The UML Extension for Business Modeling, version 1.1, for example, allows for the subdivision of workers into *case workers* and *internal workers*:

Case worker: A worker who interacts directly with actors outside the system.

Internal worker: A worker who interacts with other workers and entities inside the system.

In this book, we will confine ourselves to the more generic term "worker."

Putting Theory into Practice

When the BA walks onto a project, some preliminary work has often already been done: Someone has had an idea for the project and developed a preliminary business case for it. Based on the business case, a decision has been made to assemble a project team. One of the first steps for the BA is to review this preliminary documentation, often in a kick-off meeting with stakeholders. The purpose of the meeting is to review stakeholder interests in the project and to identify the business use cases that the project could impact.

Here is also where our case study begins. Together, we'll walk through the B.O.O.M. steps for analyzing and documenting the requirements of this system, and in doing so, gain hands-on experience in being an OO Business Analyst. I urge you to work through each of the steps yourself, before viewing the resulting documentation. Then compare your work to the documentation I've provided in this book. It's perfectly OK for you to come up with a different result; after all, there is more than one way to analyze a system. But you should be able to justify any decision you've made.

Note to Rational Rose Users

All of the case studies in this book can be done manually. For those who use the modeling tool Rational Rose, I have included notes on the use of the software for BA purposes. To work through the upcoming case study, you'll need to know enough about Rose to create a business use-case diagram.

When you start Rose up, it asks you whether you want to use an existing framework for your new model. Select Cancel; you want to do everything from scratch.

Figure 4.2 shows the Rose screen.

The elements of the Rational Rose screen are as follows:

- *Browser window.* The Browser window contains all the model elements that appear on the diagrams. To work on the properties of an element, find it in the browser and double-click. Note that this window is divided into a number of sections, each highlighted with a Windows-like folder symbol (the UML "package" symbol). These are

  - *Use-case view.* For use-case diagrams and diagram elements
  - *Logical view.* For class specifications and diagrams
  - *Component view.* Describes the physical organization of software components (not covered in this book)

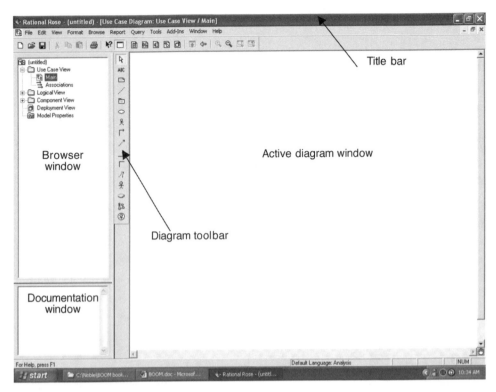

Figure 4.2 The Rational Rose screen

- *Deployment view.* For specifications of processors, devices, and connections (not covered in this book)
- *Documentation window.* Displays documentation about a modeling element that has been selected.
- *Active Diagram window.* You'll be drawing and viewing diagrams in this window. You may have many diagram windows open at one time, but only one of them will be active.
- *Diagram toolbar.* Displays tools specific to the type of diagram displayed in the Active Diagram window. You can customize this toolbar.
- *Title bar.* Displays Rose title. If the Active Diagram window has been maximized, the title bar also displays the name of the diagram.

To begin working, follow these steps:

1. Maximize the Active Diagram window. The title bar should now contain the name of the active diagram. (When Rose starts up, the main class diagram is always active.)

2. Select the Main use-case diagram: In the Browser window,

   ▪ Press the plus next to the Use-Case View package to open it up.

   ▪ Then double-click on the icon to the left of Main. The title bar should now read, Use Case Diagram/ Use Case View/ Main.

3. Customize the toolbar: Right–click on the diagram toolbar. Add the following tools, if they are not already there:

   ▪ Association

   ▪ Unidirectional association

   ▪ Include use case

   ▪ Extend use case

   ▪ Business actor

   ▪ Business worker (Rose does not come with a "worker" tool, so we'll use this instead.)

   ▪ Business use case

You won't be using all of these tools right away, but you will need them in future case study problems.

Case Study D1: Business Use-Case Diagrams

In the following case study, you'll be introduced to the Community Peace Program (CPP) project—a project you'll follow throughout this book as you learn to apply B.O.O.M. steps in practice. In Case Study D1, you'll see an example of BRD documentation based on the template you saw earlier in this chapter. As the BRD is a living document, it will change as the project progresses. Case Study D1's version is a draft produced during the initiation phase of the project.

Problem Statement

As a Business Analyst assigned to a new project, you've convened a kickoff meeting with stakeholders to discuss their interests in the project and to identify the business processes potentially impacted by it. Based on what you learn at the kickoff meeting, you put together the following first draft of a BRD (Business Requirements Document). In order to summarize stakeholder interests, you will create a business use-case diagram, showing business use cases and the business actors and workers involved in each use case.

Suggestions

Read through the following BRD. Then identify the stakeholders as workers or business actors and document their involvement with each business use case in a business use-case diagram. Do not include systems in your model at this stage; your focus should be on the activities that need to occur and the humans involved.

CPP Business Requirements Document (BRD)/Initiation

Project No.   1000

Production Priority High

Target date: _____

Approved by:

_____   _____

Name of user, department   Date

_____   _____

Name of user, department   Date

Prepared by: _____

Date: _____

Filename: _____

Version no.:   0.1 (1st draft)

Table of Contents

- *Version Control*
  - *Revision History*
  - *RACI Chart*
- *Executive Summary*
  - *Overview*
  - *Background*
  - *Objectives*
  - *Requirements*
  - *Proposed Strategy*
  - *Next Steps*
- *Scope*
  - *Included in Scope*
  - *Excluded from Scope*
  - *Constraints*
  - *Impact of Proposed Changes*
- *Risk Analysis*
  - *Technological Risks*
  - *Skills Risks*
  - *Political Risks*
  - *Business Risks*
  - *Requirements Risks*
  - *Other*
- *Business Case*
  - *Cost/Benefit Analysis, ROI, etc.*
- *Timetable*
- *Business Use Cases*
  - *Business Use-Case Diagrams*
  - *Business Use-Case Descriptions (Text and/or Activity Diagram)*
- *Actors*
  - *Workers*
  - *Business Actors*
  - *Other Systems*
  - *Role Map*

- *User Requirements*
    - ▲ *System Use-Case Diagrams*
    - ▲ *System Use-Case Descriptions*
- *State Machine Diagrams*
- *Nonfunctional Requirements*
    - ▲ *Performance Requirements*
        - ◆ *Stress Requirements*
        - ◆ *Response-Time Requirements*
        - ◆ *Throughput Requirements*
    - ▲ *Usability Requirements*
    - ▲ *Security Requirements*
    - ▲ *Volume and Storage Requirements*
    - ▲ *Configuration Requirements*
    - ▲ *Compatibility Requirements*
    - ▲ *Reliability Requirements*
    - ▲ *Backup/Recovery Requirements*
    - ▲ *Training Requirements*
- *Business Rules*
- *State Requirements*
    - ▲ *Testing State*
    - ▲ *Disabled State*
- *Static Model*
    - ▲ *Class Diagrams: Entity Classes*
    - ▲ *Entity Class Documentation*
- *Test Plan*
- *Implementation Plan*
    - ▲ *Training*
    - ▲ *Conversion*
    - ▲ *Scheduling of Jobs*
    - ▲ *Rollout*
- *End User Procedures*
- *Post Implementation Follow-Up*
- *Other Issues*
- *Sign-Off*

Version Control

[Completing the following table makes it easy to come back later and track what changes were made to the requirements at each point in the project, who made them, and why they were made. This is a way of implementing change control on the BRD.]

Chart 4.1 Revision History

Version #	Date	Authorization	Responsibility (Author)	Description
0.1	06/05		Mbuyi Pensacola	Initial draft

RACI Chart for This Document

[This chart identifies the persons who need to be contacted whenever changes are made to this document. The codes below describe the involvement of individuals in the creation of this document. They are adapted from charts used to assign roles and responsibilities during a project.]

Chart 4.2 RACI Chart

Name	Position	*	R	A	S	C	I
C. Ringshee	Director, CPP	×					
J. Carter	Manager, Operations			×			
Mbuyi Pensacola			×				

Each person's connection to the BRD has been documented in the above chart as *, R, A, S, C, I. The following chart explains the meaning of each of these codes.

Chart 4.3 Codes Used in RACI Chart

*	Authorize	This individual has ultimate signing authority for any changes to the document.
R	Responsible	Responsible for creating this document.
A	Accountable	Accountable for accuracy of this document (e.g., Project Manager).
S	Supports	Provides supporting services in the production of this document.
C	Consulted	Provides input (interviewee, etc.).
I	Informed	Must be informed of any changes.

Executive Summary

[The Executive Summary should be a precis of the entire document. It should summarize, in a page or two, the context for the document (why it was written), the main issues raised within, and the main conclusions of the document. The purpose of the Summary is to provide just enough detail for a high-level stakeholder (who may not have time to read the whole thing) and to help any other potential reader ascertain whether it is worth reading the rest of the document.]

Overview

This project is for a software system to govern the tracking and reporting of cases by the Community Peace Program (CPP).

Background

The project is being developed for the Community Peace Program (CPP), a South African non-profit organization that provides infrastructure for community-based justice systems based on the model of restorative justice.[4] The main objective of the CPP is to provide an effective alternative to the court system. Its advantages are improved cost-effectiveness and a decreased recurrence rate, since problems are treated at their source. All parties to a dispute must consent to having the case diverted to the CPP. The advantage to the *perpetrator* is the avoidance of incarceration and other severe punishment; for the *complainant*, the advantages lie in the possibility for a true resolution to the problem and a decreased likelihood that the problem will recur. The advantages to the *justice system* are

- A reduction in case volume due to the offloading of cases to the CPP and a decrease in recurrence rates, and
- A decrease in the cost of processing a case.

The system is being deployed in the townships of South Africa under the auspices of the CPP and with the support of the Justice Department. Similar approaches are being used throughout the world, for example, the "Forum," in use by Canada's Royal Canadian Mounted Police (RCMP).

The CPP operates by working with local communities to set up Peace Committees. Most of these are currently in townships on the Cape Town peninsula. Each Peace Committee is composed of "peacemakers"—members of the community who are trained in conflict resolution procedures based on principles of restorative justice. The complainants and accused must all agree to adhere to the procedure, or the case is passed on to the state justice system.

Due to increasing demand for its services in conflict resolution, the CPP is undergoing a rapid expansion. Current manual practices will not be able to keep up with the expected rise in case volume.

[4]The principles of restorative justice were developed by Terry O'Connel.

Objectives

The most urgent need is for timely statistics regarding cases handled by the CPP. Because of the anticipated increase in caseload, these statistics will be difficult to derive using the current, manual systems. Timely statistics will be essential in justifying the project to its funders. Also, the tracking of funds disbursement and monitoring of cases will become increasingly difficult as the program expands.

Requirements

The project will leave current manual systems in place for the initial recording of case information up to and including the conduct of a Peace Gathering and the completion of subsequent monitoring. Workflow after that point will be within the scope of the project, that is, recording of case data, validation of CPP procedures, disbursement of payments, and the generation of statistical reports.

Proposed Strategy

An iterative SDLC will be employed as follows: The Business Analyst(s) will analyze all use cases at the start for the project (Analysis phase); the design and coding will proceed iteratively. In the first iteration, general administration and case tracking will be developed. In the second iteration, payments will be disbursed and reports generated.

Next Steps

> *Action*: Select software developer
> *Responsibility*: J. Carter
> *Expected Date*: One month after acceptance of this document

Scope

The scope section defines what is to be included and excluded from the project, what has been predetermined about the project (constraints), the business processes affected by the project, and the impact of the project on stakeholders.

Included in Scope

The system will provide statistical reports for use by funders. Also, it will provide limited tracking of individual cases, to the degree required for statistics and, wherever possible, in a manner that will facilitate expansion of the system to include complete case monitoring. The project includes manual and automated processes. The system will encompass those activities that occur after a case has been resolved. These are primarily: the recording of case data, disbursement of payments, and the generation of reports. CPP members will be the only direct users of this system.

Excluded from Scope

The system becomes aware of a case only when it has been resolved. All activities prior to this point are not included in this project; i.e., it excludes the tracking of cases from the time of reporting, convening of Peace Gathering, and monitoring of cases. The activities will continue to be performed manually, although the manual forms will be changed to comply with new system requirements.

Constraints

1. Eighty percent match (minimum) between CPP's needs and OTS (off-the-shelf) product(s).
2. One integrated solution is preferred. No more than two OTS products should be needed.
3. Mbuyisela Williams will be main liaison for the project.
4. Final approval for a system is estimated to take six weeks to two months.

Impact of Proposed Changes

Table 4.2 lists the end-to-end business processes that stand to be impacted by the project. Each process is identified as a business use case. The table documents whether the process is new (as opposed to an update to an exisitng process), what the stakeholder would like the process to do, and what the process currently does. The difference between the desired and current functionality defines the project's scope. Each business use case is linked to stakeholders and prioritized.

[Prioritization helps the project manager plan the project and, when competing software vendors are being considered, to short-list viable solutions.]

Risk Analysis

[In this section of the BRD, you describe risks. A *risk* is anything that could impact the project. For each risk, you'll note the likelihood of its occurrence, the cost to the project if it does occur, and the strategy for handling the risk. Strategies include

- *Avoid*: Do something to eliminate the risk.
- *Mitigate*: Do something to reduce damage if risk materializes.
- *Transfer*: Pass the risk up or out to another entity.
- *Accept*: Do nothing about the risk. Accept the consequences.

Analyze risks now, during initiation, and regularly as the project progresses. While you may not be able to avoid every risk, you can limit its impact on the project by preparing for it beforehand.]

Technological Risks

New technology issues that could affect the project: To Be Determined (TBD).

Table 4.2

Business Use Case	New?	Desired Functionality	Current Functionality (If a Change)	Stakeholders/ Systems	Priority
Manage administration	Yes	General administrative functions, e.g., creation/updating of Peace Committees, members, etc.	Manual systems only in place	CPP General Administration	High
Manage case	Yes	Manage a case: identify new cases, update case information, etc.	Manual systems only in place	Peace Committee, Facilitator, Monitor, Convener	High
Administer payments	Yes	Make payments to individuals that assisted in a case and to various funds.	Manual systems only in place	Convener, Peace Committee Member, AP System	Medium
Generate reports	Yes	Report on cases by region and by period; compile stats on caseload, # cases per type of conflict, etc.	Manual systems only in place	Any worker (members of the CPP), government body (any governmental organizational receiving reports), funder	High

Skills Risks

Risk of not getting staff with the required expertise for the project: TBD.

Political Risks

Political forces that could derail or affect the project include the following:

> *Cancellation of funding*: Funding for this project is provided by a foreign government and is granted only on an annual basis after yearly inspections of the organization and based on the government's policy toward foreign aid.
>
> *Likelihood*: Medium.
>
> *Cost*: Cancellation of the project.
>
> *Strategy*:
>
> - *Avoid*: Through regular project reports to funders and lobbying of government ministers.
> - *Mitigate*: Search out "plan B" funders: University of Cape Town School of Governance.

Business Risks

Describe the business implications if the project is cancelled. TBD.

Requirements Risks

Risk that the requirements have not been correctly described: TBD

Other Risks

TBD.

Business Case

[Describe the business rationale for this project. This section may contain estimates on cost/benefit, ROI (Return On Investment), payback (length of time for the project to pay for itself), market share benefits, and so on. Quantify each cost or benefit so that business objectives may be measured post-implementation

The estimates at this stage are ballpark only. Revise estimates periodically as the project progresses.]

- *Initial investment* = 2 person-years @ US$50,000/yr = $100,000. Hardware: Use existing PCs at office location

- *Annual cost*: 1 new half-time position, IT maintenance staff = US$25,000/yr
- *Annual benefits*: Reduce administration staff by 2 due to automatic generation of reports to funders and increased efficiency of case tracking = US$60,000/yr
- *ROI (Return On Investment)* = ([Annual benefit] – [Annual; cost])/[Initial investment] = (60,000 – 25,000)/ 100,000 = 35%
- *Payback period* = [Initial investment]/ ([Annual benefit] – [Annual cost]) = 100,000/(60,000-25,000) = 2.9 or approximately 3 years

These numbers are expected to improve over the years as the project expands, since the efficiencies of the IT system relative to a manual system are more pronounced the greater the volume of the cases.

Timetable

Only a ballpark timetable can be provided at this stage.

- *Analysis*: To begin 1 month after the project is approved to go beyond Initiation.
- *Execution*: To begin 3 months after the project is approved.
- *Testing*: Verification of requirements and planning of requirements-based testing to begin during Analysis. Actual tests of software to be run as modules become available.
- *Close-Out*: To begin 6 months to 1 year after project is approved. Close-out to take 1 month.

Business Use Cases

[Complete this section if the project involves changes to the workflow of end-to-end business processes. Document each end-to-end business process affected by the project as a business use case. If necessary, describe existing workflow for the business use case as well as the new, proposed workflow.]

Business Use-Case Diagrams

[Business use-case diagrams describe stakeholder involvement in each business use case.]

Business Use-Case Descriptions

[Describe the work flow of each business use case with text and/or an activity diagram. If you are documenting with text, use an informal style or the use-case template, introduced later in this book, when system use cases are described.]

Actors

[*Actors* are people, organizations, or other entities that interact with a system. In this section, describe the actors that participate in the execution of business use cases.

Workers

List and describe stakeholders who act within the business in carrying out business use cases.

Department/Position	General Impact of Project
Convener	(Member of the CPP). Will use it to update cases and administer payments.
CPP General Admin	(Member of the CPP). Will use it to perform administrative functions, such as updating Peace Committees and members in the system.

Business Actors

[List and describe external parties, such as customers and partners, who interact with the business.]

Actor	General Impact of Project
Facilitator	A member of the community trained to facilitate Peace Gatherings. Current manual processes will remain with slight changes to forms as required for reporting purposes.
Monitor	A member of the community assigned to monitor parties' compliance with plan of action agreed to during Peace Gathering. Current manual process will remain in place.
Peace Committee	An organization set up within a community and consisting of local members of the community, trained by the CPP to assist in dispute resolution. Current manual process will remain in place. Will need to report to head office about any changes to the organization, membership, etc.
Peace Committee Member	A member of a Peace Committee. A local trained by the CPP to assist in dispute resolution. The IT system will send notification of payment for services.
Government Body	Represents any government organization that receives reports from the new system.
Funder	Source of CPP funding. The IT system will send analytical reports.

Other Systems

List computer systems potentially impacted by this project.

System	General Impact of Project
AP System	Existing system for tracking accounts payable. This system must remain in place.

Role Map

[The role map describes the roles played by actors (users and external systems) that interact with the IT system.]

TBD: This section will be completed later during Initiation.

User Requirements

[Describes requirements for automated processes covered by the project from a user perspective.]

TBD: This section will be completed later. Portions of this section will be completed later in the Initiation; other portions will be added during Analysis, as described below.

System Use-Case Diagrams

[System use-case diagrams describe which users use which features and the dependencies between use cases.]

TBD: This section will be completed later during Initiation.

System Use-Case Descriptions

[During Initiation, only short descriptions of the use cases are provided. During analysis, the following template is filled out for each medium- to high-risk use case. Low-risk use cases may be described informally. This template may also be used to describe the business use cases documented elsewhere in the BRD.]

TBD: Later in the Initiation, short descriptions of the system use cases will be provided as well as detailed descriptions of selected high-risk system use cases, for example, those that are to be developed early because they involve new and poorly understood technology.

State Machine Diagrams

[Insert state-machine diagrams describing the events that trigger changes of state of significant business objects.]

TBD: This section will be completed during Analysis.

Nonfunctional Requirements

[Describe requirements not covered in the use-case documentation.] (TBD)

Business Rules

[List business rules that must be complied with throughout the system (for example, for a flight reservation system, the rule that the baggage weight on an aircraft must never exceed a given maximum). If an external rules engine is being used, this section should refer the reader to the location of these rules.] (TBD)

State Requirements

[Describe how the system's behavior changes when in different states. Describe the features that shall be available and those that shall be disabled in each state.] (TBD)

Testing State

[Describe what the user may and may not do while the system is in the test state.] (TBD)

Disabled State

[Describe what is to happen as the system goes down (that is, how it "dies gracefully"). Clearly define what the user will and will not be able to do.] (TBD)

Static Model

[During Initiation, only strategic classes are modeled.] (TBD)

Case Study D1: Resulting Documentation

The following business use-case diagram was created by the BA to summarize the business use cases potentially impacted by the project and the stakeholders involved with each one (see Figure 4.3).

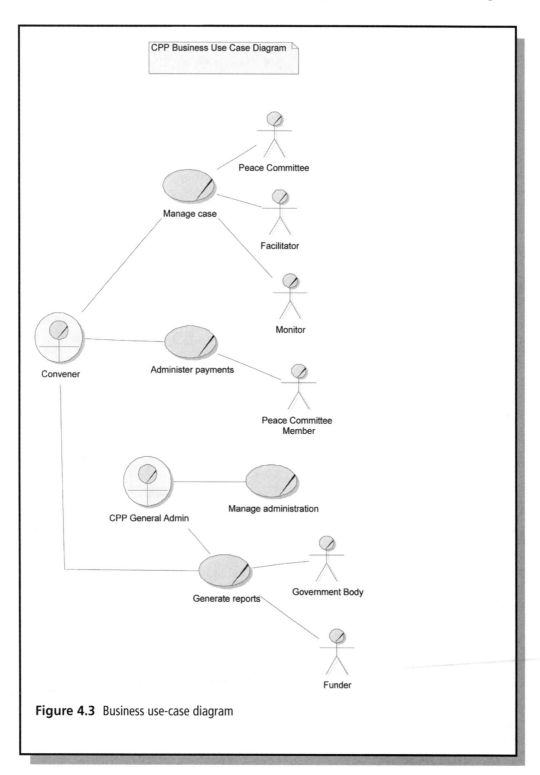

Figure 4.3 Business use-case diagram

Step 1a ii: Scope Business Use Cases (Activity Diagram)

Now that you have a business use-case diagram that matches up stakeholders with business processes, you can begin to plan the next stage of the interviews. Each interview should focus on a subset of the business use cases. Be sure to invite all stakeholders associated with the use case (as shown on the diagram) as well as off-stage stakeholders—those who do not directly interact with the process but still have a stake in it, such as regulators and high-level management.

The purpose of these interviews is to analyze the workflow of each business use case. *Workflow* means the sequencing of activities and (optionally) a clear designation of who carries out each activity. Workflow can be documented in text and/or through the use of a workflow diagram. If you are analyzing business use cases for the broad purpose of improving the business process, you may want to use a formal template for documenting the workflow. In this case, use the use-case template provided earlier in this chapter. The template is described in Chapter 5, since formal documentation is usually more critical for system use cases than for business use cases, when working on IT projects. If you are analyzing business use cases only as a means to an end—the end being the system use cases—then an informal description will probably suffice. This is the situation we are presuming for the case study.

You can use a number of diagrams to describe workflow. They are useful now, to describe business use cases, as well as later in the analysis, to describe the system use cases of the future system. Table 4.3 summarizes some of the diagrams commonly used to describe workflow.

Activity Diagrams for Describing Business Use Cases

The activity diagram is the one most useful to the IT BA for depicting workflow. It is simple to understand—both for BAs and end users. Some practitioners advocate sequence diagrams for this purpose. Despite this, don't use sequence diagrams as a BA tool: Compared to activity diagrams, they are not as readily understood by non-technical people. The best time to use sequence diagrams is during the technical design of the system, an activity that is beyond the scope of the BA.

Activity Diagram without Partitions

The following diagram describes the process *Initiate Peace Gathering*, a sub-goal of the business use case *Manage case*. *Initiate Peace Gathering* is the process of setting up a Peace Gathering to deal with a case (dispute). The diagram illustrates most of the major features of an activity diagram without partitions that are useful to the IT BA. I have added other diagrams to illustrate the remaining features.

Table 4.3   Diagrams for Depicting Workflow

Diagram	Description	Advantages	Disadvantages
System flowchart	Earliest form for depicting sequencing of activities.	■ Intuitive. Each type of input and output is clearly marked with its own symbol. ■ Includes logic symbols.	■ Not compliant with UML. ■ Can be hard to learn (many symbols).
Swimline workflow diagram	Tool used for describing process logic. UML equivalent is an activity diagram with partition.	■ Intuitive. ■ Can handle many situations in one diagram. ■ Shows who is responsible for which action (using partitions).	■ Not compliant with UML.
Sequence diagram	OO tool for describing one path (*scenario*) through a use case.	■ Part of OO standard (UML). ■ Encourages thinking in objects: Clearly specifies who does what. ■ Simplifies logic: Only one situation dealt with in each diagram. ■ Sometimes recommended for business modeling.	■ Diagramming style is often non-intuitive for Business Analysts and users. ■ Requires analyst to determine not only who carries out each activity, but who requests it.
Activity diagram	OO tool for describing logic. Used to describe entire system, a use case, or an activity within a use case. Has two versions: ■ Activity diagram without partitions: Does not show who does what. ■ Activity diagram with partitions: Shows who does what.	■ Part of OO standard (UML). ■ Can handle many situations in one diagram. ■ Intuitive. ■ Simple diagramming conventions. ■ Encourages thinking about opportunities for parallel activities (more than one activity going on at the same time).	■ Ability to handle many situations can lead to a diagram that is too complex to follow.

Activity Diagram Elements

Activity diagrams may include the following elements:

- *Initial node*: Indicates where the workflow begins.
- *Control flow*: An arrow showing the direction of the workflow.
- *Activity*: Indicates a step in the process.
- *Decision*: A diamond symbol, indicating a choice. Workflow will proceed along one of a number of possible paths, according to the guard conditions.
- *Merge*: Use this symbol if you wish to follow best practices when a number of flows lead to the same activity and your intention is that *any* of the flows would lead to the activity. Rather than terminating them at the same activity, terminate them at a merge, and draw a flow from the merge to the activity.[5] This practice is required for strict adherence to UML 2. For Business Analysis purposes, this does hinder readability, however, and you might want to consider relaxing the standard by dispensing with the merge.
- *Guard condition*: A condition attached to a control flow. When the guard condition is true, workflow may flow along the control flow. Guard conditions are usually attached to control flows that come out of a decision symbol. (However, they can also be used without the decision symbol.) A guard is shown within square brackets.
- *Event*: A trigger attached to a control flow. An event must occur for the flow to move along the control flow. Declaring something as an *event* has a stronger implication than a calling it a *guard*. An event actually *triggers* the control flow by forcing the previous activity to end, whereas a guard only governs whether a flow that was triggered for another reason (such as the completion of the previous activity) is allowed to flow along the control flow. An event is indicated without the use of square brackets.
- *Fork and join*: Bars used to document parallel activities. In the UML, parallel activities are those that may begin in any sequence—either at the same time or one before the other. A fork indicates the point after which a number of activities may begin in any order. A join indicates that workflow may commence only once the parallel activities that flow into it have all been completed.
- *Final node*: Indicates the end of the process.

---

[5]The reason for this recommendation is that, in UML 2, two incoming flows on an activity are interpreted as an implicit join, meaning that both prior activities had to have been completed.

Figure 4.4 Adding an activity diagram to a business use case

Note to Rational Rose Users

To add an activity diagram to a business use case, navigate to the business use case in the Browser window, right-click on the use-case icon, then select New/Activity Diagram, as shown in Figure 4.4.

Note that Rose does not automatically generate numbers for activities. (The numbers preceding the activity names on the diagram in Figure 4.5 were put in manually.)

To indicate guards and events in Rose, double-click on the control flow and enter the guards/events in the State Transition Specification window.

Note

The symbol that looks like a piece of paper with an end folded over is the UML *note* icon. You can use notes freely to add your own annotations to diagrams and you can tie your notes to diagramming elements as I've done in Figure 4.5.

Figure 4.6 shows the use of fork and join.

Figure 4.7 shows a control flow labeled with an event.

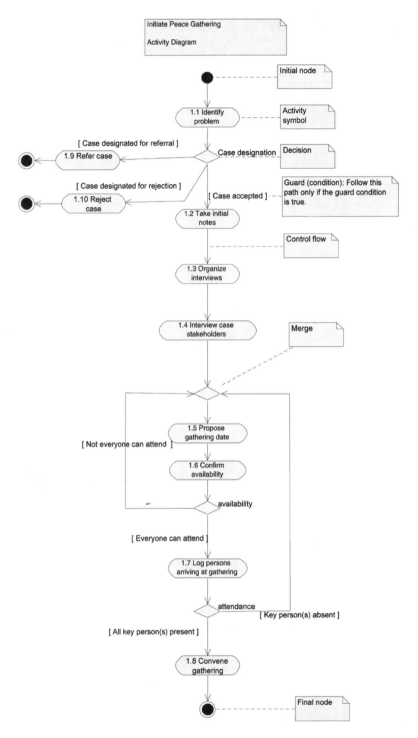

Figure 4.5 Activity diagram describing workflow for the business use case *Initiate Peace Gathering*.

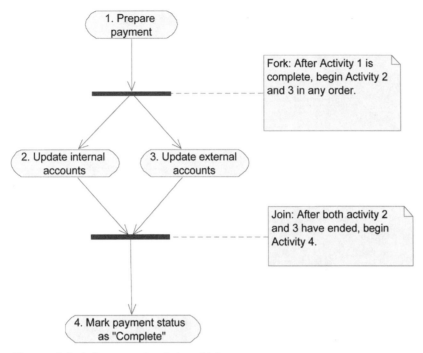

Figure 4.6 A diagram using fork and join

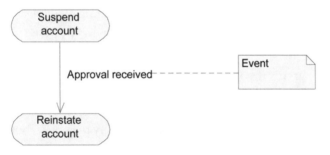

Figure 4.7 A control flow labeled with an event

Nested Activities

UML also allows you to put an entire mini–activity diagram inside an activity symbol (see Figure 4.8). The inner activities are *nested* inside the larger one.

In Figure 4.8, the initial node indicates the beginning of the activity, *organize interviews*, and the final node indicates its end.

Figure 4.8 Activities nested within an activity symbol

Object Flows

If you find the above notation communicates enough about a workflow to stakeholders, you won't need the extra notations described below. But the UML does give you the option of indicating the inputs and outputs of any activity on the diagram by adding *object flows*. (If you are a reader versed in Structured Analysis, it may help to think of object flows as the OO equivalent of the data flows in a data flow diagram.)

Add object flows to your activity diagrams if you wish to show the point at which business objects are created, changed, or required by activities. Examples of business objects that you might think of including in this way are claims, complaints, reports, invoices, and paychecks. On the activity diagram, you will not only be able to identify the object, but you can also indicate what state it'll be in at that point.

What Is a State?

Objects may be considered to be in various states during their lifetimes. For example, invoices pass through some of the following states: *Created, Due, Paid, Past 30 days, Written Off.* To find out what these states are, simply ask the stakeholders to tell you what statuses they consider a business object to be in. Anything they refer to as a *status* can generally be treated as a UML state. What makes some changes to a business object important enough to be considered changes of state? The business treats the object differently because of the change: for example, there are rules for the sequence in which the object may move in and out of the state, or the objects' response to external events differs. You'll learn more about states in the chapter that discusses state chart diagrams.

Figure 4.9 shows how object flows are depicted in the UML.

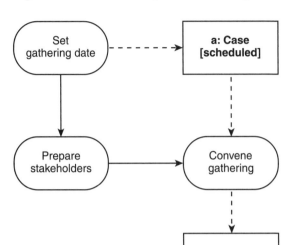

Figure 4.9 Indicating object flows on activity diagrams

Figure 4.9 indicates that the *set gathering date* activity causes a case to move into the *scheduled* state. After this, a *prepare stakeholders* activity is performed. This is followed by the *convene gathering* activity, which takes as input a case in the *scheduled* state. Once the activity has been completed, the case will be in the *resolved* state. The previous example illustrates some of the main features of object flows:

- *Object flow:* A dashed line with an open arrow-head. An object flow connects an object to an activity. When the arrow points *away* from an activity, the object flow indicates that the object (or object state) at the tip of the flow is a result (output) of the activity. When the arrow points *to* an activity, it indicates that the object at the source of the flow is required by (input to) an activity.

- *Object:* The object that is required, created, or altered by an activity. Name the object according to the format `<objectName>: <ClassName> <[statename]>`, for example, `a:Case [resolved]`. You may omit `objectName`, for example, `:Case[resolved]`. As well, you may omit the state, for example, `a:Case`.

An object may be a source or destination of an object flow, or both. One activity diagram may include objects of many classes and different objects of the same class. As well, the same object may appear more than once on an activity diagram, as in Figure 4.9.

If an activity produces an object as output, and this same object is the input for the next activity, you may omit the control flows between the two activities. In Figure 4.10, a control flow between the *set up interviews* and *interview stakeholders* activities is not required.

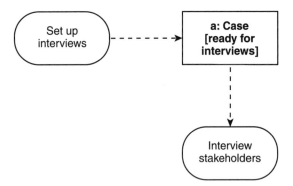

Figure 4.10 No control flow required

Figure 4.11 shows a draft of an activity diagram segment for the process *Initiate Peace Gathering*—with object flows added to indicate how a case changes its state during the process.

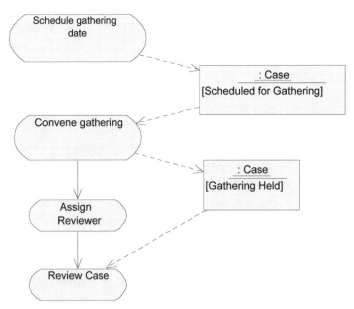

Figure 4.11 Activity diagram with object flows: draft of *Initiate Peace Gathering*

The activity diagram shown in Figure 4.11 is interpreted as follows:

- The activity, *schedule gathering date*, results in a case's state being set to *Scheduled for Gathering*.

- Next, the activity, *convene gathering*, takes a case that has been *Scheduled for Gathering* and results in it being set to the *Gathering Held* state.

- The next activity is to *assign a reviewer*.

- The next activity is to *review a case* that is in the *Gathering Held* state.

Activity Diagram with Partitions

To indicate who performs each activity, you add partitions to the activity diagram. A *partition* is a column (or row) of an activity diagram. Allocate one partition for each object that takes an active part in the process flow. Each partition represents a stakeholder (business actor or worker) that carries out some activity. Although you shouldn't spend too much time focusing on technology at this time, you may also show a computer system as a partition.

Position every activity in the partition of the object that performs it. Name each partition at the top of the column, according to the participating object, as shown in Figure 4.12.

You may use an informal, simple name for the partition, identifying the actor that carries out the task, for example, *Problem Identifier*. A better approach is to use the more formal form ⟨objectName⟩ : ⟨className⟩. className is the name of the role, that is, the worker, business actor, or external system that participates in the activities. objectName identifies a specific instance (or example) of the role. For example, *Mr. Dudu: Problem Identifier*. This format is recommended because it allows you to show the participation of more than one instance of the same actor: for example, two different *Problem Identifiers* involved in the same business case. The objectName in this format is optional. If you wish to omit it, don't forget to leave in the colon, for example, *:Peace Committee Operations*. When using a drawing tool such as Rose, the formal format has the added advantage of allowing you to conveniently name the partition by dragging actors from the browser to the partition in the diagram window.

Case Study D2: Business Use-Case Activity Diagram with Partitions

The following case study walks you through the next evolution of the CPP project. During this case study, you meet with stakeholders to discuss the workflow for two business use cases. During the meeting, you draw and revise activity diagrams in order to help stakeholders work toward a consensus regarding workflow.

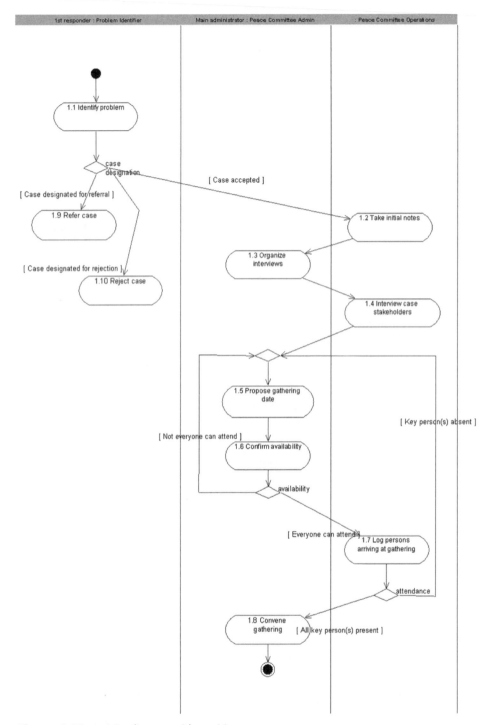

Figure 4.12 Activity diagram with partitions

Problem Statement

You've met individually with stakeholders involved in the business use cases, *Manage case* and *Administer payments,* in order to discuss workflow for these processes. Not too surprisingly, everyone has a slightly different view of how best to sequence activities, so you decide to convene a meeting to reach a consensus. In preparation for the meeting, you plan to create activity diagrams with partitions to summarize your best understanding of the workflow for these business processes. You won't be including object flows, as you wish to focus on the sequencing of the activities. You'll distribute the diagrams to interviewees before the meeting to give them a chance to preview it. During the meeting, you'll post the diagrams and make changes to them based on feedback from stakeholders.

Suggestions

Don't get uptight about creating perfect activity diagrams right off the bat. All you need is a reasonable first guess. The main value of the diagrams at this point is that they give stakeholders something concrete to bounce ideas off of. During the meeting itself, you'll come up with a consensus regarding the workflow. Following is an informal textual description of the business use cases, based on your preliminary interviews. Your immediate goal is to convert these into activity diagrams with partitions—one for each business use case.

Business Use Case: Manage Case (Dispute)

The following business use case has been written fairly informally because it is being used as a means to an end. A more formal style uses the same format as the system use-case template. For more on the formal style, including Basic and Alternate Flow sections of the template, refer to the chapter on writing system use cases.

Despite the informal style, this example does use two sections found in the formal template, *preconditions* and *postconditions.*

- A *precondition* is something that must be true before the use case begins. In the following example, a Peace Committee must already have been set up before the CPP can manage a case.
- A *postcondition* is something that will be true after the use case ends.
- A *postcondition on success* is something that will be true after the use case ends, but only if the goal (expressed in the name of the use case) is accomplished. In the example, the postcondition on success is that a case report has been prepared for the case being managed during the business use case.
- A *postcondition on failure* (not shown in the example) is a condition that will be true after the use case is over, if it ends with abandonment of the goal.

Precondition: A Peace Committee has been established in the township.

Postcondition on success (what is true after the use case completes successfully): A case report has been prepared.

Flow:

1. The Peace Committee in the area initiates a Peace Gathering.
2. The Peace Committee prepares an individual interview report for each party to the dispute.
3. Once all reports have been taken, the Facilitator summarizes the reports to the Peace Gathering.
4. The Facilitator verifies the facts in the reports with those present.
5. The Facilitator solicits suggestions from the gathering.
6. The Facilitator solicits a consensus for a plan of action.
7. If the gathering has decided to refer the case to the police, the Facilitator escorts the parties to the police station, after which the Convener prepares a case report as per Step 10.[6]
8. If, on the other hand, a consensus has been reached, the Facilitator appoints a Monitor.
9. The Monitor performs ongoing monitoring of the case to ensure its terms are being met.
10. When the deadline for monitoring has been reached, the ongoing monitoring immediately ends. At this time, if the conditions of the case have been met, the Convener prepares a case report. If the conditions have not been met, then the process begins again (return to Step 1.).

Business Use Case: Administer Payments

Precondition (what must be true before the use case begins): A case report has been prepared and submitted.

Postcondition on success(what is true after the use case completes successfully): Payments have been made to funds and to accounts of Peace Committee members involved in the case.

---

[6]The conditions described in Step 10 do not apply to cases referred to police. That is, once the parties have been escorted to the police, a case report is always prepared.

Flow:

1. The Convener reviews the case report to determine whether rules and procedures have been followed.

2. If rules and procedures have been followed:

   a. The Convener marks the case as payable.

   b. The Convener then disburses payments to the various funds and to the accounts of Peace Committee members who worked on the case.

   c. The existing Accounts Payable system actually applies the payments. (Constraint: The AP system must continue to be used for this purpose when the project is implemented.)

3. If the rules and procedures have not been followed, the Convener marks the case as non-payable.

Case Study D2: Resulting Documentation

Following are the workflow diagrams you will have created based on the previous notes. You will have included these in the preparation notes sent to each stakeholder who will be attending the interview session. During the meetings, you'll have displayed these diagrams on a flipchart, whiteboard, or projection screen and revised them based on comments from the interviewees.

Figure 4.13 is an activity diagram with partitions and describes the workflow of the business use case *Manage case.*

Figure 4.14, with partitions, describes workflow for the business use case *Administer payments.*

Next Steps

Review the diagrams with stakeholders and discuss ways that the process might be improved (if necessary) in the new system, through:

- Changes to the sequencing of activities
- Changes to which actor is responsible for each activity
- Suggestions about which of these steps to include as part of the IT automation project

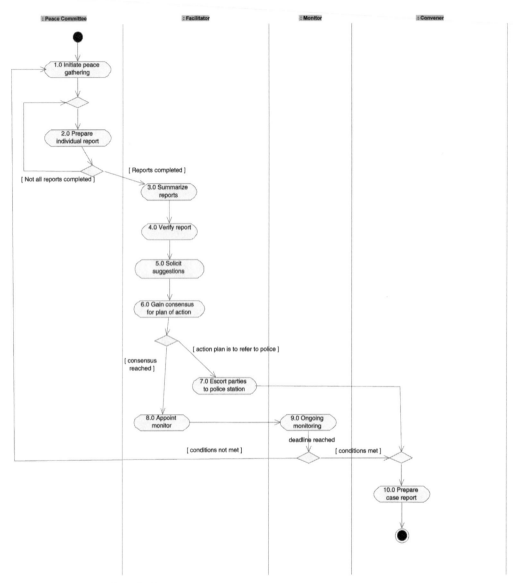

Figure 4.13 Workflow for business use case *Manage case*

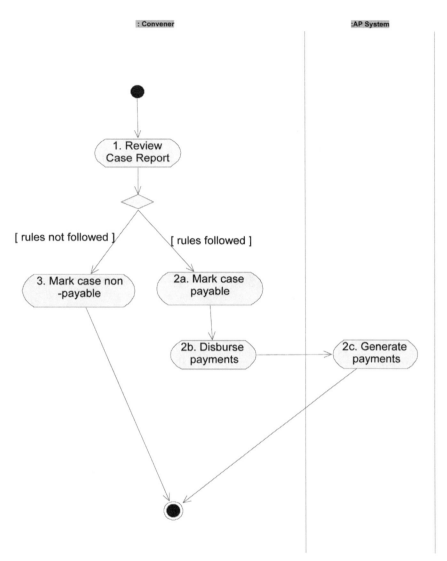

Figure 4.14 Workflow for business use case *Administer payments*

Chapter Summary

In this chapter, you learned the following concepts:

1. *Business use case*: An interaction between a stakeholder and the business, yielding a valuable result for the stakeholder; a business process.

2. *Business actor*: A stakeholder outside the business that interacts with it, such as a customer or supplier.

3. *Worker*: A stakeholder who works within the business, such as a customer service representative.

4. *Business use-case diagram*: A diagram depicting business use cases and their associations with actors.

5. *Activity diagram with partitions*: A diagram that depicts the sequencing of activities and the object that performs each activity.

6. *Activity diagram without partitions*: A diagram that depicts the sequencing of activities.

7. *Guard*: A condition that restricts flow along a transition.

8. *Control flow*: A flow line representing flow from one activity to another.

9. *Event*: A trigger that forces the end of an activity and flow along a control flow.

10. *Decision*: A diamond symbol that marks a point at which flows diverge based upon some condition.

11. *Merge*: A diamond symbol that marks a point at which flows merge. If any of the activities leading into a merge has completed, flow will continue beyond the merge. Use the merge to avoid having more than one incoming flow for an activity.

12. *Fork*: Marks a point after which parallel activities begin. Activities that are parallel may occur simultaneously or in any sequence.

13. *Join*: Marks the end of parallel activities. All parallel activities must complete before a flow moves beyond a join.

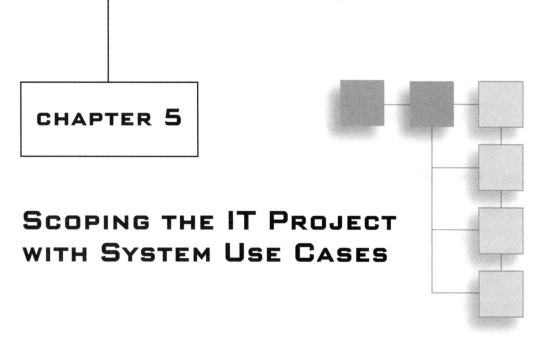

CHAPTER 5

SCOPING THE IT PROJECT WITH SYSTEM USE CASES

Chapter Objectives

By the end of this chapter, you will be able to define the boundaries of the project during the Initiation phase of the project by carrying out the following actions:

1. Initiation

　1b) Model system use cases

　　i) Identify actors (role map)

　　ii) Identify system use case packages (system use-case package diagram)

　　iii) Identify system use cases (system use-case diagram)

　1c) Begin static model (class diagrams for key business classes)

　1d) Set baseline for analysis (BRD/Initiation)

New tools and diagrams you will learn to use in this chapter:

1. Role map

2. System use-case diagram

Step 1b: Model System Use Cases

Now that you have an understanding of the end-to-end business processes, it is time to begin thinking about how the proposed IT system might help automate these processes. System use cases help you imagine the IT system from a user perspective, by focusing on the user's goals.

If the project is large, you will need to find a way to break up the work so that a number of analysts can work in parallel. First, you need to standardize common issues so that all team members handle them consistently. One of these issues is the way that users of the IT system will be documented. To address this issue, you create a diagram called a *role map*. Another issue is how to break up the user requirements into manageable pieces. You address this issue with *system use-case diagrams*.

Step 1b i: Identify Actors (Role Map)

Actors

In this step, you identify the IT system's users, or *actors*. Previously, when we spoke of actors, it was in relation to *business* use-case modeling. There we spoke of business actors and workers. From this point onward, however, we are doing *system* use-case modeling and will speak simply of actors. An actor, in this context, is a role played by a person who interacts with the IT system.

What they say:

"Actor: A construct that is employed in use cases that define a role that a user or any other system plays when interacting with the system under consideration. It is a type of entity that interacts, but which is itself external to the subject. Actors may represent human users, external hardware, or other subjects. An actor does not necessarily represent a specific physical entity. For instance, a single physical entity may play the role of several different actors and, conversely, a given actor may be played by multiple physical entities." (UML 2)

What they mean:

An actor is a type of user or an external system that interacts with the system under design.

Similar terms:

External agent/external entity. Equivalent terms used in Structured Analysis.

Stakeholder. A term more inclusive than *actor*, as it includes anyone who the project will impact even if they do not have direct contact with it.

Finding Actors

To find actors, go through your list of business actors and workers, eliminating any who don't interact with the IT system. Then add any external systems and human users who are required because of the technology. (Remember that when you performed business use case modeling, your focus was not on technology, so you may have missed some of these actors.)

FAQs about Actors

1. Why identify actors and why do it now?

   By starting with the actors, you are working toward building a system that focuses on users' needs. This is a logical step to perform now, since at this point, you need to establish a list of interviewees for eliciting the next level of requirements. The actor list gives you this.

   This step also helps you estimate the length of the analysis phase of the project. More *human actors* means more user groups to interview and a lengthier analysis. I use a ballpark figure of one day per interview—half a day to conduct the interview, the other half-day to cover preparation, analysis, and documentation. *System actors* also require increased analysis, because the interfaces to these systems need to be studied. External systems also increase the complexity of the *execution* (development) phase of the project because of the technical difficulty in getting systems to talk to each other.

   Later in the project, the actors you've identified will assist the network administrator in specifying user groups and access privileges.

2. If a user only receives reports from the system, is that user an actor?

   Yes (although there is some controversy about this question).

3. How do you handle system use cases that aren't started by anybody, but just start up automatically at a given time? Where's the actor?

   Define an actor called *Time* to act as the initiator of these use cases. (There is also controversy about this issue. Some practitioners, for example, prefer to see no actor and some prefer to see the actor who has asked that the use case be initiated at that time.)

4. If a customer calls in a request and a customer service representative (CSR) keys it in, which one is the actor?

   Only the actor who directly interacts with the computer system is considered an actor. In this case, it would be the CSR. Another option sometimes used is to name the actor *CSR for Customer*.

Stereotypes and Actors

A *stereotype* is an extension of a UML feature. Modelers can invent their own stereotypes to create extended meanings to UML model elements.

Stereotypes in the UML can be depicted either using a special symbol, such as the stick figure, or by using the regular UML symbol and including the name of the stereotype inside guillemets, as in «stereotype-name». In the case of actors, some people like to reserve the stick figure for human users and use the guillemet option for external systems. Figure 5.1 shows examples of both.

Figure 5.1 Depicting actors and stereotypes

The Role Map

A *role map* is a diagram used to standardize the treatment of users and external systems throughout the project.

A role map is a restricted form of a use-case diagram. Whereas the use-case diagram shows actors *and* their associations with use cases, the role map only shows actors. On a role map, you depict each actor using a UML icon.

Place icons for each of the actors you've identified in the role map. The role map then becomes the central diagram team members go back to whenever they want to know how to depict a user in the model. You can also use the role map to show the ways that user roles overlap.

Modeling Actors with Overlapping Roles

You document actors with overlapping roles by drawing a *generalization relationship* between actors. Any time the phrase "a kind of" comes up in the discussion of actors, think about using the generalization relationship. For example, a *Bookkeeper* and an *Accountant* are two kinds of *Accounting Staff*. Exactly how you draw the generalization depends on how the roles overlap. We'll look at two types of situations:

- Actors whose roles partially overlap
- An actor whose role completely encompasses another's

Actors with Partially Overlapping Roles

When two actors have some overlap in their roles, but each actor can do things with the system that the other can't, model the actors as specialized actors and invent an *abstract generalized actor* to represent the overlap. The term *generalized* implies that the special-ized actors inherit something from the generalized actor. In this case, the specialized actors inherit the ability to do all the things that the generalized actor can do. (Formally, the specialized actors inherit the *associations* that the generalized one has with system use cases.)

The term *abstract* means that the invented actor is not real. (In OO-speak, the abstract actor is never *instantiated*.) The generalized actor is not a true role but an abstract con-cept meant to represent the shared aspect of other roles.

Figure 5.2 shows how to depict actors with partially overlapping roles.

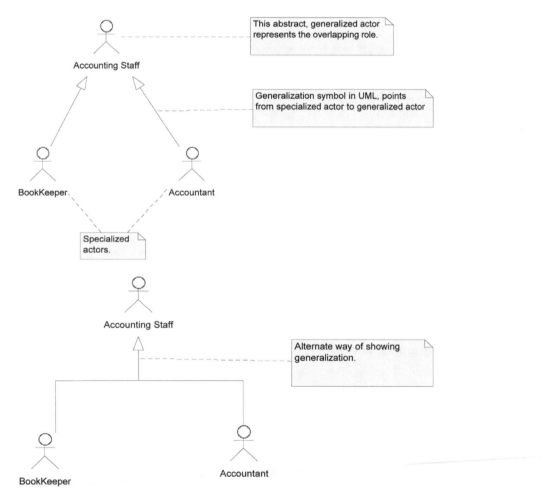

Figure 5.2 Depicting actors whose roles partially overlap

Modeling an Actor Whose Role Totally Encompasses Another's

In other cases, an actor might be able to do everything that another actor can do and more. In this situation, model the actor with the restricted role as the generalized actor, and model the actor with the larger role as the specialized actor. This may look odd at first, since the diagram tends to make the lesser role "more important." This is due to the common practice of drawing the generalized actor above the specialized actor. UML, however, does not dictate the placement of symbols on a diagram. If your users object, just draw the diagram "upside down." But make sure that the generalization symbol still points from the specialized actor to the generalized actor. Figure 5.3 shows how to depict such a relationship among actors.

Note

The generalized actor, in this case, is not an invention but a *real role*. It is therefore considered to be a *concrete* (as opposed to abstract) actor.

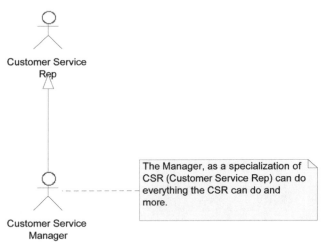

Figure 5.3 Depicting actors when one's role totally overlaps the other's

What's the Point of Defining Generalized Actors?

They simplify the drawing of use-case diagrams. Soon, you'll be creating use-case diagrams that indicate which actors are associated with each use case. If all of the specialized actors of one generalized actor are associated with the same use case, you'll be able to draw a single association line between the generalized actor and the use case instead of lines from each of the specialized actors.

Note to Rational Rose Users

To create a role map, use the following steps:

1. Expand the Use Case View (press +).
2. Right-click on the Use Case View and select New/Use Case Diagram.
3. Name the diagram *Role Map*.
4. Double-click the icon to the left of the diagram name.
5. Now add symbols from the toolbar as you need them.
6. To display an external system actor as a box instead of the usual stick figure, right-click on the actor on the diagram and select Options/ Stereotype Display/Label.

Case Study E1: Role Map

Problem Statement

You've met with stakeholders to determine which of the business actors and workers involved in business use cases will interact with the proposed IT system—either directly, by using the software, or indirectly, by receiving reports, statements, and so on, from it. Also, you've investigated the computer systems with which the proposed system needs to communicate. The results of this investigation follow. Your next step is to document your findings in a role map.

Business Actor	Interaction with Proposed System?
Peace Committee	No. (Interaction is with individual members, not with the organization.)
Peace Committee Member	Yes
Facilitator	No. (Automation begins after Facilitator's role is complete.)
Monitor	No. (Automation begins after Monitor's role is complete.)
Government Body	Yes
Funder	Yes

Worker	Interaction with Proposed System?
CPP General Admin	Yes. Role partly overlaps with Convener. (Both can generate reports.)
Convener	Yes. See above.

External System	Interaction with Proposed System?
AP System	Yes

Case Study E1: Resulting Documentation

Figure 5.4. shows the role map diagram resulting from case study E1.

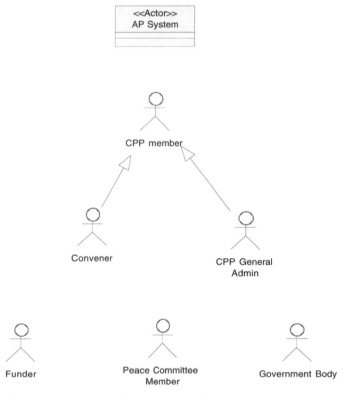

Figure 5.4 Role map for case study E1

Step 1b ii: Identify System Use-Case Packages (System Use-Case Diagram)

Managing a Large Number of Use Cases

If your project supports only one business use case, you may proceed directly to the following step, *Identify system use cases*. But if it supports a number of business use cases, consider creating system use-case packages. A *system use-case package* is a collection of system use cases and the diagrams that describe them. The UML package icon looks like (and acts similarly to) a Windows folder. By defining the packages now, you are, in effect, setting up a filing system that all members of the team will use once the analysis really gets under way.

What Criteria Are Used to Group System Use Cases into Packages?

UML does not impose any criteria, but here are some common approaches:

Group system use-cases by the main actor who uses them. For example, group together into one package all the system use cases used by General Administration.

Create a system use case package for each business use case. For example, in an insurance system, the customer sees the end-to-end process, *Make a claim*. To the customer, this represents one business goal; however, to achieve it, the company's workers require a number of discrete interactions with the computer system:

- Record claim
- Validate policy
- Adjust claim
- Pay claim

Each of these interactions qualifies as a system use case. Since they all contribute to the same high-level goal, a good way to group them is to bundle them all in the use-case package *Make a claim*.

The second option has the advantage of placing logically related system use cases together. This is the approach you'll follow as you work through the case study. Look out for system use cases that can be reused in more than one business context. Place any of those system use cases, if you find them, in special packages reserved for system use cases that transcend any one business use case. Documenting commonly used system use cases in one central place promotes reuse and consistency of treatment.

Naming Use-Case Packages

Formally, since a package is a thing—specifically, a container—then it should be named with a noun phrase. On the other hand, because of the way we are using the packages, it makes sense to name each package according to the business use case it supports. This makes tracing easier—from the business use-case model we worked on earlier to the system use-case model we are now developing. Either approach is acceptable.

Diagramming System Use-Case Packages

The diagram used to represent system use-case packages is, formally, a use-case diagram—though it looks a little odd in that it does not depict any actual use cases. Figure 5.5 shows some of the system use case packages for a credit card system and the actors who interact with them. Please note that the connecting of actors to packages, as shown in Figure 5.5, is a B.O.O.M. extension to the UML: It is not part of the standard but is a valid extension of it.

The direction of the arrow from the actor to the package indicates whether an actor initiates system use cases in the package (in which case the arrow points away from the actor) or whether the use cases initiate some action by the actor (the arrow points to the actor). Note that the arrow connecting the actors to the use-case packages is a dashed line with an open arrowhead. The dashed line indicates a *dependency*—a loose connection between modeling elements that means one element has some awareness of another one—and the arrowhead indicates the direction of the dependency. (Formally, the initiating actor is aware of system use cases in the package; in the case of non-initiating actors, it is the system that is aware of them.) You may avoid using the arrowheads but you must use the dashed line as opposed to a solid line; the UML does not allow a solid line (association) between actors and packages.

Figure 5.5 Use-case diagram showing system use-case packages and actors

This diagram indicates that a customer service representative can initiate use cases relating to card applications and that a CSR manager initiates updates to credit. In both cases, the system under design will need to be able to communicate with VERIFY (an external system that verifies the application against a person's credit record).

What If a Use-Case Package Is Connected to All of the Specialized Actors of a Generalized Actor?

Connect the package to the generalized actor. For example, suppose that VERIFY was only one of a number of systems that were able to verify a person's credit and that the system under design needed to be able to communicate with all of them. You'd indicate that as shown in Figure 5.6. (Toward the end of this book, you'll learn about another way to model this with interfaces.)

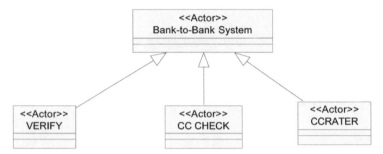

Figure 5.6 The role map updated for a system to communicate with several external systems

The use-case package diagram would now look like Figure 5.7.

In the diagram in Figure 5.7, there is no need to show the specializations of the generalized Bank-to-Bank System, since they are described in the role map shown in Figure 5.6.

Note to Rational Rose Users

To create the use-case package diagram, follow these steps:

1. Select Use Case View/Main.
2. Drag actors from the Browser window onto the diagram.
3. Create a package and dependencies using the toolbar: Select the Package tool on the toolbar, and click anywhere in the diagram window to create the package. To connect an actor to a package, select the Dependency tool on the toolbar and drag from the actor to the package or from the package to the actor, depending on which way you want the arrow to go.

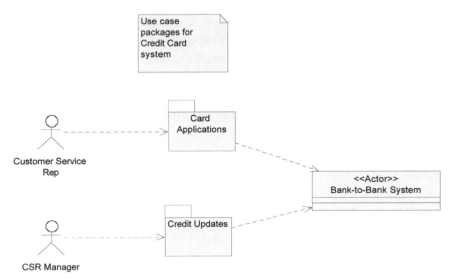

Figure 5.7 Use-case package diagram updated for a system to communicate with several external systems

Case Study E2: System Use-Case Packages

Problem Statement

Your project is large enough to justify system use-case packages. You begin by considering the business use-case model that you identified earlier. Also, you review the role map, which identifies users and external systems that interact with the IT system. (I've repeated both of these diagrams in the "Suggestions" section for convenience.) Based on these diagrams and the initial draft of the BRD, your next step is to define the system use-case packages for the project. You'll do this by creating a use-case diagram depicting actors and system use-case packages.

Suggestions

Create a system use-case package to correspond to each business use case. Figure 5.8 repeats the business use-case diagram and role map for the system.

Case Study E2: Resulting Documentation

Figure 5.9 shows the system use-case package diagram resulting from case study E2.

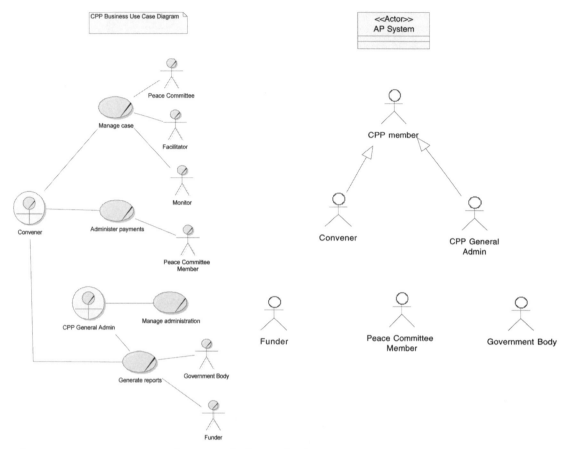

Figure 5.8 Business use-case diagram and role map for the CPP system

Note

The case study includes a *Generate Reports* system use-case package. Some analysts do not create system use cases for reports, arguing that the interaction that the user has with the computer is too trivial to warrant the use-case treatment. The arguments in favor of including report use cases are that the generation of a report is still a user goal, that a *simple* interaction is still an interaction, and that treating a report request as a use case allows the function to be managed the way other user goals are (for example, in planning what will be included in each release of the product).

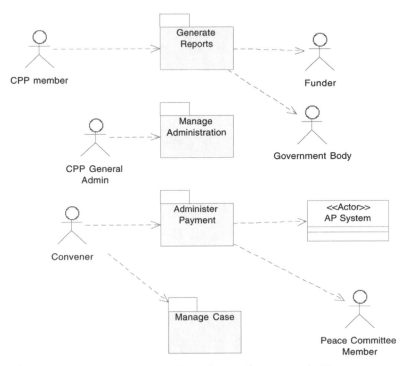

Figure 5.9 System use-case package diagram for case study E2

Step 1b iii: Identify System Use Cases (System Use-Case Diagram)

System Use Cases

The next step is to identify the system use cases that go into the packages. You do this by going back to the business use cases and reviewing the activities they describe. First try to determine, with stakeholders, which of these activities fall within the scope of the IT project. Where things are currently being done manually, you're looking for activities that could be either fully or partially automated by the IT project. Where things are being done using IT, you're looking for opportunities for improvement.

Once you've identified the activities, you'll need to group them into system use cases. Imagine the system.[1] How will someone sitting at a terminal actually use this system? What result is the user trying to achieve from the computer system with each interaction? Each of these results, expressed as a user goal, is a system use case. For example, for a Web banking system, some system use cases are *View transaction history*, *Transfer funds*, and *Pay bill*.

[1]Thanks to Tim Lloyd for introducing me to this phrase.

> Review:
>
> *System use case:* An *interaction* between an actor and a computer system.

Features of System Use Cases

A system use case is an interaction that a user (either a human or external computer system) has with the system under design. After executing a system use case, a user should be able to walk away from the terminal and feel that he or she has accomplished something of value. Purchasing stocks over the Web is a valid system use case; selecting a *From Account* is not. As a rule of thumb, use the "one user, one session" rule: Each execution of a system use case should involve only one initiating actor and should take place over a single session on the computer.

The system use-case approach involves diagrams and text. The UML provides strict rules for drawing use-case diagrams. It does not, however, standardize the writing of use-case text. Project management methodologies, such as Rational Unified Process (RUP) and books on use cases,[2] have attempted to fill the gap. (I'll discuss this further later in the book.) While textual templates for use cases differ, they are always designed in keeping with the definition of use case; they focus, therefore, on describing the *interaction* that the user has with the system, as opposed to the design. The text typically reads as a narrative: "The user does…"; "The system does…."

What Is the Purpose of Segmenting the User Requirements into System Use Cases?

System use cases become the central tool that governs the management of the project. With their user perspective, they keep the team focused on the user throughout the project. Here's how:

- *The requirements are written from the user's point of view.* Prior to use cases, requirements were often written as a list of capabilities, such as, "The system must be able to…." With system use cases, the documentation is instead written as a narrative describing the user's experience using the system.

- *System use cases help ensure that the user receives useful functionality with each release when a project is managed iteratively.* With iterative project management, the system is analyzed, designed, coded, and often released in several passes. Typically, at each pass, one or more system use cases are developed. Because each system use case achieves a meaningful goal for the user, the user is guaranteed useful functionality at the end of each iteration.

[2] A key book in this area is by Alistair Cockburn, *Writing Effective Use Cases,* 2001.

- *System use cases lead to user interfaces that are organized from a user perspective.* Most people have had experience with systems that require the user to bounce around screens or a site just to get one unit of work done. This happens because the developers have organized the user interface from their own point of view. When the interface is organized around system use cases, each option presented to the user represents a complete activity from the user's perspective.

- *System use cases yield a set of test cases that encompass the ways users use the system.* Because a system use case describes the way that an interaction plays out, it is very close to being a test script. And the way the text is typically organized, as separate "flows," makes it easy to identify test scenarios.

Modeling System Use Cases

Once you've decided what system use cases are required to support a business use case, you document your findings in a *system use-case diagram.* Create one (or more if necessary) system use-case diagram for each system use-case package.

The system use-case diagram shows which actors participate in each system use case. The diagram does *not* show sequencing; you can't tell from the diagram the order in which the system use cases should be used or the sequence of activities within each use case. (To show sequencing, use an activity diagram instead).

Figure 5.10 shows a system use-case diagram.

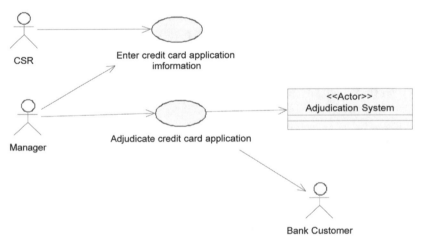

Figure 5.10 Example of a system use-case diagram

Primary actor. An actor who initiates a use-case interaction.

Secondary actor. An actor that the system initiates an interaction with, once the use case has already started.

Here's what the diagram says:

- A CSR (customer service representative) enters credit card application information.
- A Manager enters credit card application information.
- A Manager adjudicates a credit card application. The system use case, once under way, may involve an interaction with an external computer system, *Adjudication System*, for example, by requesting a maximum allowable credit limit for the customer based on application information and a credit history. The system use case may also involve an interaction with a bank customer, for example, by e-mailing the customer a letter of acceptance or rejection.

How Many Primary Actors Can a Use Case Have?

There is a difference of opinion regarding the number of primary actors use case may have. Suppose in Figure 5.10, that either a CSR or a Manager can initiate the system use case, *Enter credit card application information.* In this case, some argue that there is only one primary actor, the CSR, since the Manager would be simply acting temporarily as a CSR. What if the Manager is acting in a truly *separate* role, however, as the authorizer of information previously entered during the use case by the CSR? In that case, the Manager is documented as an additional actor for the use case. Whether the actor is primary or secondary depends on who *initiates* the interaction between the Manager and the system. If the system does—for example, by sending a request for approval to the Manager—then the Manger is a secondary actor. If the Manager does—for example by signing in and selecting the case for review—then the Manager is a primary actor. Having said this, be aware that this issue is controversial. Some analysts use multiple actors to mean that *either* one or the other may interact with the use case, while others take multiple actors to mean that all the actors are involved (in different capacities). The important thing is to set a standard for your organization and follow it consistently.

To draw a system use-case diagram, follow these steps:

1. Copy all of the actors connected to the package in the main use-case package diagram onto the new diagram. This will ensure that you don't forget any actors.
2. Draw a system use-case symbol (an oval) to represent each user goal within the package.
3. Connect the actors to the use cases using the UML *association* symbol: a solid line that may, if desired, be *adorned* (as UML puts it) with an open arrowhead. The following steps explain the rules for drawing the association.

4. Connect an actor to a system use case if the actor participates in any way while the use case plays out. If all you can say at this time is that the actor participates *somehow*, use a solid line.

5. If the actor *initiates* the system use case, draw an arrow that points from the actor to the use case. This designates the actor as a *primary actor* for the use case. Note that the direction of the arrow indicates who initiated the interaction (it always points away from the initiator). The arrow does not indicate the direction of the data. For example, a user initiates a query transaction. The arrow points away from the actor even though the data moves from the system to the actor.

6. If the actor gets involved only after the system use case has already begun, draw the arrow from the use case to the actor. In this case, it is the system (of which the use case is a part) that has initiated the interaction with the actor. This type of actor is termed a *secondary actor*.

7. If several possible actors may initiate the system use case, connect all of them to the use case as primary actors. This does not break the "one initiating actor" rule. In any particular execution of the system use case, only one of these primary actors is involved. (Keep in mind, however, the controversy around this issue: Some interpret two primary actors to mean that *both* must be involved, as opposed to the interpretation of this book, that *either* may be involved.) You may also designate more than one secondary actor for the use case, if appropriate.

8. If all of the specialized actors of a generalized actor participate with the use case, draw an association between the generalized actor and the use case. It implies association with the specializations.

Is There a Rule of Thumb for How Many System Use Cases a Project Should Have?

No. Ivar Jacobson recommends about 20 use cases for a 10 person-year[3] project. Martin Fowler reports about 100 use cases for a project of the same size.[4]

Keep in mind that one reason for splitting requirements into system use cases is to assist *the planning of releases.* Try to size the system use cases so that you can roll out one or more complete system use cases in each release.[5]

---

[3]10 person-years means the number of people multiplied by the number of years that each one works = 10; for example, 1 person working 10 years or 10 people each working 1 year.

[4]Martin Fowler, *UML Distilled*, 1997, p. 51.

[5]Releasing complete system use cases in each iteration helps simplify the management of the project, but is not a hard-and-fast rule. You may decide, for example, to release only select flows (pathways) of a use case in a particular iteration.

Note to Rational Rose Users

To begin a system use-case diagram, follow these steps:

1. Navigate in the Browser window to Use Case View/ Main and select the Main diagram. This is the diagram that should, at this point, depict the system use-case packages and the actors who use them.

2. Select (double-click on) one of the package symbols on the diagram. Rose will open up a new diagram specifically for this package.

3. Drag the actors who participate in the use cases from the Browser window into the new diagram.

4. Use the "use-case" tool of the diagram toolbar to create new system use cases.

5. Add the following tools of they are not already on the toolbar: *association* (unadorned solid line) and *unidirectional association* (solid line with open arrow). To add a tool, right-click on the toolbar, select *Customize*, find the tool among the available toolbar buttons, and select *Add*.

6. Use the *association* tool to connect an actor to a system use case if you are not sure if it is primary or secondary. If you do know, use the *unidirectional association* tool to draw the appropriate arrow between the actor and the system use case.

Case Study E3: System Use-Case Diagrams

A) Manage Case

You have just conducted a meeting with stakeholders to discuss the business use case, *Manage case.* You've circulated the following business use-case description and activity diagram to attendees.

Business Use Case: Manage Case *(Dispute)*

Postcondition on success (what is true after the use case completes successfully): A case report has been prepared.

Flow:

1. The Peace Committee in the area initiates a Peace Gathering.

2. The Peace Committee prepares an individual interview report for each party to the dispute.

3. Once all reports have been taken, the Facilitator summarizes the reports to the Peace Gathering.

4. The Facilitator verifies the facts in the reports with those present.

5. The Facilitator solicits suggestions from the gathering.

6. The Facilitator solicits a consensus for a plan of action.

7. If the gathering has decided to refer the case to the police, the Facilitator escorts the parties to the police station, after which the Convener prepares a case report as per Step 10.[6]

8. If, on the other hand, a consensus has been reached, the Facilitator appoints a monitor.

9. The monitor performs ongoing monitoring of the case to ensure its terms are being met.

10. When the deadline for monitoring has been reached, the ongoing monitoring immediately ends. At this time, if the conditions of the case have been met, the Convener prepares a case report. If the conditions have not been met, then the process begins again (return to Step 1).

Figure 5.11 shows the diagram that results from this flow.

Here's how the interview progresses from that point:

You ask stakeholders how much of this process can be automated. They tell you that there is no budget for automation in the communities themselves, but only at the head office. They clarify that a case moves out of the community to the head office when the Convener performs the activity *Prepare case report.*

Next, you ask users to rephrase this activity as a goal they would be trying to achieve through their interaction with the IT system. They say that the goal would be to update case information; that is, to open up a new case and later to add information about the case if necessary. Accordingly, you name the system use case *Update case.*

B) Administer Payments

Next, you discuss the *Administer payments* business use case with the users. The following is the document, extracted from the Business Requirements Document, that you've circulated, describing the process.

Figure 5.12 shows the diagram that results from this flow.

---

[6]The conditions described in Step 10 do not apply to cases referred to police. That is, once the parties have been escorted to the police, a case report is always prepared.

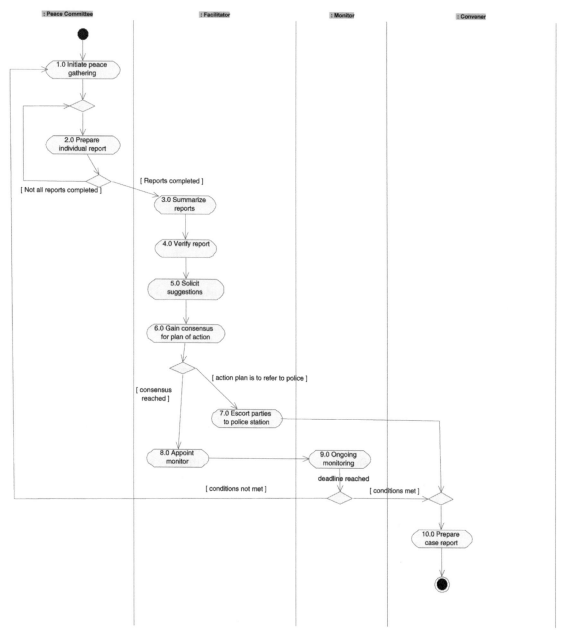

Figure 5.11 Activity diagram for business use case *Manage case*

Business Use Case: Administer Payments

Precondition (what must be true before the use case begins): A case report has been submitted.

Postcondition on success (what is true after the use case completes successfully): Payments have been made to funds and to accounts of Peace Committee members involved in the case.

Flow:

1. The Convener reviews the case report to determine whether rules and procedures have been followed.
2. If rules and procedures have been followed:
   a. The Convener marks the case as payable.
   b. The Convener then disburses payments to the various funds and to the accounts of Peace Committee members who worked on the case.
   c. The existing Accounts Payable (AP) system actually applies the payments. (Constraint: The AP system must continue to be used for this purpose when the project is implemented.)
3. If the rules and procedures have not been followed, the Convener marks the case as non-payable.

Once again, you have a discussion with the stakeholders about automation. You learn that, as originally scoped, the project will not incorporate the actual generation of payments; these will remain the responsibility of the existing AP system. However, the new system will need to interface with the AP system. Also, the new system should be able to assist the Convener in performing all of the other steps in the process.

Next you ask stakeholders to group the activities, thinking of what they would expect to accomplish in each session with the computer. You learn that the process of reviewing a case and marking it as payable or non-payable is all part of the same user goal and would happen best as one session. Stakeholders imagine a Convener reviewing a case and marking it, then moving on to the next case, and so on.

They envision a separate session for disbursing the payments for cases that have earlier been deemed payable. The transactions will be sent to the AP system at that time.

This yields the following use cases:

- Review case
- Disburse payments

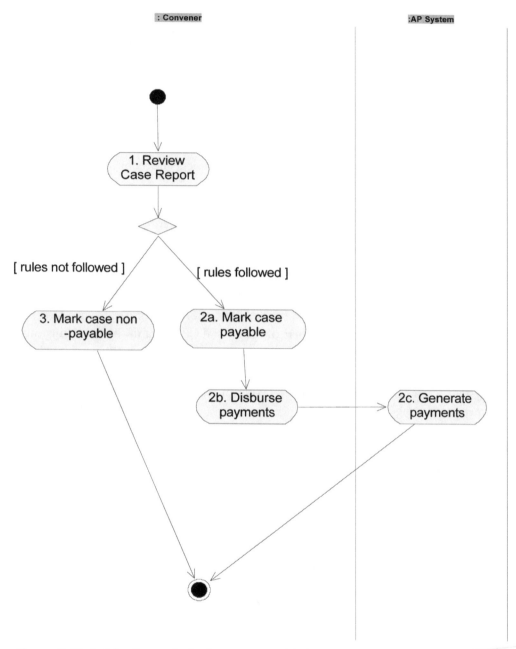

Figure 5.12 Activity diagram for business use case *Administer payments*

Note how this meeting, focused on system use cases, really keeps you in tune with the users' experience; this is the main point of the use-case approach.

C) Other Business Use Cases

In similar meetings regarding the other business use cases, you've identified the following system use cases.

Generate reports package:

- *Generate funder reports:* initiated by any CPP member. The reports are sent to the Funders.
- *Generate government reports:* initiated by any CPP member. The reports are sent to a Government Body. (This is as specific as the stakeholders can be at this time.)

Manage administration package:

- *Update Peace Committees:* initiated by the CPP General Administrator to add or update information on the Peace Committees located in the communities.
- *Update CPP Member List:* initiated by the CPP General Administrator to add or update information about members of the central CPP organization, working out of the head office.
- *Set system parameters:* initiated by the CPP General Administrator to "tweak" the system. Such parameters would include one-time setup operations as well as parameters affecting performance.

Your Next Step

Create system use-case diagrams that summarize what you learned in the meeting. You'll present these during the meeting as a way of summarizing your conclusions. Later, these diagrams will serve to direct the next phase of the project, Analysis.

Case Study E3: Resulting Documentation

Figure 5.13 shows the diagrams resulting from case study E3.

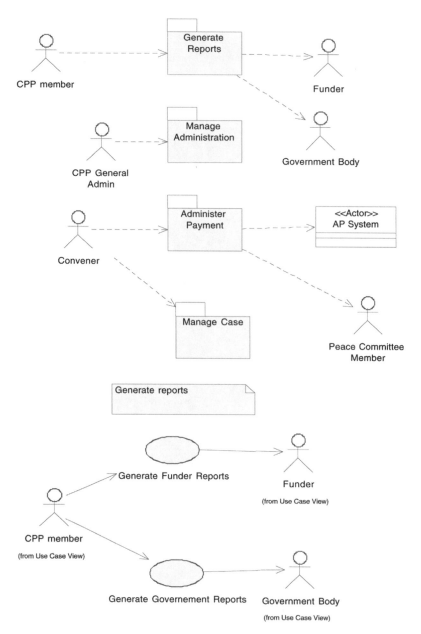

Figure 5.13 Use-case diagram depicting CPP system use-case packages and actors

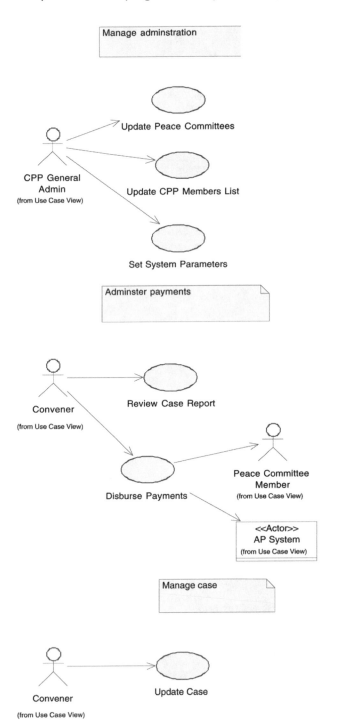

Figure 5.13 Use-case diagram depicting CPP system use-case packages and actors (continued)

Step 1c: Begin Static Model (Class Diagrams for Key Business Classes)

As you've worked through the initiation of the project, business terms such as "case" and "peace gathering" have come up. Now is an appropriate time to begin formally defining these business concepts and their relationships to each other. You do this by beginning the static model—drawing class diagrams for the main business classes. You'll explore static analysis in Chapter 8, which is devoted to the topic. But just to give you an idea of what you might expect to see at this point of time, Figure 5.14 shows a class diagram describing some of the main business classes that have come up during the Initiation phase.

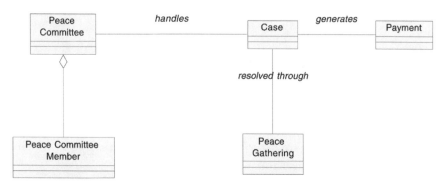

Figure 5.14 A class diagram describing several business classes discovered during Initiation

Don't be perturbed if you have trouble with this diagram right now; I've included it here only to provide context. Here's what it means:

- A Peace Committee handles a case.[7]
- A case is resolved through peace gatherings.
- A case generates payment(s).
- A Peace Committee consists of Peace Committee members.

Other information, such as the number of payments per case, can also be added to the static model at this stage.[8] Since this is still early in the project, expect changes to be made to the static model as the project progresses.

---

[7] The diagram as shown has an ambiguity regarding the direction in which it should be read. For example, it either states that a Peace Committee *handles* a Case or a Case *handles* a Peace Committee. In practice, many BAs do not worry about this, since the statement usually only makes sense in one direction. However, the UML does allow for a solid triangular arrowhead to be placed next to the association name (*handles*) to indicate the direction it should be read. More on this in Chapter 8.

[8] This type of requirement is termed a *multiplicity* in the UML. You'll learn more about multiplicity in Chapter 8.

Step 1d: Set Baseline for Analysis (BRD/Initiation)

Once the initiation phase of the project is over, you need to "baseline" your analysis. This simply means saving the state of the analysis at this point and putting it under change control. By baselining your documentation, you'll be able to check later, if changes are requested, to see whether or not they represent a change from the original scope of the project. The analysis also becomes the starting point for the next phase of the project, Analysis.

Chapter Summary

In this chapter, you completed the Initiation phase of the project by identifying and modeling the system use cases. These system use cases will now drive the rest of the analysis and development effort.

New tools and concepts introduced in this chapter include the following:

1. *Actors*: Roles, organizations or systems that use or are used by the system.
2. *Role map*: A diagram indicating actors and their relationships to each other.
3. *Use-case package*: A container that holds use cases.
4. *System use-case diagram*: A diagram describing the system use cases (uses to which the IT system will be put) and the actors who interact with them.

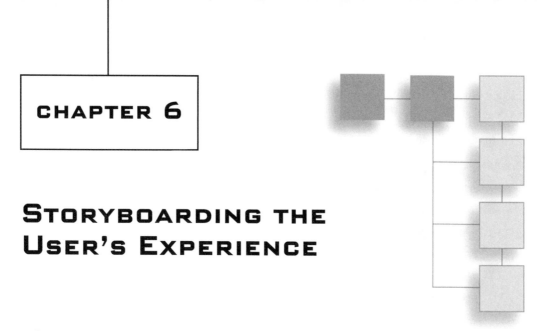

CHAPTER 6

STORYBOARDING THE USER'S EXPERIENCE

Chapter Objectives

Now that you've defined the scope of the project, you're ready to take your project "into analysis." There are various aspects to analysis. In this and the coming chapter, you'll learn how to analyze the dynamic aspects of the system in action.

You'll be able to carry out these B.O.O.M. steps:

2. Analysis

   2a) Dynamic analysis

      i) Describe system use cases (use-case description)

Tools and concepts you'll learn to use in this chapter include

- Use-case description template
- Review: activity diagram
- Decision table
- Decision tree
- Condition/response table
- Advanced use-case features

Step 2: Analysis

The Analysis phase of the project is the one that takes up most of a Business Analyst's time. Its objective is to discover and document the requirements of the proposed system. The central product of this step, the completed BRD, acts as a contract between the business and the developers. If a requirement is not in the BRD, it's not part of the contract, so it's essential to ensure that during Analysis you document all necessary requirements completely, correctly, and unambiguously. This and the following chapter will take you through a process to help you do just that.

The Analysis phase involves a number of steps:

2. Analysis

    2a) Perform dynamic analysis

        i) Describe system use cases (use-case description)

        ii) Describe state behavior (state machine diagram)

    2b) Perform static analysis (object/data model) (class diagram)

    2c) Specify testing (test plan/decision tables)

    2d) Specify implementation plan (implementation plan)

    2e) Set baseline for development (BRD/analysis)

This chapter deals with step 2a i, "Describe system use cases (use-case description template).

Step 2a i: Describe System Use Cases

At the end of the Initiation phase, you identified system use cases in the BRD. This version was baselined for Step 2: Analysis. By baselining the BRD, you ensured that you have a reference point to go back to. Updates to the BRD during Analysis are made on a new working version.

For your first changes, review the list of system use cases. If needs have changed or you have learned further information, update the system use-case diagrams and related text in the BRD. Once you've settled on a list of system use cases, your next step is to investigate and document each one thoroughly.

Deliverables of Step 2a i: Describe Use Cases

1. The BRD template contains a section for system use-case diagrams. These diagrams are updated.

2. The BRD has a section called "System Use-Case Descriptions."[1] For each system use case that appears in the system use-case diagrams, a use-case description is added that includes a completed use-case description template. The text documentation may be augmented with any of the following:

    ▪ Activity diagrams

    ▪ Decision tables

[1]The other is Project-Wide State Diagrams.

- Decision trees
- Other related artifacts containing supplementary documentation

The Use-Case Description Template

The UML, as we've learned, doesn't have a lot to say about text. The following template fills that gap, by incorporating industry best practices. If you are working for an organization that doesn't have a template, use this as your starting point, but customize it as time goes on. If you already have a template, compare it to the following template. You may find features you'd like to add.

Keep one thing in mind when using this or any other template: Its main value is as a way to institutionalize best practices in your organization. You should customize it as time goes on, based on what works for you. As an example, this template requires the BA to keep detailed rules about field verification out of the use case proper; these rules are documented in class diagrams or in a data dictionary instead. But one organization I've worked with found that it couldn't get its developers to cross-reference: if a rule was not explicitly stated in the use case, it wasn't implemented in the software. Consequently the organization decided to include such rules in its use cases. Remember that whatever choices you make, there is only one yardstick:

Does it work?

The Fundamental Approach Behind the Template

The underlying principle of this template is to describe workflow using a simple narrative style that avoids complex logic. The trick to keeping things simple is to handle variations in a separate area of the document rather than in one all-encompassing section. First, you document a normal, typical interaction in a section called the *basic flow*. Next, you describe alternative success scenarios in an *alternate flows* section. Finally, you describe error handling as *exceptional flows*.

Use-Case Description Template

1. *Use Case:* (the use-case name as it appears on system use-case diagrams)
   Perspective: Business use case/system use case
   Type: Base use case/extension/generalized/specialized
   1.1 Brief Description
       (Briefly describe the use case in approximately one paragraph.)
   1.2 Business Goals and Benefits
       (Briefly describe the business rationale for the use case.)

1.3 Actors

    1.3.1 Primary Actors
       (Identify the users or systems that initiate the use case.)

    1.3.2 Secondary Actors
       (List the users or systems that receive messages from the use case. Include users who receive reports or on-line messages.)

    1.3.3 Off-Stage Stakeholders
       (Identify non-participating stakeholders who have interests in this use case.)

1.4 Rules of Precedence

    1.4.1 Triggers
       (Describe the event or condition that "kick-starts" the use case: such as *User calls Call Center*; *Inventory low*. If the trigger is time-driven, describe the temporal condition, such as *end-of-month*.)

    1.4.2 Preconditions
       (List conditions that must be true before the use case begins. If a condition *forces* the use case to occur whenever it becomes true, do not list it here; list it as a trigger.)

1.5 Postconditions

    1.5.1 Postconditions on Success
       (Describe the status of the system after the use case ends successfully. Any condition listed here is guaranteed to be true on successful completion.)

    1.5.2 Postconditions on Failure
       (Describe the status of the system after the use case ends in failure. Any condition listed here is guaranteed to be true when the use case fails as described in the exception flows.)

1.6 Extension Points
   (Name and describe points at which extension use cases may extend this use case.)
   Example of extension point declaration:

    1.6.1 Preferred Customer: 2.5-2.9

1.7 Priority

1.8 Status
   Your status report might resemble the following example:
   Use-case brief complete: 2005/06/01
   Basic flow + risky alternatives complete: 2005/06/15
   All flows complete: 2005/07/15
   Coded: 2005/07/20
   Tested: 2005/08/10
   Internally released: 2005/09/15
   Deployed: 2005/09/30

1.9 Expected Implementation Date

1.10 Actual Implementation Date

1.11 Context Diagram
(Include a system use-case diagram showing this use case, all its relationships [includes, extends, and generalizes] with other use cases and its associations with actors.)

2. Flow of Events

Basic Flow

2.1 (Insert basic flow steps.)

Alternate Flows

2.Xa (Insert the alternate flow name.)
(The alternate flow name should describe the condition that triggers the alternate flow. "2.X" is step number in basic flow where interruption occurs. Describe the steps in paragraph or point form.)

Exception Flows

2.Xa (Insert the exception flow name.)
(The flow name should describe the condition that triggers the exception flow. An exception flow is one that causes the use case to end in failure and for which "postconditions on failure" apply. "2.X" is step number in basic flow where interruption occurs. Describe the steps in paragraph or point form.)

3. Special Requirements
(List any special requirements or constraints that apply specifically to this use case.)

3.1 Nonfunctional Requirements
(List requirements not visible to the user during the use case—security, performance, reliability, and so on.)

3.2 Constraints
(List technological, architectural, and other constraints on the use case.)

4. Activity Diagram
(If it is helpful, include an activity diagram showing workflow for this system use case, or for select parts of the use case.)

5. User Interface
(Initially, include description/storyboard/prototype only to help the reader visualize the interface, not to constrain the design. Later, provide links to screen design artifacts.)

6. Class Diagram
(Include a class diagram depicting business classes, relationships, and multiplicities of all objects participating in this use case.)

7. Assumptions
(List any assumptions you made when writing the use case. Verify all assumptions with stakeholders before sign-off.)

8. Information Items
   (Include a link or reference to documentation describing rules for data items that relate to this use case. Documentation of this sort is often found in a data dictionary. The purpose of this section and the following sections is to keep the details out of the use case proper, so that you do not need to amend it every time you change a rule.)

9. Prompts and Messages
   (Any prompts and messages that appear in the use case proper should be identified by name only, as in *Invalid Card Message*. The *Prompts and Messages* section should contain the actual text of the messages or direct the reader to the documentation that contains text.)

10. Business Rules
    (The "Business Rules" section of the use-case documentation should provide links or references to the specific business rules that are active during the use case. An example of a business rule for an airline package is "Airplane weight must never exceed the maximum allowed for its aircraft type." Organizations often keep such rules in an automated business rules engine or manually in a binder.)

11. External Interfaces
    (List interfaces to external systems.)

12. Related Artifacts
    (The purpose of this section is to provide a point of reference for other details that relate to this use case, but would distract from the overall flow. Include references to artifacts such as decision tables, complex algorithms, and so on.)

Documenting the Basic Flow

The basic flow describes the most common way that the use case plays out successfully. (Some people call it the "happy scenario.") It reads as a straightforward narrative: "The user does…; the system does…." As a rule of thumb, the basic flow should not list any conditions, since subsequent sections handle all errors and alternatives. To keep documentation consistent, employ a style guideline throughout your company for writing use-case requirements.

Use-Case Writing Guidelines

The following guidelines are compiled from standards that I have seen in practice. The template and case study adopt the numbering scheme proposed by Alistair Cockburn.[2]

---

[2] Alistair Cockburn, "Writing Effective Use Cases," Addison-Wesley, 2001.

Many other schemes are used in the industry for numbering requirements, including the practice of not numbering them at all.[3]

1. Tell a story: Write sentences that describe the unfolding narrative of the user's interaction with the system.

2. Use a simple subject-verb-object sentence structure.

3. Use a consistent tense (present or future tense).

4. Each step should contain one testable, traceable requirement.

5. Keep the number of steps in a flow small (maximum 9 to 25 steps).

6. Minimize the use of the word "if." Use alternate and exception flows instead.

7. Handle validations by writing, in the basic flow, "The system validates that…." Describe what happens when the validation fails in the alternate or exception flows.

8. Merge data fields and use the merged data name in the use case. For example, use the merged field *Contact Information* rather than the individual fields *Name*, *Address*, and *Phone Number*. Describe merged fields elsewhere. (See the "Information Items" section of the template, which links to an external document, such as the data dictionary.)

9. Do not describe the interface design within the use case. Describe the workflow only; document design details elsewhere.

10. Document the sequencing of each step clearly and consistently. For example: One step follows the other:

    2.1 User provides contact information.

    2.2 System validates user input.

    A group of steps can be triggered in any sequence:

    Steps 20 through 30 can happen in any order.

    A step is triggered at any time during a set of basic flow steps:

    At any time between Steps 7 and 9, the user may…

    Steps can be made optional:

    Steps 5 through 7 are optional.

    -OR-

    Describe optional steps in the alternate flow section (recommended).

11. Establish a standard for documenting repetitive steps:

    1 User selects payee.

    2 System displays accounts and balances.

---

[3]Some templates use named labels to avoid extensive renumbering every time the use case is amended.

    3. User selects account and provides payment amount.

    4. System validates that funds are available.

    User repeats Steps 1 through 4 until indicating end of session.

12. Standardize triggers to external systems.
The user has the system query the account balance from Interac (and does not wait for a response).

13. Label the requirements. Use a numbering scheme or text labels. (In the case study, you'll be using numbers to label the requirements.)

14. Keep the focus on the flow. Exclude anything that would distract the reader from the narrative. Document other details elsewhere, and refer to them from the use case.

Basic Flow Example: CPP System Review Case Report

1. The system displays a list of resolved cases that have not been reviewed.

2. The user selects a case.

[Steps 3 and 4 refer the reader to 12.1, a decision table that describes the rules for paying a case.]

3. The system validates that the case is payable. (12.1)

4. The system determines the payment amount. (12.1)

5. The system marks the case as payable.

6. The system records the payment amount.

7. The system checks the Cash fund records to ensure that adequate funds exist.

    7.1 No funds shall be removed from the cash fund or disbursed at this time.

8. The system records the fact that the case has been reviewed.

    [...]

12. Other Related Artifacts

(The purpose of this section is to provide a point of reference for details that relate to this use case, but would distract from the overall flow. Include references to artifacts such as decision tables, complex algorithms, and so on.)

12.1 Case Payment Decision Table: [link to table]

Documenting Alternate Flows

Document each scenario not covered in the basic flow as an *alternate flow* or as an *exception flow*. An alternate flow is a variation that does not lead to abandonment of the user goal; an exception flow involves a non-recoverable error. If your team has trouble deciding whether to list a scenario in the alternate or exception flow sections, merge the two sections into one and list both types of flows there.

Alternate flow: A scenario, other than the basic flow, that leads to success. An alternate flow may deal with a user error as long as it is recoverable. Non-recoverable errors are handled as exception flows.

Typical Alternate Flows

1. The user selects an alternative option during a basic flow step: for example, "User requests same day delivery."
2. The user selects a tool icon at any time during the use case; for example, "User selects spell-checking."
3. A condition regarding the internal state of the system becomes true; for example, "Item out of stock."
4. Recoverable data entry errors are identified. For example, the basic flow states, "The System validates withdrawal amount"; the alternate flow reports, "Funds are low."

Alternate Flow Documentation

There are a number of issues you'll need to clarify for each flow.

Trigger: The event or condition that causes the process to be diverted from the basic flow.

Divergence point: The point within the basic flow from which the process jumps to the alternate flow.

Convergence point: The point at which the process returns to the basic flow.

The following standard for naming alternate flows is advocated by Cockburn. It is not important that you use this particular standard, but it *is* important that you standardize the way you treat each of the issues described below.

Trigger: Use the triggering event to name the flow.

Example: Inventory low.

Divergence point: If the flow diverges from a *specific* step of the basic flow, use the basic flow number, and append "a" for the first alternate flow off of it, "b" for the second, and so on. For example:

> *Basic flow:*
>
> > 3. The system validates that the case is payable.
>
> *Alternate flow:*
>
> > 3a) Cash funds low but sufficient:
> >
> > > 1. The system marks the case as payable.
> > > 2. The system displays the low funds warning. (See "Prompts and Messages.")

If the flow may be triggered during a *range of steps* in the basic flow, specify the range and append an "a" for the first alternate flow off of the range, "b" for the second, and so on. For example:

> *Basic flow:*
>
> > 3. The system validates that the case is payable.
> > 4. The systems marks the case as payable.
>
> *Alternate flow:*
>
> > 3-4a. User selects option to add note:
> >
> > > 1. The user adds a note to the case.

If the flow may be triggered at any time during the basic flow, specify "*a" for the first such scenario, "*b" for the second, and so on. For example:

> *Alternate flow:*
>
> > *a. User selects save option:
> >
> > > 1. The system saves all updates made to the case in a draft folder.

Convergence point: Clearly indicate how the flow returns back to the basic flow. For example, use the following convention: If the flow returns to the step following the divergence point, do not indicate a convergence point (it's understood); otherwise, write "Continue at Step *x*."

Example of Use Case with Alternate Flows: CPP System/Review Case Report

Basic flow:

1. The system displays a list of resolved cases that have not been reviewed.
2. The user selects a case.

3. The system validates that the case is payable.

4. The system determines the payment amount.

5. The system marks the case as payable.

6. The system records the payment amount.

7. The system checks the cash fund records to ensure that adequate funds exist.

   7.1. No funds shall be removed from cash fund or disbursed at this time.

8. The system records the fact that the case has been reviewed.

Alternate flows:

> 3a. Non-payable case:
>
>> 1. The system marks the case as non-payable.
>>
>> 2. The user confirms the non-payable status of the case.
>>
>> 3. Continue at Step 8.
>
> 7a. Cash funds low but sufficient:
>
>> 1. The system marks the case as payable.
>>
>> 2. The system displays the low funds warning. (See "Prompts and Messages.")

Documenting an Alternate of an Alternate

What if there are alternate ways that an alternate flow step could play out? Document these the same way that you documented the original alternate flows. For example, suppose that in the preceding case, you want to give the user the option of overriding the non-payable status at Step 3a.2. The system use case would now read:

Basic flow:

1. The system displays a list of resolved cases that have not been reviewed.

2. The user selects a case.

3. The system validates that the case is payable.

4. The system determines the payment amount.

5. The system marks the case as payable.

6. The system records the payment amount.

7. The system checks the cash fund records to ensure that adequate funds exist.

   7.1. No funds shall be removed from cash fund or disbursed at this time.

8. The system records the fact that the case has been reviewed.

Alternate flows:

   3a. Non-payable case:

      1. The system marks the case as non-payable.

      2. The user confirms the non-payable status of the case.

      3. Continue at Step 8.

   3a.2a. User overrides non-payable status:

      1. The user indicates that the case is to be payable and enters a reason for the override.

      [. . .]

   7a. Cash funds low but sufficient:

      1. The system marks the case as payable.

      2. The system displays the low funds warning. (See "Prompts and Messages.")

Documenting Exception Flows

List each error condition that leads to abandonment of the user goal in the *exception flows*. Typical exception flows include cancellation of a transaction by the user and system errors that force a transaction to be canceled. Documentation rules are the same as for the alternate flows except that there is often no convergence point, since the goal is abandoned. In that case, the last line of the flow should read, "The use case ends in failure."

Guidelines for Conducting System Use-Case Interviews

Now that you have a solid idea of what the flows look like, let's put it all together in the context of an interview:

1. Ask interviewees to describe the basic flow.

2. Go through the basic flow, step by step, and ask if there is any other way each step could play out. List each of these as an alternate or exception flow, but don't let the interview veer off into the details of what happens within each of these flows. Your aim at this point is merely to list the flows.

3. Ask interviewees if there are any alternatives or errors that could happen *at any time* (as opposed to at a specific step) during the basic flow. Add these to the alternate or exception flows.

4. Now that you have a comprehensive list, ask interviewees to describe each flow in detail.

5. Finally, go over each of the steps in the alternate and exception flows, asking if there are any other ways those steps could play out.

Activity Diagrams for System Use Cases

The basic, alternate, and exception flows do an excellent job of describing scenarios—one at a time. If you'd like to clarify how all the flows fit together, consider using an activity diagram as a supplement to the use-case description. It clearly depicts the logic for all situations in a single picture. You draw the diagram using the same conventions you used earlier when describing business use cases.

Related Artifacts

The template contains a number of sections that point the reader to other artifacts related to the use case. For example, there are sections on *user interface, prompts and messages, business rules, class diagrams, information items,* and a catch-all *related artifacts* for anything else not included in the other sections. The point of these sections is to give you a convenient place to refer to details that are relevant to the use case, but that would distract from the overall flow. For example, at a particular point in a use case, the system may need to adjudicate a request for a credit limit increase. If the use case were to include the complex rules for doing that right in the flows, the details would distract from the narrative. The solution of the template is to describe these details in another artifact and refer to it from the use case. The flow step refers to the line number in the template where the artifact is described.

For example, in the system use case, *review case report,* there were a couple of references to a decision table.

Basic flow:

> The system determines the payment amount. (12.1)
>
> The system determines the payment amount. (12.1)

> 12. Other Related Artifacts:
>
> 12.1 Case Payment Decision Table [link to decision table]

There is an added benefit to listing details separately from the use case when they apply across a number of use cases: Changes only have to be in one place should these details ever change. For example, if a data field has a valid range that applies wherever the field is referred to, document the rule in the class model or as an information item. If the valid range ever changes, you'll only have to change the documentation in one place.

Next, you'll look at examples of some of the artifacts that supplement the use case.

People often ask me if the use cases are all of the requirements or whether they are all you need to create test cases. The answer to both questions is, "No." First of all, they are not all of the requirements because they only address the user requirements, omitting other requirements such as security requirements. Secondly, they focus on the *flow* of the conversation between the system and the actors, the storyboard of the interaction. Other issues, such as design issues (for example, screen layouts), and data validation rules are defined in other artifacts that the use case links to. To fully document and test a system, you need use cases *and* these other artifacts.

Decision Tables

One of the useful artifacts to which you can link a use case is a *decision table.* (In the template, link to this document in the section *related artifacts*).

Listen up!

Use a *decision table* to describe the system response to a number of interrelated factors. If each factor can be looked at separately, do not use a decision table; just use the alternate and exceptional flows or, alternatively, a condition/response table.

For example, the CPP use case, *review case report,* referred to a decision table that describes the logic for validating whether a case is payable and for determining the payment amount. The rules for these steps could have been described in the use case proper, but that would have made the text harder to follow. Instead, the rules are extracted into an accompanying decision table, appended to the use case.

The Underlying Concept

Instead of explaining the logic that underlies a decision, you simply list every possible situation and document how the system treats it. The method for completing the table ensures that you have accounted for every mathematically possible combination of factors.

When Are Decision Tables Useful?

Use decision tables during the interview process to ensure that you have questioned the interviewee about all possible combinations of factors that affect the outcome of a use case. Document decision tables as appendices to system use cases. During testing, use decision tables to derive test cases that cover all combinations of related factors; each column of the table represents a test case. (You'll learn more about this in the Chapter 10 on testing.)

Example of a Use Case with a Decision Table

System Use Case: Process Life Insurance Application

Basic flow:

1. User enters application information.
2. System validates eligibility. (12.1)
3. System adds application to "Adjuster" queue.

Alternate flows:

3a. Referred application:

    1. System adds application to referral queue.

    2. The use case ends.

Exception flows:

3b. Rejected application:

    1. System adds application to rejection queue.

    2. The use case ends in failure.

12. Related Artifacts:

    12.1 Validate eligibility decision table: [link to table]

A decision table, as shown in Figure 6.1, is appropriate here because all of the conditions are interrelated: You need to evaluate them together to determine how to process an application.

		1	2	3	4	5	6	7	8
C O N D I T I O N	Medical condition (<u>P</u>oor/ <u>G</u>ood/)	P	P	P	P	G	G	G	G
	Substance abuse? (Y/N)	Y	Y	N	N	Y	Y	N	N
	Previous rejections? (Y/N)	Y	N	Y	N	Y	N	Y	N
A C T I O N	Accept								X
	Reject	X	X	X		X		X	
	Refer				X		X		

Figure 6.1 Decision table: validate eligibility

A Step-by-Step Procedure for Using a Decision Table During an Interview to Analyze System Behavior

1. Prompt interviewees for conditions (factors) that may affect the outcome. List each condition on a separate row in the top-left portion of the diagram. For example, in the previous decision table example, the conditions are "Medical condition," "Substance abuse?" and "Previous rejections?"

2. Prompt interviewees for a complete list of possible values for each condition and list these next to the corresponding condition. For example, "Medical condition ('Poor,' 'Good')."

3. Prompt interviewees for a complete list of actions that the system may perform (regardless of the reason) and list each on a separate row in the bottom-left portion of the table. For example, "Reject." Do not let the interview wander into the issue of which actions are taken under what circumstances.

4. Calculate the number of cases by multiplying the number of values for condition 1 times the number of values for condition 2, and so on. This yields the number of columns you'll need to complete in the right portion of the table. For example, the preceding decision table has eight cases: two (for "Medical condition") times two (for "Substance abuse?") times two (for "Previous rejections?").

5. Start with the bottom row. Alternate possible condition values, moving from left to right until all cells are filled. For example, in Figure 6.1, the bottom row ("Previous rejections?") is *Y N Y N Y N Y N Y N*.

6. Move one row up. Cover the first set of values appearing below with the first value for the condition on the current row. Cover the second set with the second value and repeat until all cells are filled. (If you run out of values, start again.) For example, in Figure 6.1, the second row ("Substance abuse?") is filled:

   Y Y (covering one YN set of values for "Previous rejection?").

   N N (covering the next YN set).

   Y Y N N to finish off the row.

7. Move one row up and repeat until all rows are filled.

8. Each column now describes a distinct scenario. Read down each column and ask the interviewee what actions the system should take for the case it describes. Make sure that you also verify which actions the system does *not* take.

Case Study F1: Decision Table

During an interview regarding the use case *Review case report*, the user describes the requirements as follows:

1. Payments depend on whether the Community Peace Project (CPP) code of good practice was followed, whether the steps and procedures (outlined by the CPP) have been followed, and how many Peace Committee (PC) members were involved in the case.

2. If there were fewer than three PC members present during the Peace Gathering, the case is marked "not payable."

3. If the code of good practice was not followed, the case is marked as "not payable."

4. If the steps and procedures were followed and three to five PC members were present, then mark the case "payable" and pay the standard amount unless there is another reason for marking it "not payable."

5. If the steps and procedures were followed and there were six or more PC members involved, mark the case as "payable" and pay double the standard amount. (This is the preferred number of PC members.)

6. If the steps and procedures were not followed and three or more PC members were present (three to five or more than six), mark as "payable" and pay half the standard amount.

You decide that the best way to deal with these requirements is with a decision table, since a number of conditions need to be evaluated together in order to make a decision. Your plan is to create a decision table based on your notes and use this during a follow-up interview. In the follow-up, you'll go over each column with stakeholders and verify whether each scenario has been captured properly. Once verified, the decision table will be documented as a related artifact that the use case links to. The table will also act as a source document for designing test cases.

Suggestion

Follow the step-by-step procedure described earlier. First read through the interview notes looking for individual conditions and actions. Use the procedure you've learned to fill in the upper portion of the columns. Then pick a column and read through the interview notes to determine which actions apply. Continue until all columns are complete.

Case Study F1: Resulting Documentation

Figure 6.2 shows the resulting decision table.

		1	2	3	4	5	6	7	8	9	10	11	12
C O N D I T I O N	Code of good practice followed (Y/N)	Y	Y	Y	Y	Y	Y	N	N	N	N	N	N
	Steps and procedures followed (Y/N)	Y	Y	Y	N	N	N	Y	Y	Y	N	N	N
	# PC members (<3,3-5, 6+)	<3	3-5	6+	<3	3-5	6+	<3	3-5	6+	<3	3-5	6+
A C T I O N	Mark as not payable	X			X			X	X	X	X	X	X
	Mark as payable		X	X		X	X						
	Pay 1/2 amount					X	X						
	Pay standard amount		X										
	Pay double amount			X									

Figure 6.2 Decision table: validate case and determine payment amount

Decision Trees

A *decision tree* is an alternative to a decision table.[4] Instead of a table, you use a picture to describe the system's behavior, as shown in Figure 6.3.

How to Draw a Decision Tree

1. List conditions along the top. (Start a few inches to the right of the left edge.)
2. List actions down the right side of the drawing.
3. Draw an origin point at the left edge in the middle of the page.
4. From this point, draw one branch for each value of the first condition.

---

[4]An activity diagram may also be used for this purpose, but the format is different. On a decision tree, each possible value for an input condition is represented as a node; on an activity diagram, the values are represented as guards along the connecting lines. Many BAs and users find the decision tree format to be more intuitive than that of an activity diagram for requirements of this sort.

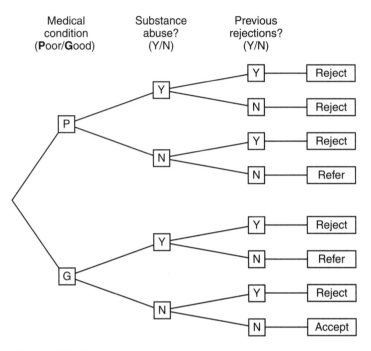

Figure 6.3 Decision tree example

5. From each of these points (or tips), draw one branch for each value of the next condition.

6. Continue until you finish the last condition.

7. Connect each final tip to the appropriate action.

8. To avoid too many crossed lines, you may list the same action separately each time it is needed.

Case Study F2: Decision Tree

You decide to provide a decision tree for the previous case to accommodate stakeholders who prefer a pictorial presentation.

Case Study F2: Resulting Documentation

Figure 6.4 shows the resulting decision tree.

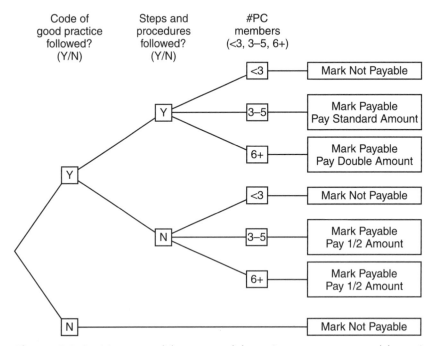

Figure 6.4 Decision tree: validate case and determine payment amount (alternative representation to a decision table)

Condition/Response Table

If the input conditions contributing to a decision can be evaluated one by one, use a condition/response table instead of a decision table (or tree). Note the following example.

System use case: *prepare taxes*

Basic flow:

   ...

11. The user enters net income.

12. The system determines tax bracket. See condition/response table that follows.

13. The system displays tax bracket.

   ...

Supplementary documentation:

Condition/response table:

Tax bracket table:

Condition	Response
Under minimum	No tax payable
Minimum – $18,000	Tax bracket A
$18,000.01–$60,000	Tax bracket B
$60,000.01–$500,000	Tax bracket C
Over $500,000	Tax bracket D

Business Rules

Business rules represent another type of documentation that should be pulled from the use case proper and referred to in a dedicated section (Section 10 of the template: *business rules*). Business rules are rules from the business area that constrain business processes. These rules are documented separately because they would distract from the flow of the use case and because they often apply to more than one system use case. For example, an airline system might include a rule that the weight of an airplane must never exceed its maximum weight capacity. This rule is active during a number of use cases, for example, *Check in passenger* and *Load cargo*. Rather than restate this rule in every use case that it applies to, list it separately as a business rule and refer to the rule from the use cases.

Business rules may be stored the "low-tech" way, for example, in a book. At the other end of the spectrum, are *rules engines*—software that manages and enforces business rules. Either way, it's not enough to record the rules—you must also specify which rules apply to which use cases. This makes it easy to identify which use cases need to be tested when a rule changes. When an automated rules engine is used, there is another advantage to linking use cases to a rule: It is inefficient to have the software, at run time, check all business rules for every use case when only some apply.

Advanced Use-Case Features

Once you have written up some system use cases, you may notice that certain *steps* appear in more than one use case. For example, the same steps for obtaining a valid policy may show up in the use cases *query policy, amend policy,* and *make a claim against a policy*. Keep an eye out for cases like this; they represent opportunities for reuse. Reuse is a good thing. It means that you only have to go through the effort of documenting the steps once; it means that if the steps ever change, you'll only have to change the documentation in one place; and it means that the steps will be treated consistently throughout the documentation. Often these inconsistencies arise when, due to a change in requirements, one of the affected use cases is changed but the other is not.

The UML has provided some advanced use-case features to help you increase reuse in the use cases. Use the advanced features for internal documentation; don't show them to the users. For example, show *business stakeholders* use-case diagrams that include only the basic system use cases discussed up to this point; distribute diagrams with the added, advanced features to the *internal team*. Finally, don't go overboard. The addition of an advanced use-case feature adds complexity to the model; use it only when necessary. In some organizations, teams can get bogged down in theoretical discussions about whether to use this or that advanced feature. Rather than *theoretically* working out which feature to use, *just write out the system use cases*, as proscribed in B.O.O.M.[5]

The advanced features described below have an impact on diagrams and on the written documentation. The purpose of the diagrams is to help the team *organize* (or *structure*) the requirements documentation. The diagrams later serve as a reference: They tell the reader which use-case documentation refers to other use-case documentation and the nature of the reference. These diagrams are also invaluable when changes are made to the textual documentation of a use case: The diagram clearly points out which other use cases are potentially affected.

Some organizations have a bias against use-case diagrams, especially when they contain advanced features. In my experience, this is often because they don't have a clear understanding of the purpose of the advanced diagramming features, mistakenly assuming, for example, that they are for the benefit of users rather than for organizing documentation. But if your organization is adamant about this issue, use the advanced features only for textual documentation and ignore the diagramming component.

The UML includes the following advanced use-case features:

- *Includes*: Extract the common requirements into a "mini use case." The main use cases are said to *include* this mini use case. This approach is useful whenever a set of steps appears in more than one system use case.
- *Extends*: You leave one main system use case intact and create a new use case that *extends* the original one. The extending use case contains only the requirements that differ from the original. This approach is useful, for example, for enhanced versions of earlier software releases.
- *Generalization*: You create a new generalized use case that contains general rules. Other use cases are created as "specializations"; they contain the non-generic requirements. This approach is useful when a set of system use cases represents variations on a theme.

Now let's have a closer look at each of these options.

---

[5]Thanks to Brian Lyons for his contribution to the sequencing of B.O.O.M. steps on this and other issues.

Includes

Use this feature when a sequence of steps is performed *exactly* the same way in different use cases.

How It Works

You avoid repetition by extracting the common steps into a separate use case. (If you're a programmer, it helps to think of an *inclusion use case* as a routine, called by the base use case.)

Terminology

The original use cases are referred to as *base use cases*. The new use case is called the *inclusion use case*. Each of the other original use cases is said to *include* this new use case.

Formal Definition

Include: "A relationship from a base use case to an inclusion use case, specifying how the behavior for the base use case contains the behavior of the inclusion use case. The behavior is included at the location which is defined in the base use case. The base use case depends on performing the behavior of the inclusion use case, but not on its structure (i.e., attributes or operations)." (UML 2)

Examples of Inclusion Use Cases

A Web-based banking system has two base use cases: *Pay bill* and *Transfer funds*. Each of these includes the use case *Debit account*.

In an air travel system, a *Make reservation* use case and a *Change reservation* use case both include the use case *Check available seats*.

How to Draw an Inclusion

Figure 6.5 shows how to diagram an inclusion use case.

Inclusion Rules

1. An inclusion use case is triggered by a step in a base use case.
2. An inclusion use case does not have to be a complete task (and it usually isn't).

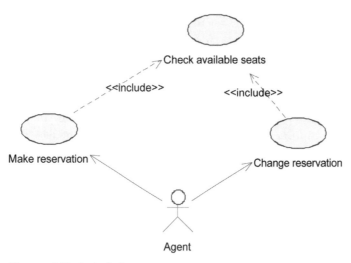

Figure 6.5 An inclusion use case

3. A use case that appears in one context as an inclusion use case may, in another context, act as a base use case triggered directly by an actor. (Be aware, however, that there is some controversy surrounding this issue.)[6]

4. An inclusion use case may include other inclusion use cases for as many levels as necessary.

5. The base use case may include as many inclusion use cases as necessary.

6. The inclusion does not have to be triggered *every* time the base use case is executed. (This issue also has some controversy associated with it.)[7] For example, the base use case may trigger the inclusion within an alternate flow scenario that is only conditionally executed.

---

[6]Some analysts insist that an inclusion use case must *never* represent a complete user goal. Others allow it. (See Schneider and Winters, *Applying Use Cases*, 2nd edition, Addison Wesley, 2001). I side with those who allow it, because BAs often encounter processes that in one context are a "side-goal" and in others are main goals. For example, a licensing system has a *Renew license* use case. As a side-goal, the use case includes steps for changing the address if the licensee has moved. On the other hand, the system also has a *Change address* use case to handle situations where the licensee calls a CSR specifically to report a move. This is most elegantly treated by defining a use case *Change address* that is included by the *Renew license* use case but that also appears in the model as a base use case that interacts directly with the CSR actor.

[7]I have also seen this handled differently in different organizations. Some show an includes relationship only if the base use case activates the inclusion every time. I don't see the benefit in restricting the use of such an effective feature in this way.

7. An *includes* step of a base use case should be accompanied by an alternate or exception flow to handle cases where the inclusion ends in failure—unless the inclusion *always* ends in success.

8. Write the inclusion so that it will apply regardless of which base use case triggers it.

How Does an Includes Relationship Affect Use-Case Documentation?

To grasp the consequence of the *includes* relationship, it is important to understand its effect on the textual documentation. The following example shows how a base use case refers to an inclusion use case in the text, and how the inclusion use case is written. (Keep in mind that UML does not dictate a standard way to handle the text.)

In the example shown in Figure 6.5, a base use case, *Make reservation,* includes the inclusion use case *Check available seats.* This is documented in the base use case, *Make reservation,* as follows:

Basic flow:

1. The agent selects a trip.
2. Include *(Check available seats).*
3. The agent confirms the reservation.

Exception flow:

2a. No available seats: (this flow handles the failure of the inclusion use case)

  .1   Cancel the transaction

The inclusion use case *Check available seats* is documented as follows:

Description: Other reservation use cases reference this inclusion use case.

Basic flow:

1. The system verifies that seats are available.
2. The system determines and displays the maximum number of seats for the trip.
3. The system determines and displays the number of seats currently reserved.
4. The system determines and displays the number of seats currently available.

Exception flow:

1a. Seats not available: (This flow handles failure of Step 1 of the basic flow.)

  .1   The system displays a "seats unavailable" warning message.

  .2   Continue basic flow at Step 2.

Extends

Use this feature whenever you need to add requirements to an existing use case *without changing the original text*. The following are some common reasons for an extension:

- *Seldom-used options that the user can choose at any time (known as* asynchronous interruptions): An extension use case will allow you to handle these options in separate extension use cases and keep the base use case free of the seldom-used requirements. Aside from the clarity this provides, it is also useful for planning software iterations: You may plan to implement the base use case in an early iteration and add the extension use cases later.
- *Customization of a generic product:* The generic product is described in the base use case. The extension use case describes the customization.

How It Works

The base use case is written as a normal use case. It describes the interaction, except for the steps that are in the extension. (If you're a programmer, it helps to think of an *extending use case* as a "patch"[8] on the base use case.) The base use case does not contain any reference to the extension use case. However, it does contain labels within the textual documentation that mark points at which it might be extended. The extension use case contains all of the steps that are inserted at these points.

Terminology

- The original use case is referred to as the *base use case.*
- The use case that is based on it is called the *extension use case.*
- A point at which the base use case might be extended is called an *extension point.*
- The circumstance that causes the extension to be activated is the *condition.*

Formal Definition

Extend: "A relationship from an extension use case to a base use case, specifying how the behavior defined for the extension use case augments (subject to conditions specified in the extension) the behavior defined for the base use case. The behavior is inserted at the location defined by the extension point in the base use case. The base use case does not depend on performing the behavior of the extension use case." (UML 2)

---

[8]This turn of phrase was coined by Rebecca Wirfs-Brock.

Examples of Extension Use Cases

Word processing example: A word processing system has a base use case *Edit document* that is extended by the extension use case *Check spelling*. The condition is *User selects spell-checking option.*

Academic system example: A school's tuition package has a base use case *Assign tuition fee* that is extended by *Apply subsidy*. The extension point is *Calculate final amount*, a label that marks the point just before a final fee is calculated. The condition is *Student is eligible for subsidy.*

Another Way to Think of Extensions

Recall that the system use-case template contains a *basic flow*, describing the normal success scenario, *alternate flows* for alternate pathways, and *exception flows* for paths that lead to abandonment of the goal. Instead of putting all of the alternate and exception flows in one base system use case, you can extract some of them into an extension.

> An *extension use case* represents one or more alternate or exception flows that are *executed due to the same condition.*

How to Draw an Extension

Figure 6.6 shows how to draw an extension use case.

The example in Figure 6.6 shows the following:

- The base use case is *Make reservation.*
- The extension use case is *Make 1st class reservation.*
- The extension point is *Set seat class.*
- The condition is *Passenger requests 1st class seating.*

Extension Rules

1. The base use case must be complete on its own.
2. A base use case may have more than one extension use case.
3. The extension use case interrupts the flow of the base use case at defined extension points and under specified conditions.
4. An extension use case may interrupt the base use case at more than one extension point.

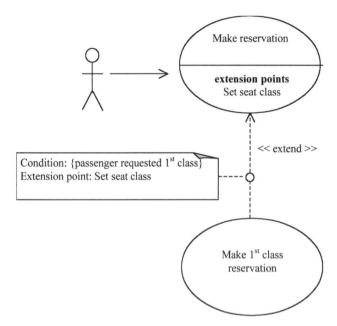

Figure 6.6 An extension use case

5. The conditions attached to the extension are evaluated once, when the first extension point is reached inside the base use case; the conditions are not reevaluated
   when subsequent points are reached.

6. Once the system confirms that the extension applies, the extension use-case will be
   invoked at all its extension points.

7. The base use case must not refer to the extension use case or even "know" that it is
   being extended. Exception: A section in the base use case documentation may
   describe extension points.

8. Connect actors to the base use case; they automatically apply to the extension.
   Exception: If the extension introduces a new actor, connect the new actor to the
   extension use case.

How Does an Extends Relationship Affect Use-Case Documentation?

The original use case should not make any reference to the new extending use case.
However, the original use case must contain extension points—marked spots in the document to which the extending use case may refer.

The following example shows how the textual documentation of a base use case indicates
an extension point and how an extension use case refers to an extension point.

Base use case: *Make reservation*

Extension points

    Set seat class: Step 3.

Basic flow

  ...

  3. Assign coach seat

  ...

Extension use case: *Make 1st class reservation*

Description: This use case extends the *Make reservation* use case. It contains changes to the flow when the reservation is first class.

Flows:

    Set seat class:

    Assign 1st class seat

Generalized Use Case

Use this feature when a number of use cases represent variations on a theme. Common reasons for a generalized use case are the following:

- *Technology variations*: The same user goal is achieved using different technologies. Define a generalized use case to hold rules that apply regardless of technology; handle the technology variations as specialized use cases.

- *Similar process but different business artifacts*: The business has a standard process for handling different kinds of artifacts (for example, different kinds of applications forms), but the process differs slightly depending on the artifact. Handle the generic rules in a generalized use case and describe the peculiarities in specialized use cases—one for each artifact.

How It Works

Write workflow steps that apply across a group of use cases in a generalized use case. Specify variations on how the steps are handled in the specialized use cases.

Terminology

- The generic use case is referred to as the *generalized use case.*
- Each variation is called a *specialized use case.*
- Each specialized use case has a *generalization* relationship with the generalized use case. The relationship points from the specialized use case to the generalized one.
- The specialized use cases *inherit* features of the generalized use case.

Formal Definition

> *Generalization* [between use cases]: "A taxonomic relationship between a more general classifier [use case] and a more specific classifier [use case]. Each instance of the specific classifier [use case] is also an indirect instance of the general classifier [use cases]. Thus, the specific classifier [use case] indirectly has features of the more general classifier [use case]."[9] (UML 2)

Examples of Generalized Use Cases

Banking example

Generalized use case: *Pay bill.*

Specialized use cases: *Pay bill through ATM, Pay bill over the Web, Pay bill through teller.*

CRO (Clinical Research Organization) example

Generalized use case: *File documents.*

Specialized use cases: *File case documents, File regulatory documents.*

How to Draw a Generalized Use Case

Figure 6.7 shows how to draw a generalized use case.

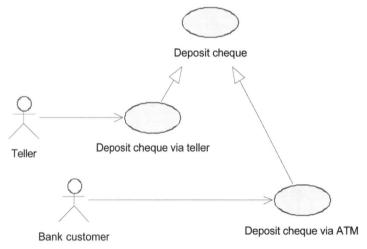

Figure 6.7 A generalized use case

[9]The definition is written so that it applies to any generalization. I've added the phrase "use case" in brackets after each use of the term "classifier" so you can see how the rule applies to use cases.

In Figure 6.7, *Deposit cheque* is a generalized use case containing generic steps for depositing a cheque. Any overriding or additional steps are described in the specialized use cases *Deposit cheque via teller* and *Deposit cheque via ATM.*

Rules for Generalized Use Cases

The UML does not provide much guidance regarding textual documentation. The following rules comply with the spirit of the UML generalization relationship and are useful extensions to the standard:

1. The specialized use cases must comply with requirements documented in the generalized use case (including all sections: Actors, Flows, and so on).

2. The specialized use case may not exclude any flows or steps inherited from the generalized use case. However, it may override them or add to them.

3. The generalized use case should be *abstract.*

   - According to the UML, the generalized use case may be either abstract (conceptual) or concrete (real). An *abstract use case* is an invention used to pool together common requirements; a *concrete use case* is a full-blown, actual use case, containing everything necessary to describe the interaction. Since the extension relation is the widely accepted mechanism for creating a new use case from a concrete one, I suggest that all your generalized use cases be abstract.

How Does a Generalization Relationship Affect Use-Case Documentation?

One practice is to write generic steps in the generalized use case and write only the overriding and additional steps in the specialized use cases. Alternatively, you can write each specialized use case in its entirety, as long as it conforms to the rules set out in the generalized use case.

The following example demonstrates the first approach.

In the diagram shown in Figure 6.7, a generalized use case *Deposit cheque* holds generic rules for cheque deposits. The specialized use cases contain overriding or extra steps. The generalized use case, *Deposit cheque,* is documented as follows:

Description: This generalized use case contains a generic workflow for depositing cheques.

Basic flow:

The user identifies the deposit account and the amount of the cheque.

(Hold cheque) The system places a hold on the cheque, blocking withdrawal of the cheque amount for the period of the hold.

The system credits the account with the cheque amount.

The specialized use case *Deposit cheque via ATM* is documented as follows:

Description: This use case is a specialization of the use case *Deposit cheque*. Only steps that override or are inserted into the generalized use case are documented herein.

Basic flow:

> *(Hold cheque)* Hold cheque for one business day.

The specialized use case *Deposit cheque via teller* is documented as follows:

Description: This use case is a specialization of the use case *Deposit cheque*. Only steps that override or are inserted into the generalized use case are documented in *Deposit cheque via teller*.

Basic flow:

> *(Hold cheque)* Hold cheque for five business days.

Note to Rational Rose Users

The default toolbar for use-case diagrams does not have tools for *includes* and *extends*. If you neglected to do so earlier, customize the toolbar now by adding these tools.

Case Study F3: Advanced Use-Case Features

Problem Statement

You can now examine the system use cases, looking for places where the same steps apply to more than one system use case. You note that while carrying out the system use case *Update case*, the user may become aware that the case involves a new Peace Committee or that information about an existing committee has changed. Users of that use case want the option of updating *Peace Committee* information without leaving the *Update case* function. They also want to add or update *CPP members* without leaving the *Update case* function. There is a redundancy here due to the fact that the *Manage administration* package has already described both of these functions, *Update Peace Committees* and *Update CPP Members*, as system use cases.

Your Next Step

You review existing system use-case diagrams in order to restructure the use cases for maximum reuse. You'll be making changes to the use-case diagram for the *manage case* package.

Figures 6.8 and 6.9 are the existing diagrams relevant to case study F3.

Case Study F3: Resulting Documentation

Figure 6.10 shows the diagram developed for case study F3.

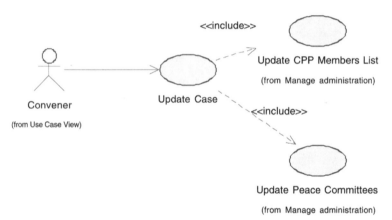

Figure 6.9 Existing diagram: *Manage case* package

Figure 6.8 Existing diagram: *Manage administration* package

Figure 6.10 Updated use-case diagram for *manage case* package containing advanced features

Chapter Summary

In this chapter, you performed the following B.O.O.M. steps:

2: Analysis

    2a) Dynamic analysis

        i) Describe system use cases (use-case description template)

You learned about the following new tools and concepts in this chapter:

1. *Use-case description template*: A format for describing a system use case.
2. *Decision table*: A table format for describing requirements when conditions need to be evaluated together.

3. *Decision tree:* A graphic alternative to a decision table.

4. *Condition/response table:* A simpler table you can use when you can evaluate conditions one by one.

5. Advanced use-case features:

Inclusion use case: For steps that occur the same way in more than one use case.

Extension use case: To add flows to an existing use case while leaving the original documentation intact.

Generalized use case: To be used when a number of use cases represent variations on a theme.

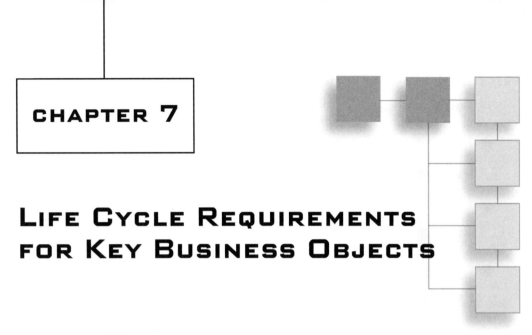

CHAPTER 7

LIFE CYCLE REQUIREMENTS FOR KEY BUSINESS OBJECTS

Chapter Objectives

In this chapter, you'll learn how to define the life cycle of critical business objects.

You'll be able to carry out the following steps in bold:

   2a) Dynamic analysis

      i) Describe system use cases (use-case description template)

      ii) Describe state behavior (state machine diagram)

            1. Identify states of critical objects

            2. Identify state transitions

            3. Identify state activities

            4. Identify composite states

            5. Identify concurrent states

Tools and concepts that you'll learn to use in this chapter include the following:

1. State machine diagram
2. State
3. Transition
4. Event
5. Guard
6. Activity
7. Composite state
8. Concurrent states

What Is a State Machine Diagram?

A *state machine diagram* is a picture that describes the different statuses (states) of an object and the events and conditions that cause an object to pass from one state to another. The diagram describes the life of a single object over a period of time, one that may span several system use cases.[1] For example, a state machine diagram might show the different statuses of an insurance claim (Received, Validated, Adjusted, Paid, Not Paid, and so on).

> *State:* "A condition or situation during the life of an object during which it satisfies some condition, performs some activity, or waits for some event." (UML 2)
>
> *State machine diagram:* "A diagram that depicts discrete behavior modeled through finite state-transition systems. In particular, it specifies the sequences of states that an object or an interaction goes through during its life in response to events, together with its responses and actions." (UML 2)
>
> *State machine:* "A behavior that specifies the sequences of states that an object or an interaction goes through during its life in response to events, together with its responses and actions." (UML 2)

The terms *state machine* and *state machine diagram* are almost synonymous: The state machine is the behavior, and the state machine diagram depicts it. Other names for the diagram are *state diagram* and *statechart diagram*. The diagram was originally developed by David Harel.

Why Draw a State Machine Diagram?

The behavior of an object over time *could* be surmised by analyzing system use-case descriptions, activity diagrams, and so on. For example, one could gain an understanding of an *Insurance Claim* object by noting how it is handled during the system use cases *Receive claim*, *Validate claim*, *Adjust claim*, and *Pay claim*. But if the state of the object is critical to the system, it is helpful to be able to get the full picture for the object as it passes through the system.

---

[1]Unlike many of the other concepts in the UML, there is no single programming equivalent to a state—but they can be programmed. An object's state is often tracked with a state attribute; the object's operations can then be written so that they depend upon this state attribute. Other programming mechanisms involve design patterns that use a combination of associations and generalizations to model states.

State Machine Diagram Example: Credit Card Application

In the next steps, we'll walk through the creation of a state machine diagram. To give you an idea of where we're headed, Figure 7.1 shows an example derived from a credit card system.

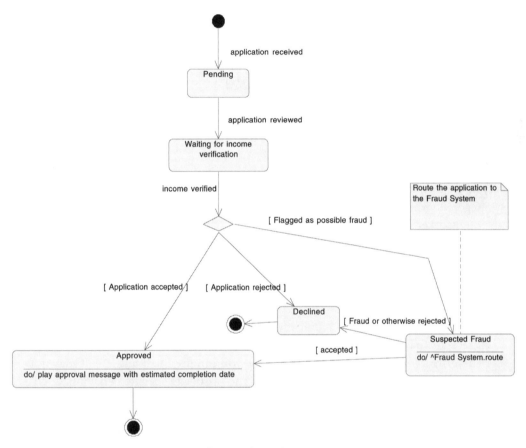

Figure 7.1 A state machine diagram for a credit card system

Step 2a ii: 1. Identify States of Critical Objects

Define a new state for the object if the system treats the object differently because of a change or if the object itself behaves differently. If there is no difference, then only a piece of information about the object has changed. You can modify a piece of information about the object by using attributes (which you'll learn about later in this book).

Examples of states include the following:

- *Red* and *Blue* are not two states of a *Product* object, but merely indicate different values of a color attribute.

- However, *Sold* and *Unsold* may be considered as states since they affect how the product is handled.

Other examples of states include the following:

- Telephone line states: *Busy, Off-the-Hook, Not-in-Use*
- Invoice states: *Entered, Paid, Unpaid, Canceled*
- Student registrant states: *Wait-listed, Pre-screened, Accepted, Attending, Graduated, On leave, Left institution*

Types of States

Many of the elements that appear on a state machine diagram fall into one of the following categories, which are shown in Figure 7.2. Thinking in terms of these categories will help you discover states.

- *Initial pseudostate*: This is shown as a "dot" on the diagram. This is the "start" point for the object. The UML classifies this, as well as some other modeling elements, as *pseudostates* rather than *states. Pseudostates* mark points that transitions may leave from or go to, but they do not represent actual states of the object.

- *Final state*: This appears as a bulls-eye. It represents the final state of the object. The final state may be named, and there may be more than one final state for an object. There are a number of restrictions on how you can use the final state: It may not have any outgoing transitions, and you cannot associate specific behaviors, such as entry, exit, or ongoing activities. (You'll learn how to specify these activities for other kinds of states later in this chapter.)

Other states are shown as a rounded rectangle. These typically fall into one of the following categories:

- *Wait state*: The object isn't doing anything important; it is simply waiting for an event to happen or a condition to become true. In the credit card example in Figure 7.1, the state *Waiting for Income Verification* is of this type.

- *Ongoing state*: The object is performing some ongoing process and stays in this state until some event interrupts the process. For example, a system to manage the work of health inspectors has an inspector state *Monitoring compliance* that ends only when management instructs the inspector to discontinue.

- *Finite state*: The object is performing some work that has a definite end. Once the work is over, the object passes out of the state.

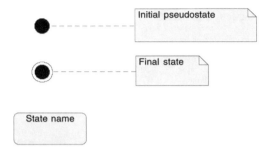

Figure 7.2 Drawing states in UML

Note to Rational Rose Users

To create a state machine diagram for an object:

1. Define a class for the object in the Logical View (see Figure 7.3). Position the cursor on the Logical View icon in the Browser window, right-click, and select New/Class.

Here's where you add the state machine diagram for a case.

Figure 7.3 The Logical View of Rational Rose

2. Position the cursor on the new class, right-click, and select New/Statechart Diagram.

3. Select and name the new diagram.

4. You can now begin drawing states using the diagram toolbar.

Case Study G1: States

During interviews with the CPP, you've identified a *Case* (a dispute handled by the CPP) as a critical business object tracked by the system. You ask the interviewees what states a case can be in, and learn that they are

- *Initiated* when the initial report has been made.
- *Scheduled for gathering* once a Peace Gathering has been scheduled.
- *Gathering held* once a Peace Gathering has been held.
- *Monitored* while it is being monitored.
- *Resolved/no gathering*
- *Referred to police*
- *Awaiting review* indicating the case has been resolved and is awaiting a review to determine if it is payable.
- *Under review* while it is being reviewed.
- *Payable* once the case has been reviewed and deemed payable.
- *Not payable* once the case has been reviewed and deemed not payable.
- *Paid* once all payments for the case have been made.
- *Final state*

Your next step is to begin the drawing of a state machine diagram by depicting these states.

Case Study G1: Resulting Diagram

Figure 7.4 shows the diagram that results from these interviews.

Step 2a ii: 2. Identify State Transitions

The next step is to establish what causes the object to pass—or *transition*—from one state to another. There are two ways that this transition may occur.

Listen up!

A *transition* is a change of state.

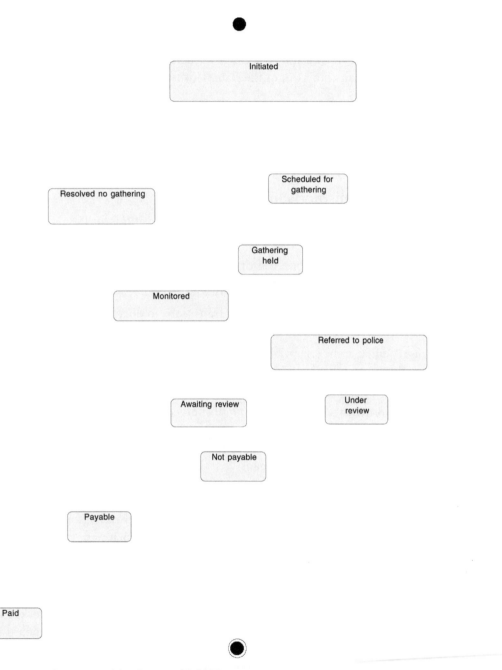

Figure 7.4 Diagram resulting for case study G1

A transition may occur automatically when activities occurring while it was in a previous state have been completed. For example, while an insurance claim is the state *Under adjustment*, it is evaluated by an adjuster. As soon as the adjuster completes the evaluation, the object automatically transitions out of the state. This type of transition is called a *completion transition*.

Alternatively, a transition may occur because an event *interrupts* the previous state. For example, an application in the state *Waiting for income verification* stays there indefinitely until it receives the event *Income verified*. This type of transition is a *labeled transition*.

Depicting State Transitions in UML

Figure 7.5 shows a first draft of a diagram showing state transitions for the *Case* object. The example shows a number of elements involved in documenting a transition.

The model elements that appear on this diagram are the following:

- *Transition*: A change of state, indicated with an arrow.
- *Event*: A trigger that fires—or forces—a transition. To document an event, simply write the event name beside the transition symbol.
- *Activity*: A quick, uninterruptible activity that happens whenever the transition occurs. To document an activity, precede the activity name with a slash, as in */Assign temporary case number*.
- *Send event*: A message that is sent to *another* object whenever the transition occurs. To document a send event, identify the *target* (the object receiving the request) and the event (or message) that is sent as follows: ∧*Target.Event*. For example, ∧*Convener.Notify central office* means "Tell the convener to notify the central office." You can also identify any information (parameters) that you need to send to the object. For example, if the Convener needs to know the temporary case number, then specify ∧*Convener.Notify central office(temporary case number)*. If you find the notation of a send event cumbersome, don't use it. Document it as a regular event and clarify who performs the job with a note if necessary.
- *Guard*: A condition that must be true for the transition to occur. A guard is somewhat like an event in that both determine whether a transition may occur. The difference is that an event *forces* the previous state to end; a guard is only checked once the previous state has already ended for some other reason. Show a guard in square brackets, as in *[Consensus reached]*.

You can also use the diamond decision symbol the same way you used it in activity diagrams, as shown in Figure 7.6. The official UML term for this is *choice pseudostate*.

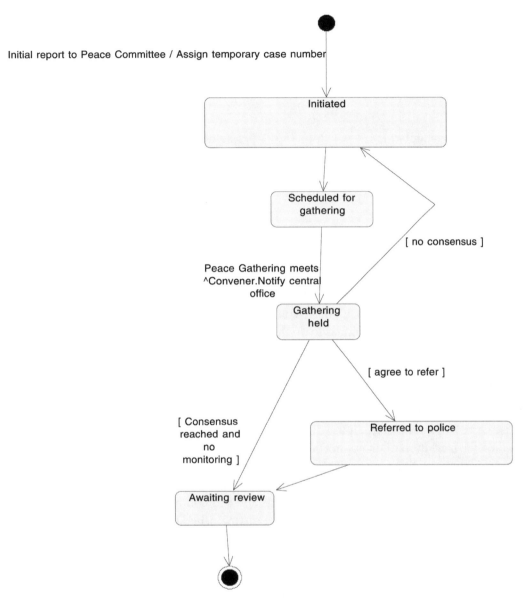

Figure 7.5 Draft of a diagram depicting state transitions for the *Case* object

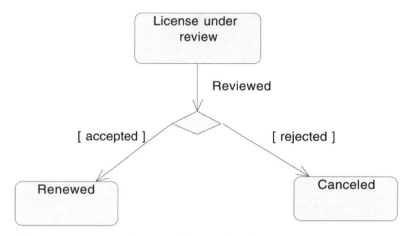

Figure 7.6 Using a choice pseudostate when documenting state transitions

Mapping State Machine Diagrams to System Use Cases

You can use state machine diagrams to compile a comprehensive picture of how system use cases change the states of objects. To do this, use the names of the system use cases for the events, and the names of flows for the guards. For example, a transition labeled *Review report [not payable]* means that the transition occurs when the *Not payable* flow of the system use case *Review report* is executed.

This naming convention can also lead to preconditions and postconditions for the relevant use case. For example, in Figure 7.7, the system use case *Review application* is used to name the transition of an application from *Pending* to *Waiting for income verification*. A precondition for this use case is that the application is in the *Pending* state. A postcondition is that the application is in the state *Waiting for income verification*. You can also explicitly document other use-case preconditions and postconditions right on the transition label. These look like regular guards but are distinguished by where they appear relative to the use-case name. Use the form *[precondition] use-case name/[postcondition]*. For example, if the transition in Figure 7.7 were labeled *[valid reviewer has been identified] review application/[request for income sent]* the implication is that, for the use case *review application*

- The preconditions are that a *valid reviewer has been identified* and that the application is *pending*.

- The postconditions are that a request for income had been sent and the application is waiting for income verification.

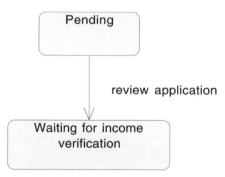

Figure 7.7 Naming a transition as a use case

Note to Rational Rose Users

To add a label, guard, or send event to a transition, select (double-click) the transition and enter the requirements in the State Transition Specification window, as shown in Figure 7.8.

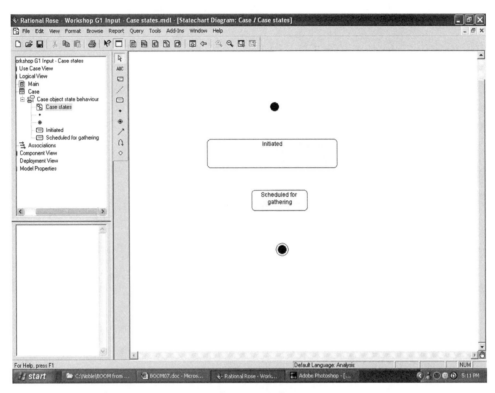

Figure 7.8 Rose's State Transition Specification window

Case Study G2: Transitions

You continue your interview, with the aim of identifying state transitions for the *Case* object. Here's what you find out:

1. The CPP first becomes aware of a case when someone makes an initial report to a Peace Committee. Once that happens, the case has the status *Initiated*. Whenever a case makes the transition to the "*Initiated*" state (from the *initial pseudostate*), a temporary case number is assigned to the case.

2. The case then moves automatically to the *Scheduled for gathering* state.

3. When a Peace Gathering meets to deal with the case, the case moves to new state: *Gathering held*. Also, whenever the Peace Gathering meets, the Convener must notify central office.

4. If, during the gathering, no consensus was reached, the case returns to the *Initiated* state so that it can make its way through the system again.

5. If, during the gathering, the parties agreed to refer the case, the case passes from *Gathering held* to *Referred to police*.

    a. After the police have dealt with a case, the case status changes automatically to *Awaiting review* (see Step 10).

6. If, during the gathering, a consensus was reached and no monitoring was required, then the case passes from *Gathering held* to *Awaiting review* (see Step 10).

7. If a consensus was reached during the gathering and monitoring is required, then the case status moves from *Gathering held* to *Monitoring*.

8. While a case is being monitored, when the deadline for compliance comes up, the case transitions out of the *Monitoring* state.

    a. If the monitoring conditions have not been met, the case is put back into the system, returning to the *Initiated* state.

    b. If the monitoring conditions have been met, the case passes from *Monitoring* to *Awaiting review*.

9. A case remains in the *Awaiting review* state until the case report is selected for review, at which time it is placed *Under review*.

10. At the end of the review, the case will have either been deemed payable or non-payable:

    a. If the case was deemed payable (as a result of the review), the case state becomes *Payable*.

    b. On the other hand, if case was deemed *Not Payable*, its status becomes *Not Payable*. From there it moves to its final state.

11. Once a cheque has been issued for a *Payable* case, it becomes *Paid*. From there, it moves to its final state.

12. If, at any time while a case is *Initiated* or *Scheduled for a gathering*, the parties agree to dismiss the case, then its status is recorded as *Resolved/no gathering*. From there it moves to its final state.

Your next step is to document these transitions on the state machine diagram you began earlier.

Case Study G2: Resulting Documentation

Figure 7.9 shows the state machine diagram that you've developed for the *Case* object.

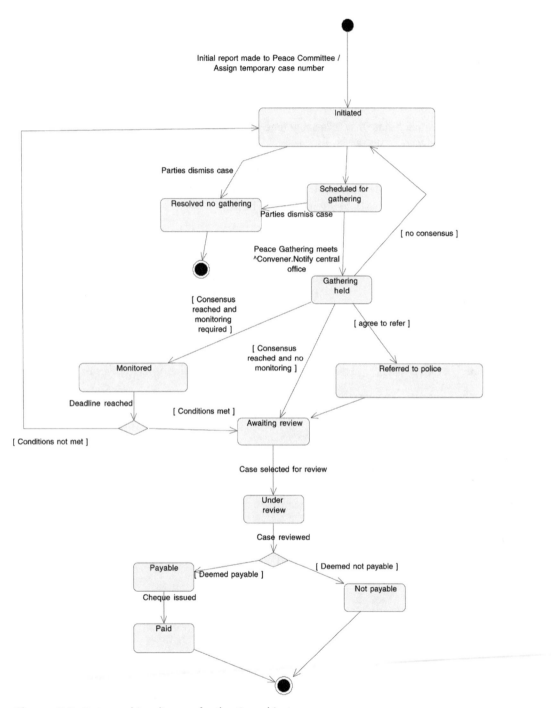

Figure 7.9 State machine diagram for the *Case* object

Step 2a ii: 3. Identify State Activities

The next step is to identify what activities occur while the object is in each state.

Listen up!

A *state activity* is a process that occurs while an object is in a certain state.

An *activity* within a state may take some time. (This is in contrast to an *activity* on a state transition, which always occurs quickly.)

List activities inside the state symbol. You'll need to identify when each activity occurs with a prefix, as follows (the UML keywords are in bold):

Entry/ activity	The activity occurs whenever the object *enters* this state.
Do/ activity	The activity occurs while the object *is in* this state
Eventname/ activity	The activity occurs *in response to an external event.* (Deviating from the UML standard, Rational Rose uses the keyword *event* before this phrase. Some of the diagrams in this book were produced from Rose and use this keyword inside the state symbol.)
Exit/ activity	The activity occurs whenever the object *leaves* the state.

Name the activity informally, such as *Monitor case.* If you want to specify that a different object carries out the activity, handle it as a send event, as in ^*monitor.monitor case.* (As before, if you find the notation of a send event cumbersome, don't use it. Document it as a regular event and clarify who performs the job with a note if necessary.) Figure 7.10 shows the various types of activities associated with the *Monitored* state of a *case* object in the CPP system.

Figure 7.10 Documenting the *Monitored* state

Note to Rational Rose Users

To add activities to a state, use the following steps:

1. Select (double-click) the state to bring up the State Specification window.

2. Select the Actions tab, position the mouse within the window, and right-click. Select Insert.

Rose will start the activity off as an *entry/*. To change it, double-click on the word *entry/* and make your changes in the Action Specification window, as shown in Figure 7.11.

Figure 7.11 The Action Specification window of Rational Rose

Case Study G3: State Activities

Further interviews with the users reveal that the following activities are carried out for a case based upon its state:

- *Initiated state*: While a case is in this state, the Peace Committee interviews the parties to the dispute and sets a date for the Peace Gathering.

- *Referred to police*: When a case enters this state, the Peace Gathering escorts the parties to the police station.

- *Resolved no gathering*: As soon as a case enters this state, a case report must be entered.

- *Under review*: While a case is in this state, the Convener reviews the case.

- *Monitored*: Whenever a case enters this state, the Convener is asked to appoint a Monitor. While the case is in this state, the Monitor provides ongoing monitoring. If the monitor becomes ill while the case is in this state, the Convener is to appoint a temporary monitor. Whenever the case leaves this state, the Monitor is to submit a monitoring report.

Case Study G3: Resulting Diagram

Your next step is to add these activities to the state machine diagram you have been developing, as shown in Figure 7.12. Please note that this diagram was produced using Rational Rose and, therefore, uses the *event* keyword for activities in a state that are triggered by an external event. As noted earlier, the UML does not advise the use of the *event* keyword in this context.

Step 2a ii: 4. Identify Composite States

If a number of states share one or more transitions, you can simplify the drawing by using composite states.

Listen up!

A *composite state* is a state that contains other states. It represents a general state for an object that encompasses any number of more specific states, called *substates*. A *substate* inherits the transitions of its *composite state*.

Place an initial *pseudostate* inside the composite state so that you can indicate the first state that the object moves to as it enters the composite state.

For example, an ATM transaction initially passes through the states *Checking access*, *Getting input*, and *Checking balance*. If the user cancels the transaction while it is any of these states, the transaction immediately changes to a *Cancelled* state. Rather than show three transitions, you invent a composite state, *In progress*, and use it as shown in Figure 7.13.

Note to Rational Rose Users

To create a composite state, follow these steps:

1. Use the regular "state" tool to create the new composite state.
2. Select the new state symbol in order to view the item's handles.
3. Grab a handle and stretch the state symbol.
4. Drag the substates into the composite state.
5. To include a history node (referred to in the UML as a *pseudostate*), double-click on the state to display the State Specification window, select the General tab, and check the History box.

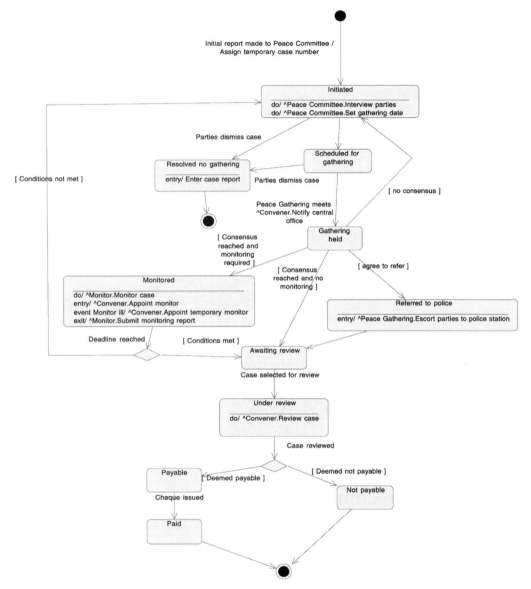

Figure 7.12 Adding state activities to the state machine diagram

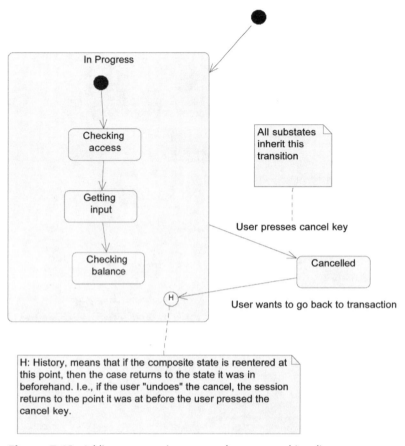

Figure 7.13 Adding a composite state to the state machine diagram

Case Study G4: Composite States

You examine the state diagram you have developed so far, looking for an opportunity to simplify it through the use of composite states.

Suggestion

Look for two transitions that have the same label and that go to the same state. Model the states at the origin of these transitions as substates.

Case Study G4: Resulting Documentation

Figure 7.14 shows the state diagram after you've incorporated several composite states.

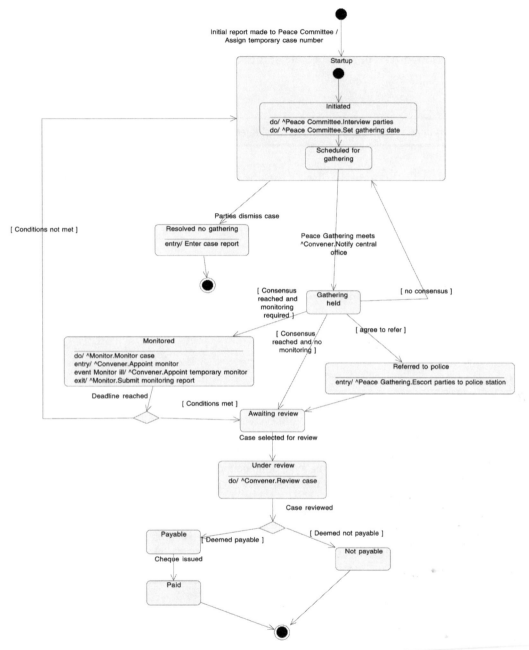

Figure 7.14 State machine diagram for a case with composite states

Step 2a ii: 5. Identify Concurrent States

If, according to one criterion, an object can be in one of a set of states and, according to another criterion, can be in another state at the same time, use concurrent states to model the object.

Listen up!

An object is in *concurrent states* when it is considered to be in more than one state at the same time.

The UML refers to the state that holds the concurrent states as an *orthogonal* state. An *orthogonal* state contains more than one region; each region holds states that can vary independently of the states in the other regions.

Concurrent State Example

If the payment on an insurance claim is large, it is not paid right away. Rather, it is scheduled for payment, during which payments are made at regular intervals. At the same time, the claim also undergoes monitoring. Once all payments have been made, no more payments are scheduled and monitoring ends. One way to model this is with concurrent states, as shown in Figure 7.15.

Note

In Figure 7.15, the claim object moves from the *accepted* state into the concurrent states if the amount of the claim is large. In this case, the vertical bar indicates a *fork*—a point after which the following transitions occur in any order: a transition to *Payments scheduled* and a transition to *Monitored*. Once all payments have been completed, the case makes the transition out of the *Payments scheduled* state. When the monitoring period is over, it makes the transition out of the *Monitored* state. When *both* these transitions have occurred (indicated by the second vertical bar, or a *join*), the object moves into the *Payments issued* state. On the other hand, if the amount of an accepted payment is small, it immediately goes into the *Payment issued* state.

This is a simple example to introduce the concept of concurrent states. Concurrent states can get much more complicated. For example, each half of the diagram typically depicts a *series* of state transitions.

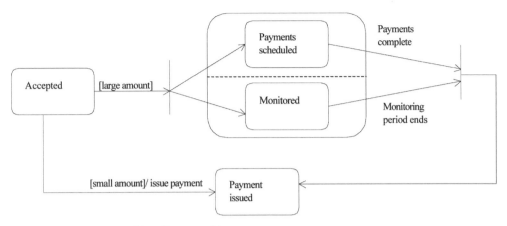

Figure 7.15 State machine diagram with concurrent states

Chapter Summary

In this chapter, you performed the following B.O.O.M. steps:

2: Analysis

2a) Dynamic analysis

      i) Describe use cases (use-case description)

      ii) Describe state behavior (state machine diagram)

            1. Identify states of critical objects

            2. Identify state transitions

            3. Identify state activities

            4. Identify composite states

            5. Identify concurrent states

New tools and concepts you learned in this chapter include the following:

1. *State machine diagram*: A picture indicating how an object changes from one state to another.
2. *State*: The status that an object may have at any given time. The state of the object determines what activities are performed, how the object responds to events, and so on.
3. *Transition*: A change of state.
4. *Event*: Something that happens, causing the state of an object to change.
5. *Guard*: A condition.

6. *Activity*: A process that occurs while an object is in a given state. It may be specified as "entry," "do," "exit," and so on.

7. *Composite state*: A general state that encompasses more precise substates. Substates inherit the transitions of the composite state.

8. *Concurrent states*: States that may occur at the same time. The state holding the concurrent states is referred to by the UML as an *orthogonal* state.

9. *Concurrent states*: States that may apply to an object at the same time.

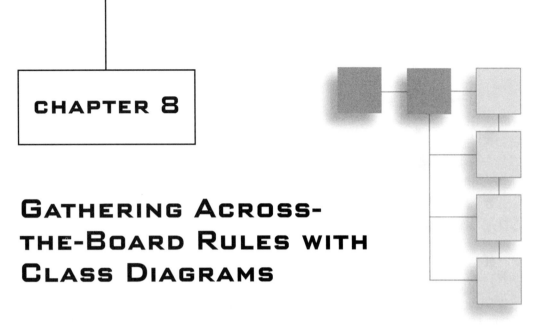

CHAPTER 8

GATHERING ACROSS-
THE-BOARD RULES WITH
CLASS DIAGRAMS

Chapter Objectives

In this chapter, you will

- Learn a step-by-step interviewing process for uncovering business rules regarding the precise relationships between business classes.
- Document these relationships in accordance with UML 2.
- Through this process, decrease the likelihood that the developers will introduce database and screen design errors.

B.O.O.M. steps covered in this chapter include the following:

2b) Static analysis

    i) Identify entity classes

    ii) Model generalizations

    iii) Model transient roles

    iv) Model whole/part relationships

    v) Analyze associations

    vi) Analyze multiplicity

Tools/concepts you'll learn to use in this chapter are the following:

1. Entity class
2. Class diagram
3. Inheritance

4. Aggregation

5. Composition

6. Association

7. Multiplicity

8. Object diagram

9. Link

Step 2b: Static Analysis

Review

In Chapter 7, you worked with state machine diagrams. You looked at state machine together with activity diagrams because those are your main options for describing the dynamic nature of the business—the sequencing of business events and activities. If you want to highlight activities, use activity diagrams; if you want to shine the spotlight on a specific object and how it changes in response to conditions and events, use the state machine diagram.

The state diagram started you thinking about the dynamic nature of business objects. Objects are the fundamental "atoms" that make up a business system. In this chapter, you'll learn to analyze the static, or structural, nature of business objects—the rules that apply *irrespective of time*. An example of such a rule is the maximum number of *Peace Committees* that can handle a *Case*. The rule about this maximum does not change over time, and is, therefore, part of the static model.

Listen up!

A *static model* is an abstract representation of what the system is. It represents the aspects of a system that are not related to time, such as the kinds of subjects tracked by the system, how these subjects are related to each other, and the information and business rules that relate to each one. The main diagram you'll be using for static modeling is the *class diagram*.

Output from this step consists of the following:

- Class diagram
- Package diagram
- Composite structure diagram
- Object diagram

FAQs about Static Analysis

Why isn't the Business Analyst's job over *after dynamic analysis?*

The dynamic requirements lack a complete description of the "nouns" of the business. Also, the precise numerical relationship between the "nouns" is undefined.

For example, in Chapter 2, you read about a municipality with a human resources (HR) system. Because they had not worked out the numerical relationship between employees and unions, they ended up purchasing an HR system that allowed an employee to belong to only one union, when in fact some employees belonged to more than one. As a result, the software could make only a single deduction of union dues for each paycheck, the data tables were set up incorrectly, and the input screens used to assign employees to unions were incorrect. Guess who had to pay for all those corrections? (Answer: the municipality.) Had the BAs performed a proper static analysis, they would have included the employee-union rule in the requirements documentation, diminishing the chances that it would be missed in the software and ensuring that, at the very least, the cost of the fix would be borne by the developers.

Aren't these issues addressed in the dynamic analysis?

It is true that many of these issues are contained within the system use-case descriptions. For example, in a banking system, the relationship between customers and accounts might be found in a system use case, *Open new account.* However, since dynamic analysis does not include a rigorous approach to examining the "nouns," it is likely that some important requirements will be missed. Also, since these rules are dispersed throughout the use cases, there is the possibility for internal inconsistency within the BRD. For example, a system use case *Open new account* might allow up to three people to co-own an account, while a system use case *Query account activity* allows for only one owner. In addition, future requirements for enhancements to the system may add new inconsistencies.

What does static analysis have to do with this?

Static analysis focuses on the "nouns" of the system. It provides a rigorous method for ensuring that all of these nouns are fully analyzed and documented. Requirements that cut across system use cases but relate to the same classes of objects (nouns) are centralized in a set of diagrams and accompanying documentation. This makes it easier to ensure internal consistency within the BRD. Each system use case description is verified against the static model. As future system use cases are added, these too are checked against the static model, ensuring that business rules are obeyed in future enhancements.

What is the context for static modeling?

Use the static diagrams as a guide for asking questions and as form of shorthand during interviews. Later, include the diagrams in the BRD. They enable a seamless transition to development, since they present the business model in a form widely understood by OO developers.

What issues are addressed during static analysis?

OO static analysis provides a step-by-step procedure for documenting the attributes and operations that apply to each business and the numerical relationships between business objects, such as the fact that many customers may own a particular account.

Step 2b i: Identify Entity Classes

Listen up!

An *entity class* is a *category* of business object, tracked by the system.

Rules about Objects and Classes

All objects of the same class must share the same operations, methods, and attributes.

FAQs about Entity Classes

Why use the term *entity* class? Why not just class?

The term *entity* is used to differentiate these classes from other types of classes introduced into the system during the development stage.[1] An *entity class* describes objects that are tracked by the business. Since all the classes we'll be interested in as BAs are entity classes, I will sometimes just use the simpler term *class*.

What are some examples of entity classes?

Payment and *Customer*.

---

[1]These include control classes, which encapsulate process logic; boundary classes that act as interfaces; utility classes, like *Date*; special design classes to support multitiered architecture; and so on. In the UML, the kind of class can be shown with a *stereotype*. The stereotype may be shown as <<Control>>, <<Entity>>, and so on, when the class appears on a class diagram, or special symbols may be used.

What attributes are specified for a class?

The attributes specified for an entity class are information items typically stored by the business for a long period, such as the *date* and *amount* of a *Payment,* the *name* and *address* of a *Customer,* and the *price* of a *Product.* Attributes usually show up in the user interface as field names on screens and reports. In the database, they show up as data fields (also called *columns*).

How do you come up with a list of entity classes?

Review the system use-case documentation and human interface requirements (screen mock-ups, report layouts, and so on). Any noun phrase appearing in these, such as *Wholesale customer,* is a candidate class. (I use the term *candidate class* because the noun may represent something else, such as an attribute.) Consider also conducting interviews specifically for the purposes of static analysis. Hints to guide the interview follow later in this chapter.

Indicating a Class in UML

Figure 8.1 shows how to indicate classes in UML.

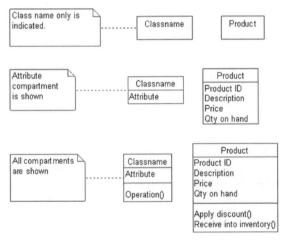

Figure 8.1 Classes in UML

Naming Conventions

Name a class with a singular noun phrase, such as *Invoice* or *Retail customer*. Though the UML includes more formal naming conventions, these are more relevant to developers than to Business Analysts. As a BA, your prime interest is to enhance communication between business stakeholders and the technical team, and an informal naming convention works best for this purpose.[2]

Grouping Classes into Packages

If the model contains a large number of classes, it's worth grouping them so they'll be easier to manage. The UML provides the package symbol to stand for a container. We've seen this before with respect to use cases. Here, we will use the package to contain classes and class diagrams. Class packages may contain other packages for as many levels as necessary.

It's helpful to depict all of the packages on a single diagram—a simple form of the class diagram. When using a modeling tool such as Rational Rose, it is a good practice to make this the top-level *main* diagram. Used this way, the diagram acts as a navigation map—each package icon links to the class diagram that depicts all of the classes in the package.

There is no rule (although there are suggestions[3]) for how to group the classes into packages. One recommended approach, applicable to many business contexts, is to define packages according to the common "flavors" of business classes: *People and Organizations, Products and Services,* and *Events/Transactions.* Figure 8.2 shows this approach, which you'll use in the case study.

---

[2]The UML does include other naming conventions for classes, attributes, and operations. Use these during the design stage. These standards include

- For a *class* name: Begin the name with an uppercase letter.
- For an *attribute* name: Begin the name with a lowercase letter.
- For an *operation* name: Begin the name with a lowercase letter. Follow the name with parentheses; these will be used to surround parameters and help identify the name as an operation.
- For any name: If there are two or more words to the name, join the words into a single name; mark the beginning of each new name with an uppercase letter.

[3]Some methodologies use a package for each group of classes within an inheritance or aggregation arrangement. Others design packages so that collaboration between classes in separate packages will be at a minimum and/or unidirectional.

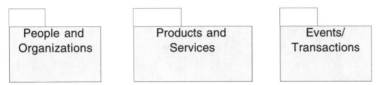

Figure 8.2 Example: Class packages for business entities in the CPP system

Figure 8. 3 A package diagram for a telecommunications company

The Package Diagram

A *package diagram* is simply a large package symbol with the package's classes drawn inside it. This form of diagram was valid in previous versions of the UML standard, but the name for the diagram, *package diagram,* is new to UML 2.[4] Figure 8.3 is an example of an early draft of the *Product and Services* package diagram for a telecommunications company.

The best way to organize the diagrams is to use the package diagram to show only classes, generalizations, attributes, and operations; show other relationships between the classes on separate diagrams. Don't try to say too much on any one diagram. Instead, draw a new diagram to highlight a specific aspect of the system, such as a particular aggregation. This way, each diagram gets across one main idea, making it easy to interpret.

Interview Questions for Finding Classes

Tip

Dedicate interview time specifically for the purpose of static modeling. This helps you learn the business terminology relevant to the project.

[4]Previously, the diagram was treated as a form of the class diagram.

> I once worked with a group who were developing a model for a telecommunications system. They kept talking about *Product Groups*. It was only after I began to develop the static model that it became apparent there was no consensus on the meaning of this business term. Half the people on the project thought it referred to a group of products and services marketed together under one package price; others thought it referred to a particular telephone line and all the services attached to it. This type of ambiguity often crops up in the requirements and can lead to serious errors in the software. By creating a static model, you'll ensure that there is a clear understanding of each business noun that appears in the requirements.

The first step of static modeling is to identify the classes of objects that comprise the business. Use the following questions during the interview. The same rules also help you derive classes from the system use-case descriptions.

To find candidate classes, ask these questions:

1. What *people and organizations* does the system keep track of? Examples include *Customer*, *Card holder*, and *Board member*.
2. What *events and transactions* does the system keep a record of? An example is *Sale*.
3. What products and services does the system keep a record of? Examples include *Chequing account (product)* and *Cheque return (service)*.

Challenge Questions

Ask these follow-up questions about candidate classes:

1. Is it important that the business track this class?

   If not, then exclude it from the list of classes. For example, in a point-of-sale system for a corner grocery store, you would exclude the class *Customer* because the store doesn't keep track of its customers.

2. If two candidate classes appear similar, is there any attribute, operation, method, or relationship that applies to one class but not the other?

   If the answer is "yes," treat each candidate as a separate class.[5] Otherwise list one class only for both. For example, *Digital cell phone* and *Analogue cell phone* each have specialized attributes, although they also share others. List them as two separate classes.[6] On the other hand, *Green cell phone* and *Blue cell phone* share the same

---

[5]You may also add a new class to act as a generalized class for common attributes, though you will focus on this later.

[6]A new class "Cell phone" may also be added to contain rules applying to all cell phones. More on this when we discuss inheritance.

attributes and operations and do not represent distinct classes. (A *color* attribute in the *Cell phone* class will suffice to distinguish between them.)

3. Is the candidate class merely a piece of information about something else?

   If the answer is "yes," you are not dealing with a class at all, but an attribute. For example, *Customer name* is not a class; it's an attribute of the *Customer* class.

4. Is it an alias for a previously recorded class?

   Sometimes business stakeholders use two names for the same thing. If this is the case, ask them to settle on one phrase as the main name; document this as the *class name*. Treat the other one as an *alias*—an alternative name for the class.[7] For example, *Client* is an alias for *Customer*. If your BRD includes a business glossary (a dictionary of business terms), then add the alias to this glossary.

Note

Remember, the goal of Step 4 is to produce a simple list of classes. Anything else you pick up at this stage is "gravy." For example, if you pick up any attributes now, by all means record them but don't spend too much time on them.

Here are some follow-up questions to ask users about selected classes:

1. Could you provide a brief description of the class? (The description should be one paragraph.)

2. Could you provide a couple of examples of the class?

3. Could you tell me a few pieces of information (attributes) that you'd track about each example (object)?

Supporting Class Documentation

Document the following for each class:

- Class (use a singular noun phrase to name the class)
- Alias
- Description
- Examples
- Sample attributes

---

[7]There must be a one-to-one association between two terms or they are not aliases but separate classes. For example, an Account and Customer cannot be considered aliases if a customer can have more than one account. Additionally, if different operations apply to each or they are used in different contexts, they must be considered as separate classes rather than aliases.

Here is an example:

Class:	*Customer*
Alias:	*Client*
Description:	Person or company that does business with us
Examples:	Stan Plotnick, Minelli Enterprises
Sample Attributes:	*Name, Mailing address, Credit rating*

Note to Rational Rose Users

When you open a Rose model, Rose displays a class diagram listed in the Logical View of the Browser window under the name Main. This is a good diagram to use to indicate the class packages, as follows:

1. To add a package to the diagram, use the Package tool.

2. To create a class diagram for one of these packages, first select (double-click) the package icon in the Active Diagram window for the Main diagram. This will open a new diagram that you can use to model the classes in the package. Unfortunately, you won't be able to draw a true package diagram since Rose (at the time of this writing) does not support this feature. However, you will be able to depict the classes themselves without the package icon.

3. To add a class to the diagram, click on the Class tool on the toolbar, then click anywhere in the diagram.

4. To add documentation to a class, click once on the class's icon and enter your notes in the Documentation window (at the bottom-left of the screen).

Case Study H1: Entity Classes

Seeking to define the "nouns" used within the CPP, you conduct an interview with business subject matter experts. You ask them what types of *people and organizations* are tracked by the CPP, what types of *events or transactions* occur, and what *products and services are* offered by the CPP. Here's what you learn:

■ The organization consists of CPP members who work for head office. It administers a network of Peace Committees throughout South Africa.

■ When a Peace Committee member is informed about a case (dispute), he or she alerts the Peace Committee, which then meets with each party to the dispute and organizes a Peace Gathering.

■ Various attendees participate in the Peace Gathering. An attendee may be a person or represent an agency involved in the case.

- All attendees at a Gathering must be recorded. Extra information is kept about attendees who are there as Observers. (For example, information about the Observers' relationship to the parties involved in the dispute is recorded.)

- When a case has been dealt with, various payments are disbursed to the personnel involved in dealing with the case and to various community funds. (The next several items explain the disbursement of funds.) Payments are not made to the parties involved in the dispute.

- The Peace Committee members involved with the case are paid.

- Also, payments are made into three fund accounts, which the system tracks internally: Admin Fund Account, Peace Building Fund Account, and Microenterprise Fund Account. The same fields are tracked for each of these funds.[8]

- Payments are also deposited into Peace Committee (PC) Member Accounts for each PC member involved in the case.

- Internal Accounts are kept so that the CPP is aware of the current balances and payments for all Fund Accounts, Peace Committee Member Accounts, and the Cash Account.

Your Next Step

Start developing the static model, showing only the classes you've derived from the notes.

Suggestions

First, create a Main diagram showing only the packages *People and Organizations*, *Products and Services*, and *Events/Transactions*. Then create a package diagram for each package. Use the interview questions and challenge question you learned earlier to pick out the classes mentioned in the preceding notes. When you discover a class, add it to the appropriate package diagram.

Case Study H1: Resulting Documentation

Figure 8.4 shows the diagrams that you've developed after determining the entity classes.

Notes on the Model

The model includes classes such as *Person* and *Agency* because they came up during the interviews, and it seems likely that they will each have special attributes. For example, every

---

[8]Note that while the Fund Manager *actor* referred to elsewhere represents an external software system, the listed fund accounts (Admin Fund Account, Peace Building Fund Account, and so on) refer to the internal records of the accounts.

People and Organizations

Person

Agency

Party to Dispute

Peace Committee

Attendee

Peace Committee Member

Observer

CPP Member

Products and Services

Internal Account

Peace Committee
Member Account

Cash Account

Fund Account

Figure 8.4 Diagrams reflecting the entity classes for the CPP system

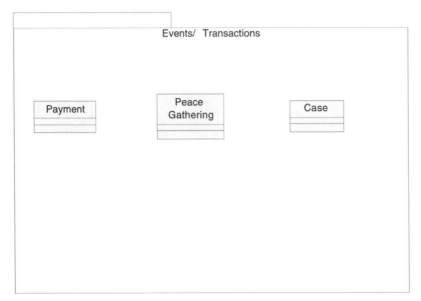

Figure 8.4 Diagrams reflecting the entity classes for the CPP system (continued)

Person in the system is likely to be tracked with attributes (such as *name* and *address*) that stay with the person, whether that person is a CPP Member, Party to Dispute, or so on.

Only one *Fund Account* class is included, because the system treats all fund accounts the same way: a single process for calculating payments to a fund could be described, the attributes kept on each fund are the same, and so on. The *Cash Account* is treated as a separate class because it is different from other funds and accounts. For example, payments are *not* deposited to a cash account when a case is processed, whereas payments may be deposited to all the other accounts and funds.

A PC member and his or her corresponding account could have been modeled with a single class, but two classes were used since the organization often treats them separately; there are many instances where account information is irrelevant and only biographical information and operations should be accessible.

Step 2b ii: Model Generalizations

Subtyping

The upcoming steps deal with the issue of subtyping.[9] A subtype is a smaller category within a larger category. Subtyping is useful because it allows the Business Analyst to

---

[9] I use the word "subtype" here instead of "subclass" because I don't yet want to dictate the OO relationship to be used.

make statements about general types that automatically apply to all subtypes. You'll need to distinguish between two kinds of subtypes: full-time and part-time.

Full-Time Subtypes

A general category can be split into a number of full-time subtypes if objects cannot change from one subtype to the other over their lifetime. For example, in a non-coed dormitory, where dormers are processed differently according to their sex, *Male Dormer* and *Female Dormer* are two full-time subtypes of *Dormer*. Use the generalization relationship to describe full-time subtypes.

Part-Time Subtypes

Part-time subtypes are unstable. Use part-time subtypes to model objects that change from subtype to subtype during their life span. For example, in a welfare system, there are two subtypes of *Client*: an *Employed Client* and *Unemployed Client*. Since a client might change from one to the other, the two subtypes are part-time. The UML does not have a specific relationship icon for part-time subtypes. B.O.O.M. uses the UML *association* relationship, stereotyped as *plays role*, and refers to the relationship as a *transient role*. (More on this relationship later.)

Generalization

> ### Memory Jog: Generalization
>
> If class *x* is a (kind of) class *y*, then class *x* is said to be a *specialized class* (or specialization) of the *generalized class y*. Objects of class x inherit all of the features of class y, such as attributes, operations, and relationships.
>
> To this definition, we now add the following: For proper use of generalization, the subtypes must be full-time. An object cannot change from one specialized class to another during its lifetime.[10]

Why Model Generalizations?

Use of generalization reduces redundancy in the requirements: requirements that apply across a number of classes may be stated only once. Also, generalization allows you to specify rules that extend into the future; rules stated for a generalized class apply to all current and *future* specialized classes.

---

[10]Some Object-Oriented languages, do, in fact, allow an object to change its type during its lifetime, but even in these cases, you'll need to let the developers know whether a subtype is full-time or part-time, so that they can design an appropriate solution.

Sources of Information for Finding Generalizations

Ask leading questions during your interviews:

- Use the initial class diagrams you drew in the previous step as a guide for questions. Ask interviewees if any of the classes are variations on others. (A more detailed guide to questions follows in this section.)
- Review the system use-case documentation. Anywhere the documentation indicates that there is more than one "kind of" something (for example, two kinds of accounts), generalization may be indicated.

Rules Regarding Generalization

1. The specialized class inherits all the attributes, operations, and relationships of the generalized class.
2. The specialized class may have additional attributes, operations, and relationships beyond those inherited from the generalized class.
3. The specialized class may have a unique *polymorphic*[11] method for carrying out an operation it inherits from the generalized class.
4. According to the UML, a specialized class may inherit from more than one generalized class. This is called *multiple inheritance*. Many IT organizations limit the use of multiple inheritance because it can lead to ambiguities. (For example, if a specialized class inherits two methods for the same operation from two generalized classes, which one applies?) Check with your organization before using multiple inheritance.

Generalization Example from the Case Study

An *Observer* is an (that is, a kind of) *Attendee*.

The specialized class is *Observer*; the generalized class is *Attendee*. The specialized class *Observer* inherits all the attributes, operations, and relationships of the generalized class, *Attendee*. *Observer* may also have additional attributes, operations, and relationships. Also, through polymorphism, an *Observer* may perform an operation inherited from *Attendee* in its own unique way.

Don't Go Overboard

Remember that the use of generalization is meant to make life easier for the BA (ultimately). If the addition of a generalized class doesn't "buy you" anything, there is no reason to model it.

---

[11]Polymorphism allows a number of classes to have different implementations of the same operation.

If you are *unsure* whether or not to list a generalized class, include it for now and reassess your decision later. If toward the end of analysis there are no generic attributes, operations, or relationships that you can specify for the generalized class, you may discard it then.

Remember that the specializations must be full-time: An object of a specialized class cannot change into a different specialization. For example, a *Fund Account* does not turn into a *Peace Committee Member Account*. (Part-time subtypes are dealt with in the next step.)

Indicating Generalization in the UML

Figure 8.5 demonstrates how you express generalization in a diagram.

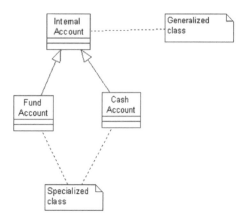

Figure 8.5 Indicating generalization in the UML

Interview Questions for Finding Generalizations

Use the following list of questions during an interview to identify *possible* cases of generalization. (Verify any decision made at this point using the *challenge questions* that follow.)

1. Can the following statement be made about any two classes?

   Class A *is a kind of* class B.

   If the answer is "yes," model class A as a specialized class of B. Model B as the generalized class.

   For example, a *Cash Account* is a kind of *Internal Account.*

2. Are any classes the same in some respects but different in others?

   If the answer is "yes," the two classes are specializations of a generalized class.

   For example, *Peace Committee Member Account* and *Fund Account* are similar but different. Both are specializations of *Internal Account.*

3. Is there any point where the business treats two otherwise distinct classes in a generic fashion?

If the answer is "yes," the two classes are specializations of a generalized class.

For example, a report on account activity for all *Internal Accounts* prints the same information about all kinds of accounts, regardless of whether they are *Fund Accounts*, *Cash Accounts*, or *Peace Committee Member Accounts*.

Challenge Questions

1. Can you substitute a specialized class wherever the generalized class is used in the requirements and still have valid specs? (This is called the *rule of substitution*.)

   If the answer is "no," then don't use generalization.

2. Is there at least one generic rule (an attribute, operation, or relationship) that can be stated for the generalized class?

   If not, it may not be a worthwhile generalization. For example, a *Telephone Line* and *Gas Line* are two kinds of *Line*s but they're treated as *specialized classes* of *Line* only if they have some things in common. If you think that you may uncover some commonalities later in the analysis, keep the generalization for now and reassess your decision later.

Advanced Challenge Questions

With generalization, the subtype of an object must be full-time—that is, stable during its lifetime—otherwise, a transient role is indicated. The following challenge questions can help determine whether the subtyping can be treated through generalization:

1. Can the object change its subtype during its lifetime?

   If it can, then don't use generalization or specialization to describe the relationship between the classes. For example, an *Employee* changes from being *On leave* to *Working*. These are not considered as specializations of *Employee*.[12]

2. Can an object be more than one subtype at the same time?

   If it can, don't use generalization or specialization. For example, a *Person* might be a *CPP Member* and a *Peace Committee Member* at the same time. *CPP Member* and *Peace Committee Member* are *not* treated as specialized classes of *Person*.[13]

3. Can an object act as more than one instance of the subtype?

   If it can, then don't use generalization. For example, a *Person* might be a *Party to Dispute* twice, once for each involvement; you cannot use generalization to describe the relationship between *Person* and *Party to Dispute*.[14]

---

[12]They might be viewed as *Transient Roles* or merely distinguished by a *Status* attribute.

[13]They would be viewed as *Transient Roles* of a *Person*.

[14]"*Party to Dispute*" is a *Transient Role* of a *Person* and of an *Agency*.

Note to Rational Rose Users

You may add the generalization relationships to existing diagrams, or you can create new diagrams—one for each generalization/specialization hierarchy.

1. To create a new diagram for a package, right-click the package icon within the Browser window and select New/Class Diagram.

2. To add an existing class to the new diagram, drag it from the Browser window onto the Active Diagram window.

3. To create a new class, first add it to the Main package diagram, using the Class tool. Next, drag the newly created class from the Browser window onto the new diagram.

Case Study H2: Generalizations

Interviews to identify generalizations yield the following notes:

1. An *Observer* is a special kind of *Attendee* (at a *Gathering*). Extra data is tracked about *Observers* over and above that kept for other *Attendees*.

2. A *Person* may be a *CPP Member* as well as a *Peace Committee Member*. The person may become a *CPP Member* or a *Peace Committee Member* at any time.

3. A *Person* or *Agency* is a *Party to Dispute*. One *Person* may be viewed as many *Parties to Dispute*. For example, if one person were a party to five disputes in five different cases, that person would be considered as five separate instances of a *Party to Dispute*. One record of biographical information is kept for the *Person* and one for *each* involvement.

4. All *Internal Accounts* are identified with a generic *Account Number*, and some common information is kept for all accounts (account balance and so on). However, additional information is kept on an account based on its type, which would be either *Cash Account*, *Fund Account*, or *Peace Committee Member Account*.

Your next step is to model the generalization relationships that these notes infer.

Suggestions

Create a new diagram for each grouping of full-time subtypes. Use the challenge questions to ensure that you've used generalization properly. If you discover any part-time subtypes, make a note about them; you'll add them to the model later.

Case Study H2: Resulting Documentation

Figure 8.6 shows the resulting diagrams for each group of full-time subtypes.

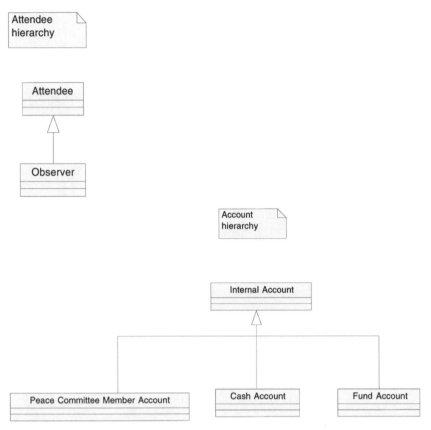

Figure 8.6 Full-time subtypes

Notes on the Model

The numbers in the following list correspond to those used earlier for the interview notes:

1. An *Observer* is a specialized class of *Attendee*.

2. A *CPP Member* is not a specialized class of *Person* because the same person may also be a *Peace Committee Member*[15] and because the subtype is not full-time.

3. Generalization does not apply. To be a specialization, a particular *Person* could only be viewed as at most one *Party to Dispute*, which is clearly not the case here.

4. Generalization applies. *Internal Account* is the generalized class, with each *Account* type being a specialization.

---

[15]An object may not belong to two specialized classes simultaneously. Another mechanism (role) must be used to model the relationship.

Step 2b iii: Model Transient Roles

Next, you model the part-time subtypes that you skipped over in the previous step.

A *transient role* is a part-time subtype representing a role that an object may play at one time or another during its existence—but may not play at other times.[16] (The term is not part of the UML.)

Is it a *state* or a *transient role*?

You may be wondering if you can handle part-time subtypes as *states* on a state machine diagram. The answer is that, in fact, a part-time subtype can be modeled both ways—in the state machine diagrams as a state and on class diagrams as a transient role. It's a question of what you want to communicate. If you want to get across how the object changes in response to events, use the state diagram; if you want to communicate the rules that govern how an object, acting in a given role, is related to other objects, use the class diagram with transient roles.

For example, in the case study, it is important to describe the life cycle of a *Case* as it goes from the *Initiated* state, through its intermediate states, and all the way to *Paid* and *Not Payable* in response to events and conditions. The state machine diagram explains this best. On the other hand, it is not important to explain how a Case's relationships to other classes change based on its evolving states—so there is little value in treating these states as transient roles in the static model.

The situation is different for a *Participant*. Here, there isn't much to be gained by explaining the life-cycle of a *Participant* as he or she changes from being a *CPP Member*, to *Peace Committee Member*, and so on, since the events that cause these changes are fairly self-evident. (For example, a *Participant* becomes a *Peace Committee Member* by joining a *Peace Committee*.) For that reason, a state machine diagram of a *Participant* adds little value. However, it *is* important to nail down exactly how the various *Participant* roles—such as *CPP Member*, *Peace Committee Member*, *Attendee*, and so on—are related to other classes, such as *Case*, *Peace Committee*, and *Peace Gathering*. This is best explained by including these roles in the class diagrams.

---

[16]Booch, Rumbaugh and Jacobson, in their book *The Unified Modeling Language User Guide* (Addson-Wesley, 1999, p. 165), refer to this concept as a dynamic type. They suggest modeling this situation by showing the primary class (in their example, *Person*) as a specialized class and the roles as generalized classes. The important thing is not *how* you model part-time subtypes, but that you have a consistent and clear way of indicating them. B.O.O.M. uses transient roles because they lend easily to the analysis of association, multiplicities, etc. (as discussed later in this chapter) right on the class diagram.

Example of Transient Role

An *Employee* is assigned the role of a *Business Analyst* when hired but later changes roles to become a *Systems Analyst*. *Business Analyst* and *Systems Analyst* are *transient roles* of an *Employee*.

How Does a Transient Role Differ from a Specialization?

- An object's specialization cannot change during its lifetime; an object's transient role may.

- Objects of a specialized class *inherit* properties from the generalized class. Inheritance does not apply, however, to transient roles.

Some Terminology

If objects belonging to class A have a part-time role, B, then

- A is the primary class
- B is the transient role
- The relationship between A and B is "plays a role"

(These terms are not part of the UML.)

Why Indicate Transient Roles?

The developers need to know whether the subtyping you indicate is full-time (generalization) or part-time (transient role). Different design and coding solutions apply in each case.[17] The only people who really know how stable the relationship is are the users—and as their ombudsperson, you are in the best position to find this out.

Also, by indicating a subtype as a transient role rather than as a specialization, you are signaling to yourself that you need to follow up with extra questions that do not apply to specializations. (These involve *multiplicity*, discussed later in this chapter.)

Rules about Transient Roles

1. It is possible (though not necessary) for objects of the primary class to have more than one transient role at a time.

---

[17]Technical note: In the code, transient roles may be handled as aggregations; the aggregate object is composed of an object of the primary class plus objects representing each of its roles. Inheritance does not apply, but special operations (referred to as *wrapper* operations) may be written to allow public access to role operations.

2. An object may change its transient role during its lifetime.

3. By indicating that a primary class plays a role, you are not specifying that every object of the primary class *has* to play this role—only that it might do so.

Indicating Transient roles

The concept of a transient role is not part of the UML. However, UML allows for extensions to the language through specialized use of its symbols, referred to as *stereotyping*. We'll invent a <<*plays role*>> association stereotype to convey this relationship, as shown in Figure 8.7.

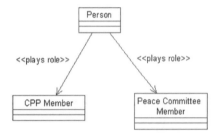

Figure 8.7 Indicating a transient role as an association stereotype

Sources of Information for Finding Transient Roles

Interview the stakeholders regarding the classes that you discovered in the previous steps. A guide to questions follows.

Interview Questions for Determining Transient Roles

To find transient roles, ask the following questions:

1. Can an object "wear many hats"?

   If the answer is "yes," each "hat" is a transient role. For example, can an employee have more than one role in the organization? If so, create a new class for each transient role, and draw a *plays role* relationship between the primary class and the roles.

2. Can an object of a given class change its subtype during its life span?

   If the answer is "yes," the subtype is a transient role. For example, any *Person* in the CPP organization may change from being a *CPP Member* to a *Peace Committee Member*, so these are considered transient roles of *Person*.

What If a Group of Specialized Classes Can All Play the Same Role?

If *all* specializations of a generalized class can play the same role, indicate the generalized class as the primary class.[18] For example, if both *Persons* and *Agencies* (two specializations of *Participant*) may attend a Peace Gathering, indicate that a *Participant* (generalized class) plays the role of *Attendee*. It is understood that this means that a *Person* can be an *Attendee*, and that an *Agency* can be an *Attendee*.

Note to Rational Rose Users

Indicate transient roles on existing diagrams or create new diagrams to highlight the relationships.

1. To model a transient role between two classes, use the *unidirectional association* tool: an arrow consisting of a solid line and an open arrowhead.
2. Open the specification window for the association (by double-clicking on it).
3. Enter **plays role** in the stereotype field.
4. After you have done this the first time, Rose adds *plays role* to the stereotype field pick list for the association specification window.

Case Study H3: Transient Roles

You continue your interviews, intending to elicit requirements about transient roles. You review the classes in the *People and Organization* package that relate to a role that a person or agency plays when involved with the CPP. You verify that there are no additional roles. Your next objective in the interview is to find out whether each role can be played only by a *Person*, only by an *Agency*—or either a *Person* or an *Agency*. To simplify the next series of questions, you work with stakeholders on defining a term that means *either a Person or an Agency*. You settle on the term, *Participant*. To record and explain this new class, you draw a new class diagram. (Hint: The diagram should treat *Person* and *Agency* as two kinds of *Participants*.) Next, referring to the existing *People and Organization* package, you select each class that represents a role and ask stakeholders whether it can be played by only by a *Person*, or only by an *Agency*, or by any *Participant*. You record each answer on the model as you get it, by drawing the appropriate transient role relationship. Here's what you learn in response to your questions:

1. Any participant (that is, a person or an agency) may be a party to a dispute. Each time a participant acts as a party to a dispute, separate statistics and data are recorded about the involvement.

[18]If only some of the specialized classes can play the role, indicate those specializations as primary classes.

2. Any participant (that is, a person or an agency) may be an attendee at a Peace Gathering. Each time a participant is an attendee at a gathering, separate statistics and information are tracked.

3. Only a person may be a CPP member or a Peace Committee member (that is, an agency may not be a member). Furthermore, a person may cease being a CPP member at any time and become a Peace Committee member. A person may also be a member of both organizations at the same time.

Your next step is to finalize the class diagrams describing the new class, *Participant*, and the new transient roles.

Case Study H3: Resulting Documentation

Figure 8.8 shows the diagrams that describe the transient roles that you identified.

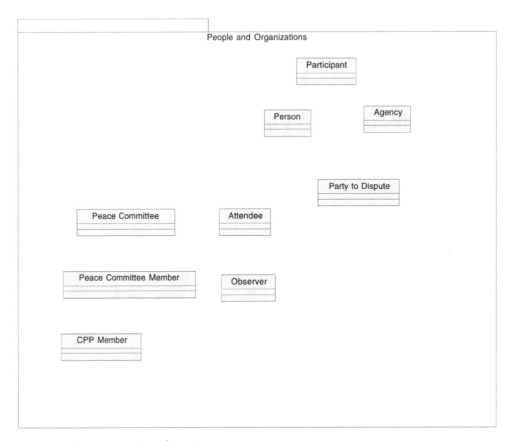

Figure 8.8 Transient roles of participants

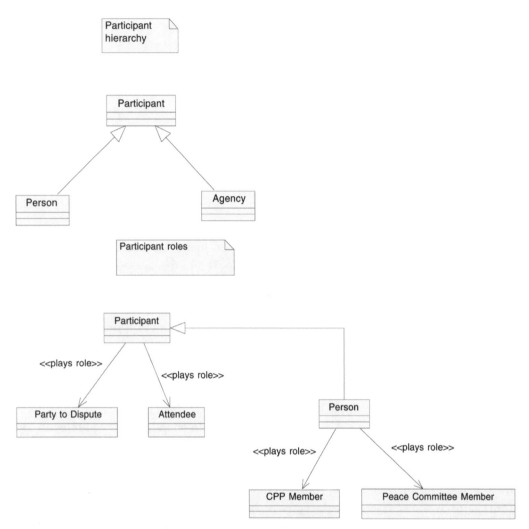

Figure 8.8 Transient roles of participants (continued)

Step 2b iv: Model Whole/Part Relationships

Some objects consist of other objects. In OO, you model these relationships using *aggregation* and *composition*.

The "Whole" Truth

Aggregation and composition describe the relationship between a whole and its parts. Aggregation is the more general term: It just means that there is *some* kind of whole/part relationship. Composition is more specific: It means that the whole owns the part entirely;

the part may not belong simultaneously to any other whole. Use the following guidelines to decide which of these relationships to use:

- If a part can belong to more than one whole and the part continues to exist when the whole is destroyed, specify the relationship as aggregation. Words that suggest aggregation include *collection*, *list*, and *group*.
- If a part is totally "owned" by the whole and the part ceases to exist when the whole is destroyed, specify the relationship as composition. Words that suggest composition include *composed of* and *component*.
- If you are not sure, specify aggregation.

Examples of Whole/Part Relationships

The relationship between a *catalogue* and the *products* that it includes is aggregation. On the other hand, the relationship between the *catalogue* and the *catalogue line items* (that refer to these products) is composition since, if the catalogue is discontinued, so are its line items.

The relationship between a travel booking and its flight, hotel, and car rental reservations is composition, since the cancellation of a booking also removes its reservations.

Why Indicate Whole/Part Relationships?

Aggregation is a strategy for reuse. If the same kind of part is used in more than one whole, the requirements for the part's class only need to be written once. Later, if requirements for the part change, they need to be specified only once to apply throughout the project.

These relationships also help the Business Analyst to distinguish between properties that are important for the whole and properties that are relevant to the parts. For example, in a mechanic's garage system, requirements that apply to a vehicle might include the attribute *Assembly date* and the rule that each vehicle may be owned by one or more owners; requirements that apply to vehicle's part might include the attributes *Replacement date* and *Part #*.

How Far Should You Decompose a Whole into Its Parts?

Take things as far as the business requires. For example, a used car lot might have only a *Vehicle* class to describe its inventory, whereas a service garage might require a *Vehicle* class as well as a *Vehicle Component* class. The difference is that only the service garage needs to keep track of the components of a vehicle.

Sources of Information for Finding Aggregation and Composition

Conduct interviews with stakeholders. Base your interview questions on the list of classes you compiled in the previous steps. A guide to questions follows. You can also discover whole/part relationships by reviewing screens, reports, layouts, and so on. Parts are often displayed along with the whole to which they belong. Also, review the system use case descriptions; if you discover any reference to parts, part attributes, or business operations related to parts, include the parts in the model. For example, a system for an auto repair shop may include a system use case *Service vehicle* that refers to the next inspection dates for various parts of an automobile.

Rules Regarding Aggregation and Composition

1. Parts do not inherit attributes, operations, or relationships from the whole—or vice versa.[19]

2. Aggregation and composition do not infer full-time links between objects. The whole can drop or add parts during its lifetime.

3. If a part dies when the whole dies, specify the relationship between them as *composition*. For example, the relationship between a policy and the riders attached to a policy is composition.

4. Specify any other whole/part relationship, for which rule 3 does not apply, as *aggregation*.

5. Don't lose too much sleep over whether a whole/part relationship is aggregation or composition. If you're not sure, specify aggregation.

Indicating Aggregation and Composition in UML

Figure 8.9 shows how to indicate aggregation and composition in a UML diagram.

The Composite Structure Diagram

UML 2 has introduced a new diagram for indicating composition, the *composite structure diagram*,[20] which gives a more intuitive view of a composite. The idea is simply to show the component parts inside the icon representing the whole, as shown in Figure 8.10.

This type of diagram is useful for describing the connections between component parts. For example, Figure 8.11 shows some of the component parts of a *Vehicle*.

---

[19]To make component (part) operations usable at the aggregate (whole) level, you need to define special operations, called *wrapper* operations, for the aggregate. A wrapper operation may have the same name as that used by the component(s). The wrapper asks the components to execute their version of the operation.

[20]Prior to UML 2, an equivalent diagram could have been constructed using context diagramming.

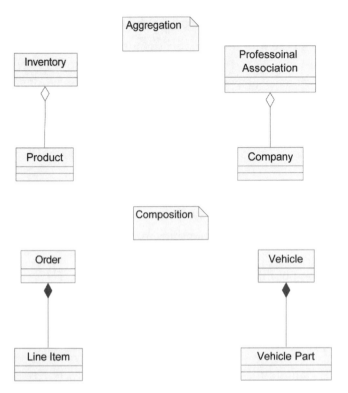

Figure 8.9 Aggregation and composition

Figure 8.10 Composite
structure diagram

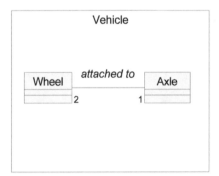

Figure 8.11 Showing component parts

The lines between the components indicate that the parts are connected. The numbers in the diagram are *multiplicities*, which are covered later in this book. The diagram in Figure 8.11, for example, specifies that each wheel is attached to one axle, and each axle to two wheels.

Interview Questions for Determining Aggregation and Composition

1. Is one object a part of another object?

   If the answer is "yes," indicate either composition or aggregation.

2. Is one object a collection or list of other objects?

   If the answer is "yes," then a whole/part relationship is indicated. Questions 4 and 5 below will help you decide whether to use aggregation or composition. As a rule of thumb, in most cases a list or collection is handled with aggregation. For example, an inventory is a collection—that is, an aggregation—of products.

3. Is one object an organization consisting of individual members?

   If the answer is "yes," then indicate a whole/part relationship. Whether you use aggregation or composition depends on the precise nature of the two classes involved. If you are specifying the relationship between the organization and a membership in the organization, use composition. If you are specifying the relationship between the organization and the independent bodies that belong to it, specify aggregation. If you're not sure, use aggregation.

4. When you destroy the whole, do you destroy its parts?

   If the answer is "yes," use composition. For example, when an invoice is removed from the system, all line items must also be removed.

5. Can one object be a part of more than one group?

   If the answer is "yes," then indicate aggregation. For example, a passenger might be part of two passenger manifests (lists)—one for each flight. *Passenger List* is an aggregate of *Passengers*.

Remember: If you are still not sure what to specify for a whole/part relationship, specify aggregation.

Challenge Question

1. Does it really make sense to say that A is a part of B?

   If the answer is "no," then you may not be dealing with aggregation or composition but with a more general relationship called an *association* (which is discussed later). For example, an *Insurance Policy* is linked to a *Customer,* but one is not part of the other.

Keep This in Mind

It is not a "big mistake" to confuse aggregation and another relationship you'll soon learn about, *association*. In fact, sometimes it's just a matter of semantics.

Note to Rational Rose Users

The default toolbar in Rose does not include the Aggregation tool. To add it, customize the toolbar as follows: Right-click on the toolbar and select Customize. Find and select the Aggregation tool in the available toolbar buttons and click Add.

Rose does not have a tool for *composition*. To model composition, first select the Aggregation tool on the toolbar, then move to the active diagram window and drag the mouse from the *whole* class to the *part* class. Rose will respond by displaying an aggregation relationship between them. Next, position the mouse on the aggregation line, close to the class representing the part. Right-click and select Containment of [part]. Next, select By value. Figure 8.12 shows what the screen will look like as you perform this operation.

If you need to mix classes from various packages together on one diagram, simply find the classes in the Browser window and drag them onto the diagram. Rose will indicate *from [package-name]* to remind you that you have "borrowed" a class from elsewhere.

Figure 8.12 Modeling composition with Rose

Case Study H4: Whole/Part Relationships

You continue your static modeling session with subject matter experts, now focusing on whole/part relationships. First, you examine your model for organizations and notice the *Peace Committee* class. You ask stakeholders if it is important for the CPP to track the *Peace Committee Members* that belong to each *Peace Committee*. Next, you look for objects that might be composed of other objects. Noting that a *Case* is a record of everything that happens with respect to a dispute, you ask stakeholders to identify what its components might be—using existing classes as your guide. You also note that a *Peace Gathering* is a collection of *Attendees* and ask stakeholders if it is important for the CPP to track which *Attendees* showed up at which *Gatherings*. This is what you find out:

1. The *Peace Committee* is an organization composed of *Peace Committee Members*.
2. A *Case* is a conglomerate of everything that is known and all actions taken with respect to a dispute. This includes *Peace Gatherings*, which are held as many times as necessary for a *Case*. Each *Case* also consists of the *Parties to the Dispute*.
3. Every time a *Peace Gathering* is held, the CPP must keep track of all the *Attendees* who made up the gathering.
4. One *Case* may require many *Peace Gatherings*. Only one *Case* is ever discussed during a *Peace Gathering*.

Your next step is to create a draft of the diagrams required to document your findings. Consider creating a separate diagram to describe each whole object's relationship to its parts.

Case Study H4: Resulting Documentation

Figure 8.13 shows the diagrams resulting from the information your interviews discovered about whole/part relationships.

Notes on the Model

1. When a *Peace Committee* disbands, all of its memberships are meaningless. Consequently, composition was used between *Peace Committee* and *Peace Committee Member*.
2. A *Case* is a record of everything that happened with respect to the dispute. This includes actions taken to deal with the dispute, such as *Peace Gatherings*. Since without a *Case* there is no *Peace Gathering*, and a *Peace Gathering* cannot be component of more than one *Case*, composition was used. This situation is similar to the composition relationship between a *Call* taken in a *Call Center* and all of the *Actions* resulting from the call.

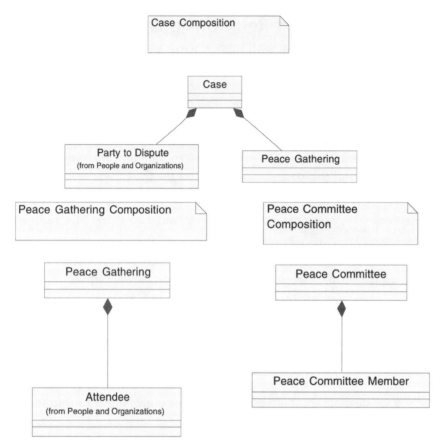

Figure 8.13 Diagrams reflecting whole/part relationships

3. If there is no *Case*, there are no *Parties* to it. Consequently, the *Case* is a composition of *Party to Dispute*.

4. There is no meaning to an *Attendee* unless there is a *Peace Gathering* to attend; consequently, composition was used.

Step 2b v: Analyze Associations

The next step is to discover all of the remaining ways that the system tracks one class of business objects against another. Each of these relationships is called an association.

Examples of Association

1. Information about one object refers to information about another object. For example, invoice data refers to product information (such as description and price), so *Invoice* is associated with *Product*.

2. To carry out a business operation relating to one object, an operation relating to another object must be performed. For example, when a booking is canceled (an operation of *Booking*), flights must be updated to reflect the newly available seat. *Booking* is thus associated with *Flight*.

Why Indicate Association?

Associations become part of the user's contract with the developers, ensuring that the software supports the business requirement to link business objects.

Second, the modeling of associations is a necessary preliminary step toward getting more detailed requirements (known as *multiplicity*, discussed later in this chapter).

Finally, associations are an important input for design. In the design phase, associations impact both the code (as pointers) and the database (as foreign keys). Keep in mind, though, that you are not dictating to the developers *how* to design the software; you are merely instructing them, through the associations you model, that the software needs to support the relationships—for example, that the software needs to track a case to the payments made against it.

Why Isn't It the Developers' Job to Find Associations?

You can't know what the associations are without knowing the way the business works. For example, only the business side knows whether payments are made against individual bills or against an account. It is the *BA's* role—not the developers'—to discover and document the rules that govern the business.

Discovering Associations

- Conduct interviews focused on the issue. Use the class diagrams you compiled in the previous steps for this purpose. Starting with key classes, interview users about possible associations to other classes.

- Review the system use-case descriptions. A requirement of the form *[noun] [verb] [noun]*—where both nouns represent classes—often suggests an association. For example, *Customer makes claim* implies an association between *Customer* and *Claim*; the association is labeled *makes*.

Rules Regarding Associations

1. Most associations are *binary*—an object of one class is related to an object (or objects) in a different class. For example, each *Case* object is associated with *Payment* objects.

2. An association may be *reflexive,* meaning that an object of the class is associated with another object of the same class. For example, one employee (the manager) manages other employees (team members).

3. An association does not have to be named—but it is a good idea to do so in order to clarify its meaning. If you do name the association, make sure that the name is not already used by any other association or class in the package. You may also add a small triangular arrowhead (▶) after the association name to indicate to the reader the direction in which to read the association.[21] This arrowhead is not required by the UML. It is often omitted by Business Analysts because the associations usually only make sense when read in one direction and because, by convention, the associations are read from left to right and top to bottom. (Keep in mind, though, that the UML standard does not attach any formal significance to the relative placement—left, right, etc.—of an element on a diagram.) It is recommended that you use the arrowhead wherever you feel there might be any confusion about how to read the association.

4. As an alternative (or in addition) to an association name, you may specify role names,[22] such as *manager* and *team member* (see Figure 8.14).

5. Indicate associations "as far up" an inheritance hierarchy as possible. For example, if a transaction log were kept for all internal accounts, indicate an association from *Transaction Log* to the generalized class *Internal Account*, not to the specialized classes *Fund Account, Peace Committee Member Account,* and so on.

6. If you are not sure if something is an aggregation or association, specify it as an association.

Figure 8.14 shows how to indicate associations in the UML.

The Association Must Reflect the Business Reality

It all sounds so easy! And it often is. However, be careful; sometimes there are subtleties. For example, Figure 8.15 shows a diagram modeling a system that manages credit card accounts.

In Figure 8.15, a payment is made against an account, not against a bill. One consequence is that the system will not be able to track which bills have been paid and how much was paid on each bill. This may be adequate for credit card payments, since they are not targeted to specific bills.

---

[21]At the time of this writing, Rational Rose does not support this feature.

[22]Don't confuse the UML role name—which defines the role an object plays in an association—with *plays role*—a B.O.O.M. stereotype.

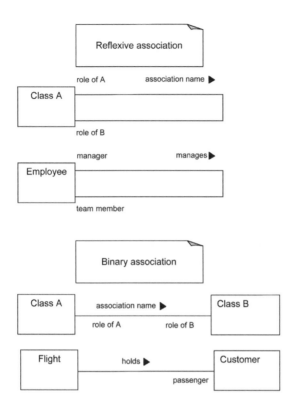

Figure 8.14 Indicating associations in UML

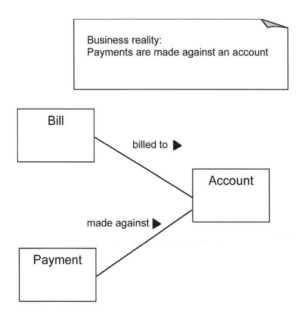

Figure 8.15 Diagram modeling credit card accounts

Contrast this with Figure 8.16, which shows the model for a small business's accounts receivable system.

Figure 8.16 A small business accounts receivable system

In Figure 8.16, the tracking of payments is more detailed; each payment is linked to a specific bill (or to specific bills). This type of tracking is usually required in an accounts receivable system.

Redundant Association Rule of Thumb

As a rule of thumb, if your model includes an indirect way to get from class A to class B and a shortcut that goes right from A to B, throw out the shortcut. Figure 8.17 illustrates this type of redundancy.

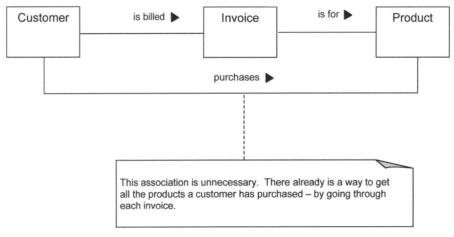

Figure 8.17 An example of redundant association

In Figure 8.17, the associations that run along the top of the diagram require the system to track all of the invoices billed to a customer and for each invoice, to track all of the products appearing on it. This implies that the system is required to track the products purchased by each customer. The shortcut adds nothing new, so it is removed.

Exception to the Rule of Thumb

Don't throw out the shortcut if it adds a new rule. Figure 8.18 shows an example.

In Figure 8.18, the top path requires that the system track all of the *Sales* made by a *Salesperson,* and for each *Sale* the *Customer* to whom it was billed. This implies that the system is required to track all the *Customers* to whom a *Salesperson* has made sales. But that's not what the shortcut says. It requires the system to associate *Salespersons* with the *Customers* for whom they are the prime contact. This is not the same as the first rule. For example, a salesperson may make sales to customers for whom he or she is *not* the prime contact—perhaps because the prime contact was away that day. As well, a salesperson may be the prime contact for a customer yet not have made any sales to that customer—perhaps because the customer was only recently assigned to the salesperson. Since the two rules are distinct, the shortcut is retained.

Figure 8.18 An example of a non-redundant association

Modeling Object Links with Object Diagrams

Sometimes, you can get an idea across better by diagramming a connection between objects, rather than a connection between classes. For example, suppose that you wanted to show that a *Transfer* is debited from a *From Account* and credited to a *To Account*. You could show the requirement using classes and associations, as shown in Figure 8.19.

Figure 8.19 Showing requirements using classes and associations

However, since *from account* and *to account* belong to the same class but play quite different roles, it might be clearer to diagram the business rule as shown in Figure 8.20.

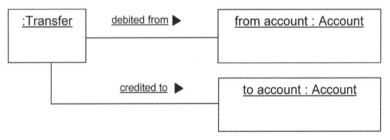

Figure 8.20 Diagramming objects of the same class with different roles

Because the diagram in Figure 8.20 shows objects rather than classes, it is not a class diagram but another static UML diagram called an *object diagram*. Note the following ways that this diagram differs from a class diagram:

- The names inside the boxes are names of objects, not classes. The following rules apply to object names:
  - Object names are underlined.
  - The full format of an object name is *object-name: class-name*. An example is *from account: Account*.
- You may omit the object name, as in *:Transfer*.
- Alternatively, you may omit the class name, as in *to account*.
- The relationship between the objects is referred to as a *link* (as opposed to an association, which relates classes). The link name should be underlined.

Tip

Use an *object* diagram instead of a *class* diagram if the situation you are trying to describe involves two objects that belong to the same class but act in different roles.

How to Discover Associations

1. During system use-case interviews, look out for statements of the form *X [verb] Y,* where *X* and *Y* represent business objects. They often reveal associations. For example, in "A *Peace Committee supervises* a *Case,*" *Peace Committee* is *associated* with *Case*; the association name is *supervises.*

2. Conduct interviews focused on associations, using existing class diagrams. Try to match each class symbol with each of the other classes. Ask interviewees, "Do you need to be able to track one of these [objects] against one of those?" If the answer is "yes," model the connection as an association on the diagram. Although this can be tedious when there are many classes, it does ensure that no associations slip through the cracks. For example, looking at *Payment,* you ask, "Do you need to match up a *Payment* to a *Peace Gathering,* a *Case,* a *Peace Committee Member Account,* an *Observer…?*" From the answers, you note that *Payment* is associated with *Case,* since each payment must be tracked to a specific case. You also find out that *Payment* is associated with *Peace Committee Member Account,* since a payment will be deposited into the account of each Peace Committee member who worked on a case. There is no direct association, however, between a *Payment* and a *Peace Gathering,* since a payment is not tracked to each *Peace Gathering* of a *Case.*

3. Examine screens, report layouts, and so on. If a screen or report ties together information about two objects, the objects are probably associated with each other.[23] For example, an invoice form includes a box for customer information: *Customer* is associated with *Invoice.*

4. Look out for redundant associations. Use the rule of thumb you learned in this chapter: If there is a long, indirect route to get from one class to another and a shortcut, the shortcut is probably redundant. Just to be sure, ask whether the shortcut expresses anything new. If it does, keep it; if not, remove it.

5. If there is a fine point about an association that you can't get across with the notations you've learned, add a note to explain the issue and attach it to the association. For example, in the following case study, a *Payment* may be associated with either a *Peace Committee Member Account* or a *Fund Account*—but not both at the same time. There are sophisticated UML features, such as the Object Constraint

---

[23]Be careful not to include redundant associations, that is, ones that can already be derived indirectly.

Language (OCL), that allow the modeler to formally make these kinds of distinctions. These UML features are of great value to the developers, particularly if they are intending to generate code from UML design diagrams. However, features such as OCL are of limited use to the Business Analyst, who can best get across these distinctions to his or her audience with simple, informal notes.

Case Study H5: Associations

Next, you try to elicit from stakeholders the *associations* the CPP needs to keep track of. To do this, you use the existing class diagrams as your guide, asking stakeholders to identify any time one object needs to be tracked against another. For example, you ask, "Does the CPP need to keep track of what *Payments* go with each *Case*?" If the answer is "yes" you draw an association line between the classes and prompt stakeholders for a meaningful verb to use as its name. At this point, you may learn that a Case *generates* Payments, providing the association name *generates*. Based on this line of questioning, you learn the following:

1. Each *Case* generates a number of *Payments* (subject to certain conditions).
2. Each *Payment* is withdrawn from the *Cash Account* and deposited into one of the *Fund Accounts* or into a *Peace Committee Member Account*. Each *Peace Committee Member* has a *Peace Committee Member Account* so that these deposits can be made.

Follow-up interviews regarding the system use case *Update Cases* results in the following notes:

1. A *Peace Committee* handles a case throughout its life span.
2. There is a special requirement for *Observers* who attend a *Peace Gathering*: Each *Observer* must be related in some way to one of the parties to the dispute.

Your Next Step

Create a draft of these associations (with descriptive text, if necessary) so they can be distributed to and verified by stakeholders.

Case Study H5: Resulting Documentation

Figure 8.21 shows the diagrams you've developed in determining the associations for *the CPP*.

Please note that, in the Payments Disbursement diagram of Figure 8.21, a note was used to explain a fine point about the associations between a *Payment*, a *Peace Committee Member Account*, and a *Fund Account*.

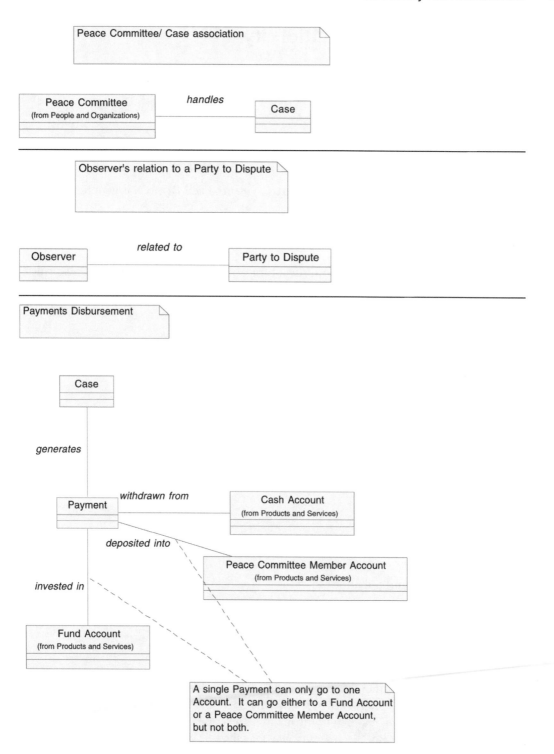

Figure 8.21 Associations required by the CPP

Step 2b vi: Analyze Multiplicity

Multiplicity: An indication of the number of objects that may participate in a transient role,[24] association, aggregation, or composition.

Example of Multiplicity

In the CPP, each *Case* generates zero or more *Payments*. Each *Payment* is generated by one and only one *Case*.

Why Indicate Multiplicity?

If you don't specify multiplicity, the software may not support important business rules, such as the number of customers who can co-own an account, or the number of beneficiaries who can be listed for an insurance policy.

Indicating Multiplicity in UML

Figure 8.22 shows how to indicate multiplicity in UML.

Rules Regarding Multiplicity

1. Indicate multiplicity at every tip of every UML symbol indicating a transient role, association, aggregation, or composition.

2. Indicate a multiplicity as follows:

   0..1   Zero or one

   0..*   Zero or more

   *   Zero or more (an alternative to 0..*)

   1..*   One or more

   1   One and only one

   a..b   From a through b, as in 1..5

---

[24]Recall, that in B.O.O.M., a transient role is an association stereotype. Multiplicity applies to transient roles since an object may, in theory, play any number of roles—even if they are of the same type. For example, a *Person* may be playing many *Attendee* roles, one for each *Peace Gathering*. Consequently, you'd indicate: "Each *Person* may play the role of zero or more *Attendees*. Each *Attendee* role is played by one and only one *Person*."

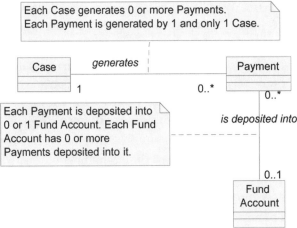

Figure 8.22 Multiplicity in UML

3. Each association generates two different sentences, one in each direction. When reading an association from class A to class B, ignore the multiplicity next to class A. When reading from left to right, piece together the sentence as follows: "Each [class name on left side of association] [association name] [multiplicity on right side] [class name on right side]." For example, Each *Case* generates 0 or more *Payments*.

   When reading from right to left, reverse the process. For example, each *Payment* is generated by one and only one *Case*.

4. Do not specify multiplicity along a generalization arrow.

5. In a composition relationship, the multiplicity adjacent to the class representing the whole must be one. (This is just the diagramming implication of the rule that, in a composition relationship, a part may not belong to more than one whole.)

Sources of Information for Finding Multiplicity

Conduct interviews, using your class diagrams as a guide for interviewing. A guide for questioning follows.

The Four Interview Questions for Determining Multiplicity

Conduct an interview using all of your existing class diagrams as source documents. The interview is over when you have answered all of the following questions, for *each* transient role, association, aggregation, or composition in the model:

1. Consider one object belonging to class A. What is the *minimum* number of class B objects to which it could be tied? (Common answers are zero and one.) Just to be sure, follow up with, "Is there any way it could be zero?"

   For example, looking at one *Case*, "What is the minimum number of *Payments* that might be posted against it? Is there any way there might be no *Payments* on a *Case?*" (The answer is that there may be zero *Payments* for two reasons: The case may not have advanced to the payment stage yet, or the *Case* was deemed "Not Payable.")

2. Consider one object belonging to class A. What is the maximum number of class B objects to which it could be tied? (Common answers are "one" and "many.")

   For example, looking at one *Case*, ask, "What is the maximum number of *Payments* that might be posted against it? (The answer is, "Many.")

3. Consider one object belonging class B. What is the minimum number of class A objects to which it could be tied? (Common answers are zero and one.) Just to be sure, follow up with, "Is there any way it could be zero?"

   For example, looking at one *Payment*, ask, "What is the minimum number of *Cases* that it is generated by? Could a *Payment* exist that was not generated by a *Case?* (Answer: A *Payment must* be generated by a *Case*, so the minimum multiplicity is one.)

4. Consider one object belonging class B. What is the maximum number of class A objects to which it could be tied? (Common answers are one and many.)

   For example, looking at one *Payment*, ask "What is the maximum number of *Cases* that might have generated it? (The answer is one.)

Note to Rational Rose Users

To indicate the common multiplicities, 0..1, *, 1, and 1..*, position the cursor at one end of the relationship, right-click and select the appropriate multiplicity. Then do the same for the other end of the relationship.

To indicate other multiplicities, such as *1..5*, double-click on the relationship to open the Association Specification window and select either the Role A Detail or the Role B Detail tab. Verify whether you've selected the right one by noting the name Rose displays to the right of the word Element; it represents the name of the class adjacent to the current association end. (If you cannot see the whole element name, click on the right border of the window and drag to the right to stretch the window.) If you've got the wrong association end, select the other Role Detail tab. Next, enter the desired multiplicity directly into the multiplicity field.

Case Study H6: Multiplicity

You conduct interviews with users in order to work out the business rules governing the numerical relationships between business objects. With your class diagrams to guide you, you inquire about the multiplicities of the associations, aggregations, compositions and transient roles that appear in the diagrams. For example, you ask, "How many *Participants* constitute a *Party to Dispute*? Could two *Participants* be considered a single *Party* if, for example, they were part of the same group? How many times can a *Participant* be involved as a *Party to Dispute*?" In this manner, you ask your stakeholders about every single relationship other than generalization that appears in the class diagrams. Here's what your interviewees tell you:

1. Some *Participants are never* involved as a *Party to Dispute*. Some *Participants* play the role of *Party to Dispute* once. Others play the role many times—once for each time they are involved in a dispute. (Considering each involvement as a separate occurrence of *Party to Dispute*, allows for a new set of business information—for example, the party's testimony—to be tracked for each involvement.)

2. Any *Party to Dispute* must be listed with the CPP as a *Participant* (either an *Agency* or *Person*).

3. A *Person* can take out only one *CPP Membership*.

4. A *Person* may be a member of more than one *Peace Committee* at the same time.

5. Each *Case* generates zero or more *Payments* (one for each fund and one for each Peace Committee member). Each *Payment* must be for one and only one *Case*.

6. Each *Case* is assigned to one and only one *Peace Committee*.

7. A *Case* must involve two or more *Parties to the Dispute*. Each involvement as *Party to Dispute* refers to one and only one *Case*.

8. An *Observer* must be related to at least one *Party* in a dispute. There is no limit to the number of *Parties* to which the *Observer* can be related. A *Party to Dispute* does not have to have any *Observers* present on his or her behalf; there is no limit to the number of *Observers* that may be related to a *Party*.

9. If a case is deemed payable, then payments are made to various accounts. Each *Payment* is withdrawn from the one *Cash Account* in the system and is deposited into one of the fund accounts (such as Microenterprise) or to one *Peace Committee Member Account.*

10. A *Peace Committee* may be set up without any members. As members join, they are added to the committee.

11. There must be at least one *Attendee* at a *Peace Gathering.* (This excludes *Parties to the Dispute,* who are expected to be at each *Peace Gathering* and are not considered *Attendees.*)

Your Next Step

Document the preceding notes as multiplicities on the existing class diagrams.

Case Study H6: Resulting Documentation

Figure 8.23 shows the diagrams resulting from your examination of the preceding multiplicities.

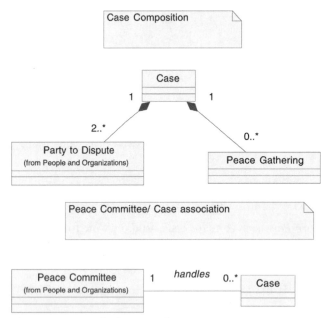

Figure 8.23 Multiplicities in the CPP system

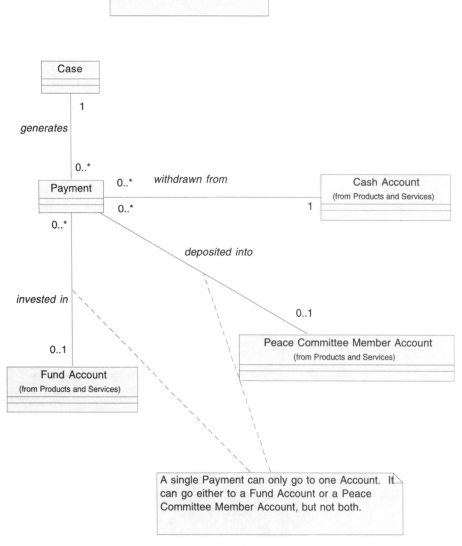

Figure 8.23 Multiplicities in the CPP system (continued)

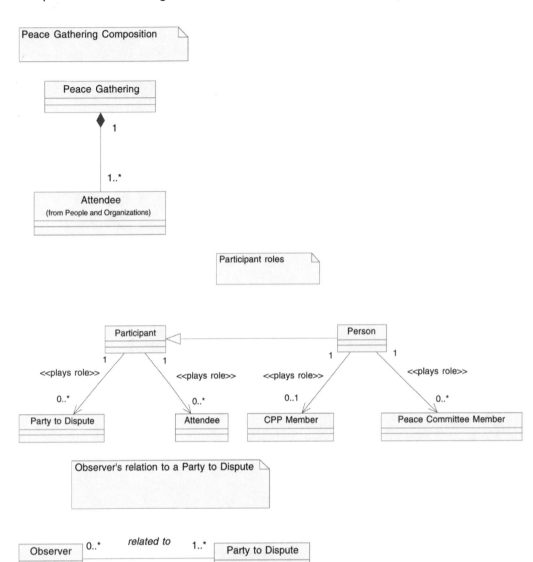

Figure 8.23 Multiplicities in the CPP system (continued)

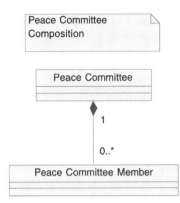

Figure 8.23 Multiplicities in the CPP system (continued)

Chapter Summary

In this chapter, you learned to complete the following B.O.O.M. steps:

2b) Static analysis

> i) Identify entity classes
>
> ii) Model generalizations
>
> iii) Model transient roles
>
> iv) Model whole/part relationships
>
> v) Analyze associations
>
> vi) Analyze multiplicity

By following these steps, you were able to elicit from stakeholders the precise meaning of business nouns and the ways that the business needs to be able to relate business objects to each other.

New tools and concepts you learned in this chapter:

1. An *entity class* is a category of business object tracked by the business.
2. A *class diagram* describes classes and the relationships between classes.
3. *Inheritance* is a property related to generalization. The specialized class is said to inherit all the atributes, operations, and relationships of the generalized class.
4. *Aggregation* is a relationship between a whole and its parts.

5. *Composition* is a special kind of whole/part relationship, where a part cannot belong to more than one whole at the same time and where the destruction of the whole causes the destruction of its parts.

6. An *object diagram* can be used in place of a class diagram to describe situations that involve more than one object of the same class acting in different roles, as in a payment that is withdrawn from a *from account* and deposited into a *to account*. In an object diagram, a connection between the objects is called a *link*.

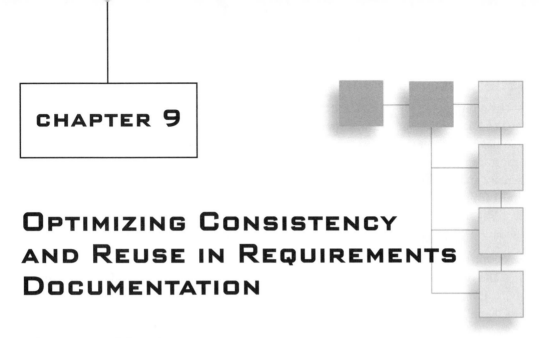

CHAPTER 9

OPTIMIZING CONSISTENCY AND REUSE IN REQUIREMENTS DOCUMENTATION

Chapter Objectives

In this chapter, you will

- Connect system use cases to the static model.
- Promote consistency and reuse of requirements by adding rules about attributes, operations, and look-up tables to the model.

B.O.O.M. steps covered in this chapter include the following:

2b) Static analysis

vii) Link system use cases to the static model

viii) Add attributes

ix) Add look-up tables

x) Distribute operations

xi) Revise class structure

Tools and concepts that you'll learn to use in this chapter include the following:

1. Association classes
2. Attribute
3. Meta-attribute
4. Operation
5. Precondition
6. Postcondition

Where Do You Go from Here?

At this point, your static model identifies the classes of objects that are used within the business domain as well the business rules dictating the relationships between them.[1] You also have documented some system use cases—a result of the dynamic modeling going on prior to and concurrently with the static modeling. This is a good time to consider the issue of traceability between the dynamic and static model. You should be able to *trace* (link) any system use case to elements of the static model because the static model contains details that apply to the use case but are not explicitly mentioned in it—for example, data validation rules.[2] The upcoming B.O.O.M. step walks you through this.

Next, you'll be adding detail to your static model by documenting rules about the attributes and operations related to each class. By adding each rule to the static model, you're giving it one centralized place to reside in the documentation, ensuring it will be consistently applied. You'll also learn to carry out this step in this chapter.

Once the static model has been set up, make sure that you actively use it. Every time a system use case is added or revised, check to see if the changes are consistent with the static model and resolve any differences.

Does the Business Analyst Need to Put Every Attribute and Operation in the Static Model?

Ideally, yes, but in practice, you'll often have to make a judgment call. Here are some factors that influence your decision:

- What is the life span of the software and how stable are the requirements?
  - If the software is to be short-lived or the business requirements are deemed to be fairly stable, you lose some of the benefit of static modeling: reduced time to identify and make changes to the business requirements documentation. Such cases would lean you toward doing less static modeling.
- Is the software going to be bought *off the shelf* (OTS)?
  - If so, concentrate on high-priority attributes and operations.
- And, of course, how much time do you have?
  - If you haven't been given enough time to do a complete model, concentrate on the high-priority attributes and operations described below.

---

[1]The static model in this state is sometimes referred to as the *conceptual* static model.

[2]Tracing in the opposite direction—from the static model to the dynamic model—is also useful as it makes it easier to identify which system use cases are impacted when changes are made to the static model.

The following considerations will help you pick out the high-priority attributes and operations to concentrate on during static modeling if time is tight. Concentrate on attributes and operations that

- Apply across a number of system use cases.
- Have a high risk of being *inappropriately* handled in the software. For example, focus on non-industry-standard attributes when buying an OTS system.
- Will have a large negative impact on the outcome of the project if incorrectly handled.

Step 2b vii: Link System Use Cases to the Static Model

In this step, you review any existing system use-case documentation for references to static modeling elements, such as classes and associations.

How do you find the modeling elements involved in a system use case?

Look out for any nouns that represent categories of business objects, such as customer and invoice; these are often classes. Next, pick out the verbs linking these nouns. For example, a Salesperson *makes* a Sale; these are often the relationships. (Later in this chapter, you'll also learn to look for fields; these correspond to attributes in the static model.)

How do you document the links between system use cases and the static model?

If you have a requirements-tracing tool, use it to tie each system use case to the static modeling elements it refers to. The approach used in this book documents the link in a special section of the system use case documentation. This section appears in the template as follows.

6. Class Diagram

   (Include a Class Diagram depicting business classes, relationships, and multiplicities of all objects participating in this use case.)

Include all classes that participate in the system use case. If any of the classes are part of an inheritance hierarchy, describe the related generalizations and specializations in the diagram or add another diagram depicting them.

If you're using a drawing tool, such as Rational Rose, a recommended approach is to create a dedicated class diagram within the tool for classes that participate in the system use case. Then add a macro in the system use-case text document to retrieve this diagram from the drawing tool when the document is opened. (If using Rational Rose, you'll need to investigate a product called SoDa for this purpose.) A second-best option is to manually copy and paste the diagram right into the text document.

There are many good reasons for providing traceability between the dynamic and static models. As mentioned at the beginning of this chapter, one reason is to be able to direct the reader to the appropriate parts of the static model that contain additional rules relevant to the system use case. Another reason is so that you will be able to identify which system use cases are impacted by a change in the static model; these are the system use cases that might need to be revised and retested if rules about the affected classes are updated in the static model. Traceability also makes it easier for you to verify that any rules that appear in the system use case comply with the across-the-board rules expressed in the static model.

Case Study I1: Link System Use Cases to the Static Model

You analyze the system use case, *Review case report*, documented below, looking for static modeling elements so that you can cross-check the models to see if there are any discrepancies between the system use-case documentation and the class diagrams.

Suggestions

1. Begin by scanning the document for noun phrases. These are often classes. Verify that each class you've identified appears in the static model. If is doesn't, add it to the static model.

2. Next scan the document for phrases of the form <class> <verb phrase> <class>, for example, A *Peace Committee* is assigned to a *Case*. The verb phrase is often a relationship—typically an association. Verify that each relationship you've identified is currently present in the model. Be careful not to add an association if there already is an indirect, but equivalent, association. If you discover a relationship that is not handled in any way in the static model, add it.

3. Next, scan the documentation for any rules regarding multiplicity. For example, a system use case might presume that there is only one *Peace Committee* assigned to a *Case*. Verify that these multiplicities are consistent with those in the static model and resolve any inconsistencies.

4. Based on your analysis, create a draft of the class diagram that depicts only the classes that participate in the system use case, and then insert it into Section 6 of the use-case documentation. If you needed to make any assumptions, document them in the Assumptions section of the template so that you will remember to verify them with stakeholders.

Following is your source document:

System use case: *Disburse payments*

...

    1.3 Triggers
        Convener selects disburse payments option.

    1.4 Preconditions

          1.4.1 The case is in the payable state and a payment amount for the case has been determined.

    1.5 Postconditions

          1.5.1 Postconditions on Success

                1.5.1.1 Payments are made into the accounts of all *Peace Committee Members* involved in the *Case* and into the *Fund Accounts.*

                1.5.1.2 The case is in the Paid state.

2 Flow of Events

Basic flow:

    2.1 The system displays a list of payable cases.

    2.2 The user selects a case.

    2.3 The system displays the amount payable for the case.

    2.4 The system displays each *Peace Committee Member* assigned to the case.

    2.5 The system displays the *Peace Committee Member Account* owned by each of the displayed *Peace Committee Members.*

    2.6 The system displays the payment amounts to be deposited into each *Peace Committee Member Account* and invested into each fund.

          2.6.1 TBD (To be determined): The formula for disbursing payments to the various accounts.

    2.7 The user approves the disbursement.

    2.8 The system creates payments for the *Case.*

          2.8.1 Each payment invests a specified amount from the *Cash Account* into one of the *Fund Accounts* or deposits an amount into one *Peace Committee Member Account.*

          2.8.2 The system sends a notice letter to a *Peace Committee Member* whenever a deposit is made to the member's account.

    2.9 The system marks the *Case* as *Paid.*

Alternate flows:

2.3a User changes disbursement amounts:

1 The user overrides the disbursement amounts.

2 The system confirms that the total payable for the case has not changed.

2.3a.2a Total payable has changed:

1 The system displays a message indicating the amount of the discrepancy.

2 Continue at step 2.3a.1.

2.8a Payment causes a withdrawal from cash that pushes balance below a specified trigger point:

1 The system sends a notice to Admin requesting new cash funds.

. . .

6 Class Diagram
(Include Class Diagram depicting business classes, relationships, and multiplicities of all objects participating in this use case.)

7 Assumptions
(List any assumptions made when writing the use case. Verify all assumptions with stakeholders before sign-off.)

Case Study I1: Results

1. Upon reviewing the system use case, you listed the following classes:

- Case
- Peace Committee Member
- Payment
- Peace Committee Member Account
- Fund Account
- Cash Account

Checking the static model, you happily noted that it includes all of the above classes.

2. Next, searching for relationships, you scanned the textual documentation for verbs connecting the classes. At this point, you discovered that the following relationships did not appear to be anywhere in the model:

- A *Peace Committee Member* is assigned to a *Case*.
- A *Peace Committee Member* owns a *Peace Committee Member Account*.

You checked to see if there were any indirect associations between the classes but nothing hit the mark. For example, although the model showed that *each Peace Committee handles a Case* and *each Peace Committee is composed of Peace Committee Members,* the model did not indicate a requirement to track which of these members is assigned to each case. Based on this analysis, you added these two associations to the model.

3. Next, you attempted to assign multiplicities to the associations.
   You guessed that each *Case* may have zero or more assigned *Peace Committee Members* because some cases are resolved without a *Peace Gathering.* You included your best guesses for the multiplicities but made a note in the Assumptions section to verify them with stakeholders.

4. Finally, you created a class diagram describing the classes involved in this system use case, incorporating the newly discovered relationships. Since the account classes belong to an inheritance hierarchy, you included a diagram depicting the hierarchy as well. Figure 9.1 shows the diagrams that you inserted into Section 6 (Class Diagram) of the use-case documentation.

5. Based on the analysis above, you have added the following to the use-case documentation:

   7 Assumptions

   7.1 Minimum *Peace Committee Members* assigned to a *Case* is zero.

   7.2 Maximum *Peace Committee Members* assigned to a *Case* is many. (There is no upper limit.)

   7.3 Each *Peace Committee Member* owns exactly one *Peace Committee Member Account.*

   7.4 Each *Peace Committee Member Account* is owned by exactly one *Peace Committee Member.*

Step 2b viii: Add Attributes

Analyzing Attributes

The next step is to find out and document the other attributes that are kept by the business for each class.

Listen up!

An *attribute* is an item of information about an object that is tracked by the business. An attribute is specified at the class level. All objects of that class have the same attributes, but the value of the attributes may differ from object to object.[3]

---

[3]You may also specify a special kind of attribute that allows one value only to be shared by all objects of the class. Such an attribute is termed a *class attribute.*

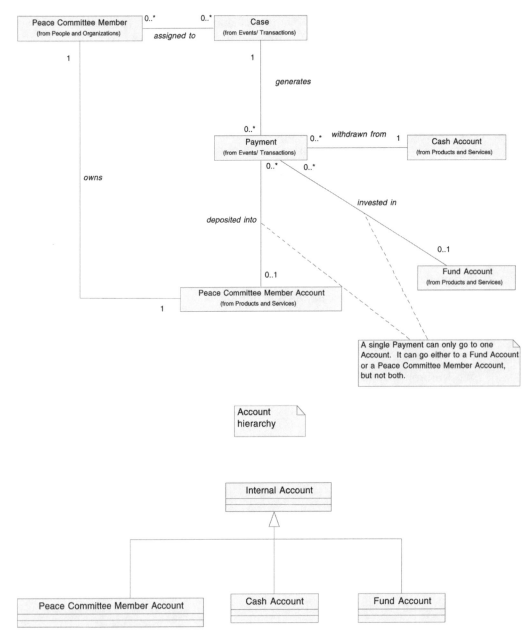

Figure 9.1 Class diagram showing classes involved in the *Disburse Payments* use case

Example

Some of the attributes the CPP might need to keep track of include

- *Peace Gathering* class: The date that the gathering was held.
- *Party to Dispute* class: The testimony given by the party.

Why Indicate Attributes?

Attributes are part of the user's contract with the developers. If you miss an attribute in your model, you run the risk that the system will not track that attribute.

Another reason to indicate attributes is that you then have a place in your model to "hang" rules about each attribute, such as valid ranges and other verifications.

Don't Verification Rules about Attributes Belong with the System Use-Case Documentation?

Generally, no. The best place to put an attribute rule is right in the static model, since it gives the rule greater scope: the class diagrams in the OO model apply across the board. On the other hand, if a rule applies to the attribute only within the context of a specific system use case, include the rule with the system use-case documentation. Yet another option for documenting these rules is along with the screens that are developed to handle the graphical user interface (GUI) for the system use case. Use this option if the rule only applies whenever the screen is used but does not apply across the board. As discussed in Point 3 in the next section, screens are not considered a Business Analysis artifact, as they relate to the solution design, but you may request the designer to add in rules you've identified.

Sources of Information for Finding Attributes

1. Using the class diagrams as a guide, interview the user about each class.
2. Inspect existing system use cases for references to attributes. For example, the system use case, *Disburse payments*, refers to a *payment amount*—an attribute of a *Payment*.
3. Inspect artifacts created by other members of the project, which include screens, reports, forms, and interfaces to external computer systems. Artifacts such as these are not formally within the scope of the BA because they deal with invention (the "how"), whereas the BA is concerned with discovery (the "what"). However, the BA should inspect them as they become available, since they provide a rich source of attributes: The fields in these artifacts typically represent attributes in the static model.

4. Also, inspect business rules expressed in the system use cases or in a separate business rules document. (These rules are sometimes stored electronically in a rules engine.) Sometimes they require new attributes. For example, the *Disburse Funds* system use case contains a rule that whenever the cash balance falls below a trigger point, a message is to be sent to Administration. This rule requires that the *Cash Account* class have a *trigger point* attribute and a *current balance* attribute.

Rules for Assigning Attributes

1. Check each candidate attribute to ensure that it isn't already listed as a class. For example, you might be tempted to list *Peace Committee Member Account* as an attribute of a *Peace Committee Member*, since it represents information tied to a member. However, there is no need to do so, since this requirement is already in the model in another form: the *Peace Committee Member Account* class is associated with *Peace Committee Member*.

2. Take care to assign the attribute to the right class. The attribute should describe a property of objects in the class. Also, the attribute should be a property that the system tracks individually for each object in the class. For example, *Dispute Date* is not listed as an attribute of *Peace Gathering* since it is constant for all gatherings related to the same *Case*; rather, *Dispute Date* is listed as a *Case* attribute. An attribute for a *Peace Gathering* is one that is kept for *each* gathering, like *Gathering Date*.

3. List an attribute as far up an inheritance hierarchy as possible. (Keep in mind that if you list an attribute in a generalized class, that it must apply to *all* specialized classes.)

4. For aggregations and compositions, take care to differentiate between an attribute that is related to the whole and an attribute that is tracked at the part level.

5. Attributes that the business tracks about an object regardless of the role are listed with the primary class. Attributes that are kept once for each role are listed with the role. For example, a person's name is kept regardless of one's role, but the date that person became a member of a *Peace Committee* is recorded once for each *Peace Committee Membership*.

Derived Attributes

A *derived attribute* is one whose values can be derived in more than one way from the model.

If an attribute can be derived from other attributes in the model, either do not include it or document it as a derived attribute. In the UML, you mark a derived attribute with a slash ("/"), for example, /extended price. The documentation for a derived attribute should explain how the attribute value is determined from other aspects of the model. For example, /extended price is a derived attribute of an invoice line item that can be calculated from other attributes as follows: /extended price = unit price x quantity.

Why Is It Important for the BA to Indicate Which Attributes Are Derived?

Derived attributes can lead to data integrity problems if they pass unnoticed from the requirements into the database design. For example, consider a student final average that can be derived directly by querying a *Final Mark* attribute and, indirectly, by calculating it from the student's individual marks. Since there are two ways to derive this mark, there is always the possibility that they will yield different results. One solution (referred to as *normalization*) prevents the problem by eliminating the *Final Mark* attribute entirely from the model. If there is no duplication, there is no inconsistency. Eliminating the redundancy also means less storage requirements, since the *Final Mark* of each student is no longer kept on file but is recalculated as needed. On the other hand, this recalculation uses up system resources at run-time. The decision on how to handle a derived attribute is up to the database designer. But for that person to do his or her job properly, the BA needs to clearly mark which attributes are derived and how they are derived.

Indicating Attributes in the UML

Figure 9.2 shows how to indicate attributes in the UML by listing them in an attribute compartment (or box) that sits just below the class-name. (The empty box below it is the operation compartment.) In the figure, /*number members* is marked as derived, since it can be determined by counting the number of *Peace Committee Members* in the *Peace Committee.*

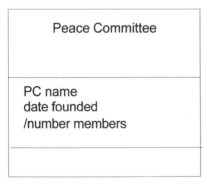

Figure 9.2 Indicating attributes in the UML

For business analysis purposes, this notation, along with supporting text, is usually sufficient. The UML does offer, however, a more formal way of declaring attributes. I'll describe it here for completeness, but you probably won't need to be this formal:

atrributeName: AttributeType [Multiplicity] = default

For example:

contactNumber: PhoneNumber [0..2] = "(416) - "

where

- *attributeName* is the name of the attribute, for example, *contactNumber*. During analysis, use informal names. Later, in design, use the formal format: one term (no spaces) beginning with a lowercase letter, with each subsequent word beginning in uppercase.
- *AttributeType* characterizes the attribute, for example, *PhoneNumber*. Use one of the following approaches to naming the *AttributeType* (listed in order of preference from a BA perspective):
  - A user-defined type, formally defined elsewhere as another class. For example: *PhoneNumber* is defined as a class with its own attributes of *areaCode and Number.*
  - Units of measurement,[4] such as *Inches.*
  - A data-type supported by the programming environment, For example:
    Integer:
    Boolean: A yes/no field.
    String: Text (any string of characters). Use this for free-form text and for codes even if they are numeric.
    Double: A decimal number.
  - Date
- *Multiplicity* is the number of times the attribute appears. Use the same notation you used when describing multiplicities for associations. For example, *contactNumber: PhoneNumber [0..2]* means that zero through two contact numbers may appear.
- *Default* is the attribute's initial value.

Once you've added the attributes and their rules to classes in the static model, ideally, you should remove these details anywhere they appear in the system use cases. For example, once you've added a rule to the *date formed* attribute (that is, the date the committee was

---

[4]This approach is particularly useful during analysis, but during design, it will be converted to one of options listed here.

established) of a *Peace Committee*, this rule should be removed from the system use case, *Manage Peace Committees*. The reader will be referred to the rule because the Class Diagram section of the use-case documentation will have included the *Peace Committee* class. This approach ensures consistent treatment and makes it easier to change rules if circumstances require it. Many organizations balk at this point, however, partly because this approach requires too much cross-referencing on the part of the reader. A second-best approach is to add the rule to the static model, include a reference from the system use case to the model, but leave the explicit rule itself in place in the system use case. While this approach means that some requirements will reside in more than one place, it still provides the benefit of a centralized reference (the static model) for verifying that each system use case is consistent with project-wide rules. Similar considerations will apply when you look at pulling operation rules out of the system use cases.

Meta-Attributes

A *meta-attribute* is an attribute of an attribute—a fancy way of referring to the verifications rules and other properties of an attribute. To document an attribute fully, you need to describe its meta-attributes. In the previous discussion on the UML declaration of attributes, you read about the following:

- Attribute Type
- Multiplicity
- Default value

These are examples of meta-attributes. You also learned to document that an attribute is derived by including a slash before its name. Other meta-attributes worth documenting include

- *Unique?*: A "yes" indicates that the value of the attribute is unique for each object in the class—in other words, no two objects may have the same value for this attribute.
- Range of acceptable values, such as:

    Quantity On Hand: Range is 0–10.

    Invoice Date: Range is (any past date) through (current date).
- List of acceptable values, such as:

    Gender: Values are Male and Female.[5]

    However, if the list of acceptable values is subject to change, define the whole attribute as a look-up table (described later in this chapter).

---

[5]This can also be defined by declaring an enumeration data type, which is not covered in this book.

- Accuracy, such as:

  Balance: 9,999.99 (stored to nearest cent).

  Length, such as:

  Name (maximum 30 characters long).

- Dependencies on other attributes, such as:

  Date Resolved (must be on or after date reported).

Document these meta-attributes using an informal style.

Note to Rational Rose Users

To add an attribute to a class, right-click on the class in the diagram, then select New attribute.

Case Study 12: Add Attributes

You ask stakeholders about the items of information the business tracks about each class that appears in your model. Also, you examine screen mock-ups and report layouts that have been created by the designers. You list each field you find and verify with stakeholders what class they describe. Through your interviews, you discover the following.

People/Organizations

1. A unique PID (participant ID) must be given to each person or agency involved with the CPP.

2. The date that a person was first entered into the system must be recorded. The system must also record the following for each person: *mailing address, last name, sex,* and *date of birth.*

3. The date that an agency was first entered into the system must be recorded. The system must record the following for each agency: *Mailing Address* and *Name.* Some reports need to indicate whether or not an agency is a government agency.

4. The testimony of each party to a dispute appears on case reports.

5. Descriptive information about each *Peace Committee* includes township and ward number.

6. For each *Peace Committee Member*, the system must record the date the person joined and a status indicating whether or not the person is active.

7. For each *CPP Member*, the system must record the date the person joined and a status indicating whether or not the person is active.

8. The system must track the type of relationship (such as neighbor, family member, and so on) each *Observer* has to a *Party to the Dispute*. If the *Observer* has a relationship with more than one party, then each relationship must be tracked.

Events/Transactions

1. A payment report shows one line per payment with a unique payment sequence number, payment date, amount, and the account to which it was paid.

2. The meeting date of each *Peace Gathering* for a case appears on the case report.

3. The case report also shows the date of the dispute, the conflict type (a predefined code), a status code describing the progress of the case, an indication of whether the rules were followed, a predefined *reason code* describing why a gathering was not held (if applicable), and whether or not monitoring was required for the case.

4. If monitoring was required, the conditions imposed appear on the case report, as well as the deadline for monitoring, and whether the monitoring conditions have been met.

5. Payable cases appear on a separate report.

Products and Services

1. All accounts are identified by a unique account number.

2. *Peace Committee Member Account:* Information items are *balance*, *date last accessed*, and *overdraft limit*.

3. *Fund Account:* Information items are *balance*, *date last accessed*, and *access code*.

4. *Cash Account:* Information items are *balance*, *date last accessed*, and *low trigger*—the balance below which new cash funds are requested.

Your Next Step

Based on these notes, you aim to discover the attributes and assign them to the appropriate classes.

Suggestions

1. If an attribute applies to all specializations of a generalized class, assign the attribute to the generalized class.

2. For any generalization hierarchy, show attributes of the classes involved on the same diagram that shows the generalization relationships. That way, the reader will be able to see which attributes are inherited by specialization classes.

Case Study 12: Resulting Documentation

Your analysis of the CPP system's attributes results in the diagrams shown in Figure 9.3.

Association Classes

The UML offers another way to treat the attribute *relationship to party,* specified for the *Observer* class. Rather than treat it as an attribute of an *Observer,* you could consider it to be an attribute of the *association* between an *Observer* and a *Party to Dispute.* The rationale for this is that the value of the *relationship to party* attribute changes for each instance of an association between one Observer and one Party. To handle the attribute this way,

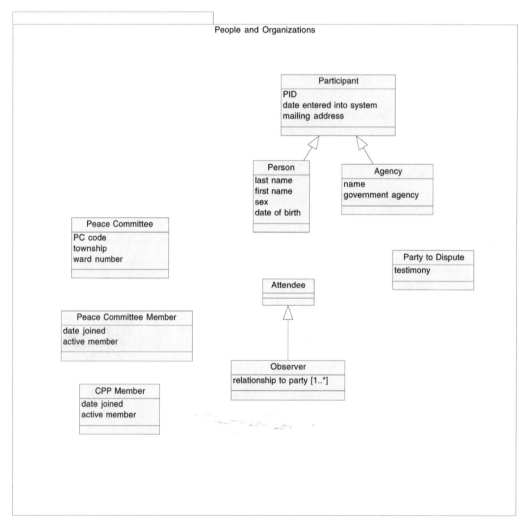

Figure 9.3 CPP system attributes

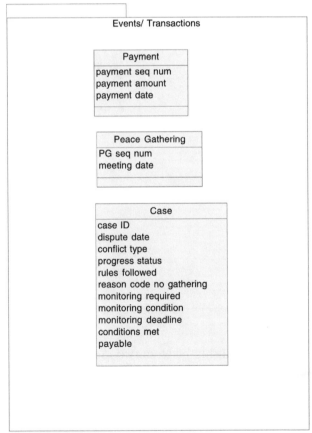

Figure 9.3 CPP system attributes (continued)

you need to introduce a new kind of class to the model; it's called an association class. An association class is considered by the UML to be both an association and a class. Each instance of the class describes one link between an object on one association end and an object at the other end. Association classes are useful at design time but are confusing during business analysis, as they are not likely to be readily understood by business stake-holders. They are mentioned in this book just in case you run into them and wonder what they're all about. Figure 9.4 shows an example of an association class between *Observer* and *Party to Dispute*. Note how the *relationship to party* attribute has been removed from *Observer* and added to the class, *Observer Related to Party*. The multiplicity of the attribute has changed from [1..*] to [1] because each *Observer Related to Party* object represents a single link between the objects at both ends; each link only requires one value of the attribute.

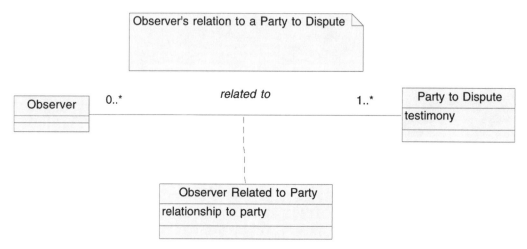

Figure 9.4 Association class

Step 2b ix: Add Look-Up Tables

What Is a Look-Up Table?

A *look-up table* is a file that lists the allowable values of an attribute. The term is not part of the UML.

An example is a relation code describing a relationship between two individuals, where PC = Parent/Child, EE = Employee/Employee, and so on.

Why Analyze Look-Up Tables?

Doing so leads to enormous savings in future modifications to the system. When implemented, look-up tables enable the user to add new acceptable values without calling on a programmer. How? For each look-up table that you identify, the developers will create data entry screens to add, change, and delete standardized codes. These screens allow users to modify codes interactively without programmer intervention.

Example

While you've been analyzing the CPP system, you've noticed that stakeholders have revised the list of allowable relationship codes (spouse, neighbor, and so on) a number of times. You verify that these codes are, in fact, subject to change, so you define a look-up table.

Rules for Analyzing Look-Up Tables

1. Look for candidate look-up tables:

   If a screen uses pull-down menus to allow the user to select the value of an attribute, the attribute is a candidate look-up table. (However, see the upcoming challenge question to determine whether the table is worth defining.) For example, the attribute *Relationship to Party to Dispute* includes a pull-down menu of relationship codes.

   If any statistics are compiled based on the *number* of objects that match a particular attribute value, that attribute is a candidate look-up table. For example, statistics based on *conflict type* suggest that you define a *conflict type* look up table.

   If the attribute appears in more than one context, and standardization of its values makes business sense, the attribute is a candidate for a look-up table. For example, in a later enhancement to the CPP system, a relationship code is used to describe the relationship of one party to another party involved in a dispute (in addition to its current use to describe an *Observer Relation to a Party*). It makes sense to standardize the relationship codes so that the same ones are used throughout the system.

2. If you have any look-up tables to add, create a package called *Look-up tables*, and add the tables to this package. For example, add the new classes *Dispute Parameter* and *Relation Parameter* to a *Look-up table* package. Another recommendation is to declare the stereotype for this new class to be <<*look-up table*>> to clarify its purpose to the reader.

3. For each new class you've added:

   a. Add attributes.
      For example, add the following attributes to *Dispute Parameter: description, criminal offence (Criminal offence* would be defined as a *Boolean* attribute, meaning it can take on the values of *Yes* or *No.*)

   b. Indicate associations to each of the classes that use the look-up table.
      For example, *Dispute Parameter* is associated with *Case.*

    c. Indicate multiplicities for each of the associations.
       For example, each *Dispute Parameter* is associated with zero or more *Cases*. Each *Case* is associated with one and only one *Dispute Parameters*.

    d. Make sure that no other attributes related to the look-up table appear in any of the associated classes. For example, *conflict type* should no longer appear as an attribute of *Case*; the requirement is captured through an association with a *Dispute Parameter*.

Challenge Question

"Can you be sure that these codes will always stay the same?"

If the answer is "yes," you don't need to define the attribute they describe as a look-up table. For example, a "Sex" code (M/F) does not require a look-up table.

Indicating Look-Up Tables in UML

Figure 9.5 shows how to indicate a look-up table in UML.

Figure 9.5 Indicating a look-up table in UML

Case Study I5: Analyze Look-Up Tables

You analyze the following report layouts, looking for opportunities to define a look-up table.

Peace Gathering Report

There is a section filled out by each observer at a Peace Gathering, which includes:

Which party are you related to? _____

How are you related? (Please select one: ____)

1: married

2: relative/near

3: relative/far

4: neighbor

5: friend

6: lover: boyfriend/girlfriend

7: acquaintance

8: stranger

9: professional: employer/employee

10: client/service provider

11: tenant/landlord

12: other agency

Governmental Report

1. Percentage of cases where no gathering was held because the dispute was resolved in the meantime: ____%.

2. Percentage of cases where no gathering was held because the relationship between the parties improved: ____%.

3. Percentage of cases where no gathering was held because someone rejected the process: ____%.

4. Percentage of cases where no gathering was held because the case was taken over by another agency: ____%.

5. Percentage of cases where no gathering was held because the case was referred to another agency by the CPP: ____%.

Dispute Frequency Report

   1: money lending % cases: _____

   2: theft (burglary of dwelling) % cases: _____

   3: failure to make payments on goods received % cases: _____

   4: assault without weapon % cases: _____

   5: assault with sharp object % cases: _____

   6: assault with blunt object % cases: _____

   7: assault with gun % cases: _____

   8: robbery with violence % cases: _____

   9: spatial dispute urination, encroachment % cases: _____

10: loan of goods % cases: _____

11: extramarital affair % cases: _____

12: other sexual affair % cases: _____

13: spousal abuse % cases: _____

14: child abuse % cases: _____

15: insult (direct disrespect or damage to identity and reputation) % cases: _____

16: housing dispute—ownership, head of house % cases: _____

17: moral issues—e.g., sister living with boyfriend % cases: _____

18: attempted rape/indecent assault % cases: _____

19: rape % cases: _____

20: gossip % cases: _____

21: drunkenness % cases: _____

22: child/spouse % cases: _____

23: witchcraft % cases: _____

Percentage of cases involving disputes representing criminally indictable offenses: ____

Case Study I3: Resulting Documentation

Figure 9.6 shows the diagrams resulting from your analysis of look-up tables.

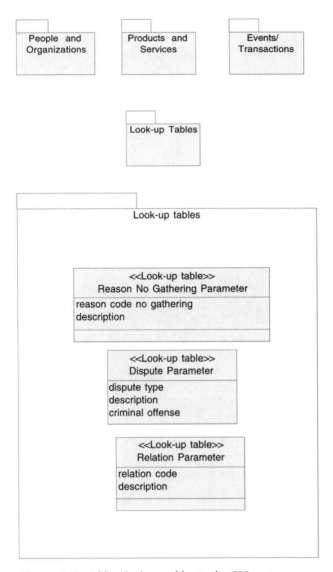

Figure 9.6 Adding look-up tables to the CPP system

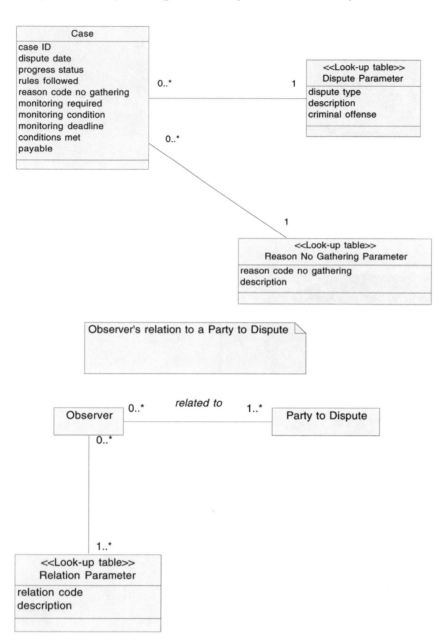

Figure 9.6 Adding look-up tables to the CPP system (continued)

Step 2b x: Add Operations

Recall that a class can hold both attributes and operations. You added attributes to the static model's classes in order to ensure that the rules for these attributes are treated consistently in the requirements. Also, by encapsulating attribute rules within the class's documentation, you created a self-contained unit of documentation that can be easily reused in other contexts. The same arguments apply to a class's operations.

An Example from the Case Study

The CPP has a business rule stating that whenever a withdrawal from cash pushes the current balance below a certain minimum (a trigger point), a notice must be sent to the Admin requesting new cash funds. This requirement now resides in the *Disburse Payments* use case. But what if this rule about the *Cash Account* must be applied to all other systems that withdraw from this account? Your solution is to add the operation *withdraw funds* to the *Cash Account* class. You attach the rule about sending a notice to Admin to this operation. In the future, any BA documenting requirements for any other system that involves the cash account will be able to include the *Cash Account* class documentation that you created, ensuring consistent handling of withdrawals and other *Cash Account* rules.

As discussed earlier in this chapter, the generally preferred approach is to remove the rule from the system use case once it's been added to the static model in order to avoid duplication. At one extreme, this would mean removing the entire alternate flow describing the low cash balance situation. However, this may place too heavy a burden on the reader; in particular a stakeholder from the business side not accustomed to this sort of cross-referencing. A workable solution is to keep the alternate flow *condition* but refer the reader to the *Cash Account* class for details on the system's *response* to the condition. For example,

> 2.8a Payment causes a withdrawal from cash that pushes balance below a specified trigger point:
>
> > 1 The system responds as described in the *withdraw* operation of the *Cash Fund* specifications. (See static model.)

This allows you to clearly describe the condition that is checked while leaving the documentation of the *response* in one place; if the required response changes later, it will still be easy to revise. If even this degree of cross-referencing is too much for your readers, then update the *withdraw* operation in the *Cash Fund* class but leave the entire rule in place (including the *response*) in the system use case. This, at least, gives you a central place to return to when writing other use cases that involve the *Cash Account* so that you can verify that withdrawals are consistently handled.

How to Distribute Operations

1. Examine the flow steps that appear in the system use case documentation. If you find an activity that pertains to a class and *needs to be handled consistently regardless of the system use case*, add it as an operation of the class. For example, add *withdraw cash* to *Cash Account*. Then attach any relevant rules to the operation, such as "When funds fall below trigger point, send notice to the Admin."

2. If the operation applies to all subtypes, list the operation with the generalized class. For example, if the rule about sending a notice to the Admin applies to all kinds of accounts, list the operation *withdraw funds* and its requirements with the generalized class *Account*.

   Each specialized class inherits this operation from the generalized class, but it may have its own method (procedure) for carrying it out (due to polymorphism). If it does, attach documentation about the new method to the specialized class.

Figure 9.7 shows how to indicate operations in UML. The operations are placed in a special operations compartment—a box below the attribute compartment. Each operation is followed by parentheses.

Figure 9.7 Indicating operations in UML

This informal naming of operations is sufficient for most BA purposes. The UML offers the following formal format for declaring operations:

```
OperationName (argument1:Argument1Type, argument2:Argument2Type, …): ReturnType
```

Example: `takeLeaveOfAbsence (effectiveDate: Date): Boolean`

The preceding operation, *takeLeaveOfAbsence*, requires an effective date, whose type is *date*. The operation returns a boolean answer (true or false) indicating success or failure.

Also, you can document a *precondition* and *postcondition* for each operation. A precondition is something that must be true before the operation begins. A postcondition is something that must be true once it has been completed.

Note to Rational Rose Users

To add an operation and its specifications to a class:

1. Double-click on the class (either in the browser or within a diagram) to display the Class Specification window.
2. Select the Operations tab.
3. Right-click within the displayed window and select Insert.
4. Enter the name of the operation.
5. Double-click on the operation name you just entered.
6. Select the General tab of the Operation Specification window.
7. Select a return type, if desired, from the pick-list.
8. To specify arguments for the operation
   a. Select the Detail tab of the Operation Specification window.
   b. Right-click inside the Arguments window and select Insert.
   c. Enter the argument name.
   d. Double-click the argument name you just entered to display the Argument Specification window, where you can specify a type and default value for the argument.
9. To specify a precondition for the operation, return to the Operation Specification window, select the Preconditions tab and enter the precondition.
10. To specify a postcondition for the operation, return to the Operation Specification window, select the Postconditions tab and enter the postcondtion.

Case Study 17: Distribute Operations

You examine the system use-case documentation, looking for operations that could be reused in other contexts, and find the following requirements in the *Disburse Payments* system use case:

System use case: *Disburse payments*

. . .

    1.3 Triggers
        Convener selects disburse payments option.

    1.4 Preconditions
        1.4.1 The case is in the payable state and a payment amount for the case has been determined.

    1.5 Postconditions

1.5.1 Postconditions on Success

    1.5.1.1 Payments are made into the accounts of all *Peace Committee Members* involved in the *Case* and into the *Fund Accounts.*

    1.5.1.2 The case is in the *Paid* state.

2 Flow of Events

Basic flow:

2.1 The system displays a list of payable cases.

2.2 The user selects a case.

2.3 The system displays the amount payable for the case.

2.4 The system displays each *Peace Committee Member* assigned to the case.

2.5 The system displays the *Peace Committee Member Account* owned by each of the displayed *Peace Committee Members.*

2.6 The system displays the payment amount to be deposited into each *Peace Committee Member Account* and invested into each fund.

    2.6.1 TBD (To be determined): The formula for disbursing payments to the various accounts.

2.7 The user approves the disbursement.

2.8 The system creates *Payments* for the *Case.*
Each *Payment* deposits a specified amount from the *Cash Account* into one of the *Fund Accounts* or into one *Peace Committee Member Account.*
The system sends a notice letter to a *Peace Committee Member* whenever a deposit it made the member's account.

2.9 The system marks the *Case* as *Paid.*

Alternate flows:

2.3a User changes disbursement amounts:

    1 The user overrides the disbursement amounts.

    2 The system confirms that the total payable for the case has not changed.

2.3a.2a Total payable has changed:

    1 The system displays a message indicating the amount of the discrepancy.

    2 Continue at step 2.3a.1.

2.8a Payment causes a withdrawal from cash that pushes balance below a specified trigger point:

    1 The system sends a notice to Admin requesting new cash funds.

. . .

6 Class Diagram
(Include Class Diagram [see Figure 9.8] depicting business classes, relationships, and multiplicities of all objects participating in this use case.)

7 Assumptions
(List any assumptions made when writing the use case. Verify all assumptions with stakeholders before sign-off.)

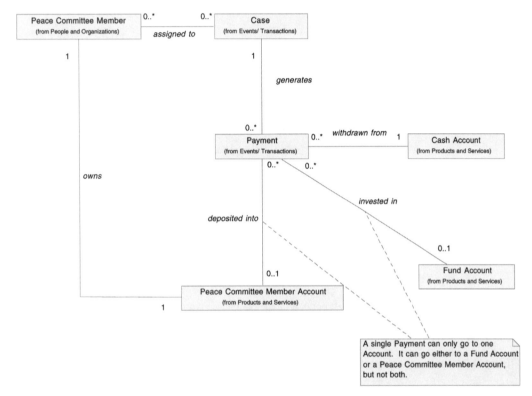

Figure 9.8

Your Next Step

You look for rules applying to the classes mentioned in this use case that might apply to other system use cases and/or systems. You add these as annotated operations of the appropriate classes.

Case Study 17: Resulting Documentation

Figure 9.9 shows the diagram that results from your addition of operations to the static model. (To illustrate your options for documenting operations, the *withdraw()* operation

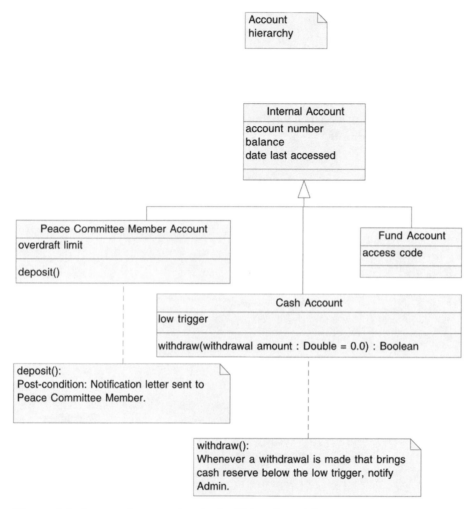

Figure 9.9 Documenting operations in the CPP static model

has been documented using the formal format; the *deposit()* operation has been documented informally.)

Step 2b xi: Revise Class Structure

As a last step, make a final review of the model and revise it if necessary. You may need to add some generalizations and drop some others. For example, you may find a generalized class with no requirements (attributes, operations, or relationships) and decide to discard it because it's simply cluttering up the model and not adding value. On the other hand, you may discover classes with shared attributes, operations, or relationships. In such cases, you'll want to consider adding a generalized class.

Rules for Reviewing Structure

1. Look for any classes that have the same associations to other classes. Consider adding a generalized class for them.

2. Look for any classes that have the same attributes or operations as other classes. Consider adding a generalized class to hold the common attributes.

3. Whenever you add a generalized class, move the common associations, attributes, and operations from the specialized classes to the generalized class.

4. Can you justify every generalized class in the model? The point of introducing a generalized class is to provide a convenient, single place to put rules that affect a number of specialized classes. *There should be at least one attribute, operation, or relationship that can be ascribed to the generalized class.*

5. As rule of thumb, *each generalized class should have at least two specializations.* There are two exceptions to this rule, however:

   - The generalized class is concrete. For example, in the case study, *Attendee* is a concrete generalized class of *Observer*.

   - You anticipate that you will need to add more specializations in the future.

Challenge Question

1. Are any of the subtypes already specializations of some other generalized class?

   If so, you have a case of "multiple inheritance." Some companies do not allow this type of structure, or do so only if certain rules are followed. Make sure your model complies with your company's policy on this.[6]

Case Study 18: Revise Structure

You review the existing class diagrams looking for generalized classes that can be discarded due to a lack of attributes, associations, and so on. Also, you are looking for classes with common attributes, operations, and/or associations.

Suggestions

Notice that that there are properties common to all members, regardless of the organization to which they belong.

---

[6]Multiple inheritance can lead to ambiguities about attributes if the same attribute is inherited from two generalizations, particularly if there is a "diamond inheritance"—that is, both parent classes inherit from the same grandparent.

Case Study I8: Resulting Documentation

Figure 9.10 shows the diagrams that result from your review of the CPP system's class structure. You've added a *Member* class as a generalized class of *Peace Committee Member* and *CPP Member* and moved the common attributes to it. This left no attributes or operations in the specialized member classes; however, you've retained these classes because they have special multiplicities and associations.

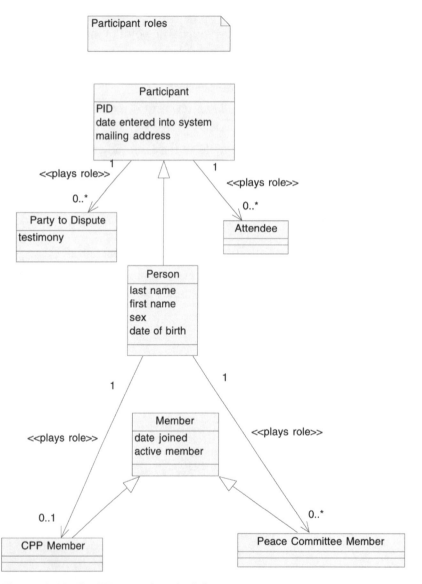

Figure 9.10 The CPP system's revised class structure

Notes on the Model

A new generalized class, *Member*, has been added to the *People and Organizations* package. The common attributes *date joined* and *active member* have been moved from the specialized classes *Peace Committee Member* and *CPP Member* to the new class, *Member*.

Chapter Summary

In this chapter, you completed the static model of the system. You linked the system use cases to the static model and you added detail to the static model by including attributes and operations. Finally, you revised the static model, adding classes to promote reuse and removing unused classes.

Tools and concepts introduced in this chapter for the first time or in a new context include the following:

1. *Attributes*: A piece of information that the business tracks about a class of objects.
2. *Meta-attribute*: A property of an attribute, such as a valid range.
3. *Association class*: A class that describes an association. Each object represents one link between instances of the classes at both ends of the association.
4. *Look-up table*: A table of codes for an attribute. The user can change the table's list of allowable values and their meanings.
5. *Operation*: An activity that all objects of a class can perform.
6. *Operation precondition*: A condition that must be true before the operation is performed.
7. *Operation postcondition*: A condition that will be true after the operation has completed.

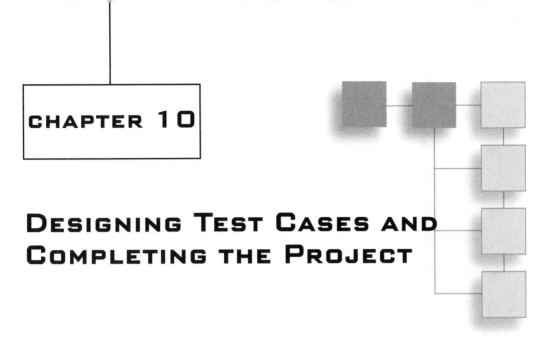

CHAPTER 10

DESIGNING TEST CASES AND COMPLETING THE PROJECT

Chapter Objectives

In this chapter, you'll learn how to design test cases that are most likely to uncover errors—an activity that should begin during analysis, before execution (design and coding). By specifying these tests up front, you add *measurable* quality requirements to your contract with the developers—clear-cut criteria that will be used to judge the acceptability of the software.

Steps covered in this chapter include the following (highlighted in bold):

2. Analysis
    a. Dynamic analysis
    b. Static analysis (object/data model) (Class diagram)
    c. **Specify testing (Test plan/Decision tables)**
        i. Specify white-box testing quality level
        ii. Specify black-box test cases
        iii. Specify system tests
    d. **Specify implementation plan**
    e. **Prepare BRD/Analysis**
    f. Set baseline for development

Tools and concepts that you'll learn about in this chapter include the following:

1. Structured testing principles
    i. Structured walkthroughs for testing

    ii. White-box testing criteria (statement coverage, decision coverage, condition coverage, and multiple-condition coverage)

    iii. Black-box testing

    iv. Use-case scenario testing

    v. Decision tables

    vi. Unit testing

    vii. Black-box test

    viii. Boundary value analysis

    ix. System tests

    x. Regression testing

    xi. Volume testing

    xii. Stress testing

    xiii. Usability testing

    xiv. Security testing

    xv. Performance testing

    xvi. Storage testing

    xvii. Configuration testing

    xviii. Compatibility testing

    xix. Reliability testing

    xx. Recovery testing

    xxi. Implementation plan

Step 2c: Specify Testing

The testing process includes technical tests of the software's components and architecture (white-box tests), tests to see if it works as advertised (requirements-based tests), and tests that see whether the software does these things "well enough" (system tests).

Who Does These Tests and How Does the BA Fit In?

Some organizations have a quality assurance (QA) team responsible for testing. The BA is often a member of this team. In fact, many organizations have people with a BA title who do nothing *but* testing. Business Analysts are particularly well suited to this work due to their role as representatives of the business stakeholders, and because they are often the authors of the business requirements that the software is being measured against.

If you're a BA involved in testing, most of your testing time will be absorbed by requirements-based testing. If your organization does not have specifically trained usability testers, you may also be asked to specify and/or run *usability* tests (discussed later in this chapter under the section "System Tests"). You'll need to know how to design effective tests and how to write them up. This chapter will give you techniques and templates to help you do that.

In general, the rest of the tests (white-box and most system tests) are too "techie" for the Business Analyst. You still need to know enough about them to know what to ask for and to be able to understand the significance of the results. You'll learn about these tests later in this chapter.

What Is Testing?

Testing is any activity aimed at proving that the software system does not do what it is supposed to. The negative phrasing is intentional. Each time a test has uncovered a "bug," it has proven itself—it means the bug won't be released to the end user. The term *quality assurance* is sometimes used because it suggests that more than the physical testing of the software may be required. For example, verifying a draft of a system use-case description with stakeholders is a quality assurance activity.

What Exactly Is a "Bug"?

We'll take the broad view. A *bug* is any variance between what the system is supposed to do and what it does. Some of these bugs are going to be introduced by the programmers. It's your job to catch them. But others are introduced earlier on by Business Analysts through inaccurate, ambiguous, or missing requirements. It's also your job to eliminate as many of these bugs as possible.

General Guidelines

Ivar Jacobson, a founder of OO, advises that you derive test cases from system use cases as follows:

- Test scenarios that cover the basic flow of each use case.
- Tests scenarios that cover the *alternate and exception flows*[1] of each use case.
- Tests of *line-item requirements*[2] in the BRD, where the requirements are traced to use case(s).
- Tests of features in the *user documentation*, where the documentation is traced to use case(s).

---

[1]Recall that an alternate flow is an alternate to the normal path of events for a use case; for example, in the use case *Withdraw Funds*, the alternate flow is *Maximum Daily Limit Exceeded*. An exception flow is a path taken when an error occurs, such as *Communications Down*.

[2]For example, over and above that in the flows described previously.

You'll need more than these suggestions to plan appropriate testing. Fortunately, much groundwork regarding testing has been done prior to OO. This pre-OO approach is called *structured testing*. In this chapter, we'll look at how Structured Analysis can be integrated with OO techniques and applied to an OO project.

Structured Testing

In 1976, Glenford Myers pioneered the field of testing with his book *The Art of Software Testing*. He laid out a discipline he termed structured testing. His work remains the basis for testing to this day.

Listen up!

Structured testing is the process of using standardized techniques to locate flaws ("bugs"). Flaws detected by structured testing include those introduced during business analysis, design, and programming.

When Is Testing Done?

Different activities occur at various stages of project development:

- *Structured walkthroughs* are performed at all stages.
- During analysis (requirements gathering), the test cases are designed.
- During execution (development), *unit testing* (tests of the individual software components) is carried out.
- At the end of execution, requirements-based (black-box) tests are performed.
- Before acceptance of the product, the developers or technical testers perform *system tests*.
- At closeout, the user performs and supervises *User Acceptance Testing* (UAT).

Principles of Structured Testing (Adapted for OO)

You begin by establishing some principles, adapted from structured testing to OO projects. Why not go directly to the techniques? A sound understanding of basic principles helps avoid the kinds of institutional problems that lead to "buggy" systems. (The real-life story in the accompanying Sidebar helps illustrate the point.)

One of my first jobs in IT was a programming stint at Atomic Energy of Canada, Ltd. (AECL). I was working on LOCA, a computer program that simulated a loss-of-coolant-accident at a nuclear power plant. I found it odd that even though I had not yet graduated from university, the company relied on me to test my own programs. Sure enough, in my first programming assignment, I introduced a new bug into the system—one that was found out only once the program had been put into production. (Fortunately, the error was minor.) This incident suggested a systemic flaw in the way the organization handled quality assurance. This was borne out a number of years later when AECL released a software-controlled medical device to deliver radiation to brain tumors. The device occasionally malfunctioned, causing a number of deaths. A testing specialist was eventually called in to determine the source of the problem. He found the bug—but he also warned of systemic problems that would continue to result in new bugs unless corrected. For example, he found that, contrary to structured testing principles, programmers were testing their own code and that there was an overall lack of understanding about the limitations of software testing.

The principles of structured testing are as follows:

1. The purpose of testing is to locate bugs.
   - A "bug" is any aspect of a system that does not meet the requirements of the business and of users.
   - A bug can be introduced at any time during the project.
   - Be a pessimist: Work under the assumption that the analysis work was incomplete and inaccurate and that the system is full of programming errors.

2. The goal of testing is to locate the maximum number of errors in the available time.
   - It is theoretically impossible to guarantee a 100 percent error-detection rate, so you have to settle for this more realistic goal.

3. Clearly define the expected results of each test, so that test results are easy to analyze.
   - If possible, create electronic versions of expected output files so that the actual outputs can be verified automatically. If not, use hard copy.

4. The more removed the test designer is from the project team, the better the test.
   - An outsider is likely to take a more critical approach than an insider, and is less likely to be operating under the same (sometimes mistaken) assumptions as insiders do.

5. A complete test plan covers:
   - Scenarios based on the basic flow of each system use case.
   - Scenarios based on all the alternate flows of each system use case—including valid but rarely occurring cases.

- Scenarios based on all the exceptional flows of each system use case—that is, all error situations.
- All line-item BRD requirements not included in the preceding (for example, general quality requirements).
- All features described in the user documentation. (The features should be traceable to system use cases.)
- The domain (valid range) of each input variable of each system use case.[3]
- All requirements regarding input/output relationships for each system use case.
- Verification of the specified relative frequency of system use cases.
- Sequential dependencies among use cases.

6. Save test plans, test cases, and test results.

- By saving tests, you can reuse them in future regression tests.

7. Concentrate on the lemons.

- If your time is limited, concentrate your testing effort on the areas of the system that have been most problematic in the past.

8. Check for unwanted side-effects.

- Unintended side-effects of a programming change are common sources of errors. When testing a programming change, make sure areas of the system that the change was not supposed to affect are still working correctly.

9. Execute tests in a safe testing environment.

Table 10.1 summarizes when to use the testing techniques covered in this chapter.

Structured Walkthroughs

A *structured walkthrough* is a peer-review process for testing the completeness and accuracy of a project deliverable, such as a portion of the BRD.

Most people think of testing as a process involving the execution of a program by the computer. This is only one type of testing, referred to, appropriately, as *computer-based testing*. Testing, however, also includes, *non-computer-based tests*. How can you test a system without actually executing it? You walk through some aspect of the system "by hand" with a group of participants. The formal method for doing this is the *structured walkthrough*.

---

[3]Boundary value analysis provides rules for selecting input values within and outside of the domain.

Table 10.1 Testing Techniques

To Do the Following:	Use These Tools:
Ensure that all of the code has been covered properly during testing	White-box techniques: statement, decision, condition, multiple condition coverage
Test the requirements for completeness and accuracy	Structured walkthrough
Test functional requirements for end-to-end business process	High-level integration tests based on business use cases
Test the system's response to simple conditions	Condition response tables
Test the system's response to a group of input conditions that might occur in any combination	Decision tables, decision trees
Design test data most likely to uncover bugs	Boundary value analysis
Test how the system handles high volume	Volume test (a type of system test)
Test how the system handles a high level of activity within a short period of time	Stress test (a type of system test)
Test for user-friendliness	Usability test (a type of system test)
Test speed	Performance test (a type of system test)
Ensure processes that should remain unaffected by the release work as before	Regression test (a type of system test)
Submit the system for final acceptance by the user	User Acceptance Testing (UAT)

Why Are Structured Walkthroughs an Important Aspect of Testing?

Errors are often thought to be exclusively due to bad programming; in fact, they can be introduced at any stage of a project. The beauty of walkthroughs is that, unlike computer-based testing, they can be performed before the software is written. *Early testing means early detection of errors.* The sooner errors are found, the easier they are to fix. Also, unlike computer-based tests, walkthroughs tend to find the *cause* of a problem, not just its symptom. For example, a computer-based test may find symptoms, such as scattered situations where credit is advanced to non-worthy applicants; a walkthrough may uncover the cause—an incorrectly documented decision table for evaluating credit applications.

Requirements-Based (Black-Box) Testing

The purpose of *requirement-based testing* is to find variances between the software and the requirements. The Business Requirements Document (BRD) acts as the reference point for these tests. The term *black-box tests* is also used for these types of tests, since the tester does not need to know anything about the internals of the software, such as the code and table structure, to design and run them.

Limitations of Testing

Since no knowledge of the code is assumed with black-box testing, the only way to know definitively the effect that a particular set of inputs will have on the system is to test the system's response to it. This means that for full coverage, you'd have to test every possible set of input values and conditions. In practice, this is an unachievable standard, so, instead, you use techniques that help you design black-box tests that will uncover the greatest number of bugs in a given amount of time.

Use-Case Scenario Testing

Use-case scenario testing is one approach to requirements-based testing, which tests the various scenarios of each use case. Use cases lend themselves well to testing. Because of the narrative style of the use-case documentation, it is already very close to being a testing script. And the way the use cases are organized—into end-to-end business use cases and user-goal system use cases—matches the way the tests are organized. However use cases are not *all* you need to design the test. To design tests, you need more detail, such as graphical user interface (GUI) screens, the static model (which provides validation rules for attributes), and the documentation on "business rules" (stored in a business rules engine or kept manually in a folder). The system use cases may *refer* to these artifacts, but the artifacts are not part of the use-case documentation itself.

Deriving Use-Case Scenario Tests

Recall that your processing requirements were grouped around system use cases, each with its own group of scenarios. The flows were chosen so that they would cover all important scenarios:

- *Basic flows*
- *Alternate flows*: Rarely occurring flows and other variations from the norm
- *Exception flows*: Errors

Use the flows of the system use case to derive scenarios, then test each scenario. For example, one test scenario might walk through the basic flow. You might be able to design another test scenario that walks through the basic flow and all of the alternate flows. At a bare minimum, you'll want to ensure that the basic flow and each of the alternate and exception flows are covered at least once in the test scenarios. But you may also be interested in designing key tests that use certain combinations of the alternate flows. For example, one alternate flow for a stock-trading site may be "non-standard lot size" and another may be "order can only be partially filled." The software may be able handle each of these alternates one at a time but not when they occur together. To test the system's response to this situation, you'll want to include a test scenario that walks through both alternate flows. If you need to ensure you've covered *all* possible combinations of a set of alternate flows, use decision tables, covered later in this chapter.

During test execution, you'll be looking to see whether or not the sequence of events during the test matches that described in the use case. One way to do this is to use the steps of the system use case as the source for the following test template. Place steps that begin with "The user…" in the "Action/Data" column of the template; place steps that begin with "The system…" in the "Expected Result/Response" column.

Test Template

Test #: _____   Project #: _____

System: _____   Test environment: _____

Test type (e.g., regression/ requirements-based, etc.): _____

Test objective: _____

System use case: _____   Flow: _____

Priority: ____

Next step in case of failure: _____

Planned start date: _____ Planned end date: _____

Actual start date: _____   Actual end date: _____

times to repeat: __

Preconditions (must be true before test begins): _____

Req #	Action/Data	Expected Result/Response	Actual Result	Pass/ Fail

Tester ID: _____

Pass/fail: _____   Severity of failure: _____

Solution: _____

Comments: _____

Sign-off: _____

(Req # is short for requirement number and corresponds to the number used to identify the requirement in the BRD. Many organizations number their requirements so that they can be traced forward to test cases and other project artifacts. The numbering may be manual, or automatically generated with the use of a tool such as Rational RequisitePro.)

Decision Tables for Testing

When the input conditions affecting a system use case are interrelated, it is not enough to test for each input condition separately; you must test all *combinations* of input conditions. An input condition is any condition that will have an impact on the system response. Examples from a Web retail site include *item on sale, customer discount,* and *fast delivery method selected.* You'll find some input conditions documented in the system use case as alternate flows, for example, the alternate flow *Non-standard lot size.* You might also see them already documented as part of the requirements in a decision table appended to a step of the use case or to the use case as a whole. In this case, you can reuse the decision table for testing purposes.

From a testing perspective, each column in the table identifies a test scenario. Keep in mind, though, that the column only *identifies* the test scenario; it does not fully *specify* it. To properly specify a test, you need to complete the test template for each test scenario you've identified from the columns. Also, as discussed below under the section "Boundary Value Analysis," you may need to create more than one test scenario per column.

The use of decision tables in this context may be complex, but that does not mean that this approach to testing is "white box." The input conditions and the expected system responses are still derived from the requirements—not from an examination of the code. This classifies the technique as "black box." (Later in this chapter, you'll learn that decision tables can also be used by programmers for white-box testing—but that is another matter.)

Case Study J1: Deriving Test Cases from Decision Tables

You are designing test cases for the system use case *Review case report.* Fortunately, you earlier created a decision table as part of the requirements documentation, as shown in Figure 10.1. Note how each column in the table identifies the nature of the input data and systems response for each test scenario.

What the Decision Table Does Not Say about Testing

The decision table shows only the net result of each test; it does not show the required sequencing of steps. For this reason, you need to complete the test template for each test scenario, indicating the expected sequence of actions. Use the system use-case description to work out the expected workflow for each case.

Also, each column tells you something about the input data for a given test, but does not specify *exactly* which data to test for. For example, for the test corresponding to column 2 in Figure 10.1, the number of *Peace Committee Members* may be three, four, or five. Which

		1	2	3	4	5	6	7	8	9	10	11	12
C O N D I T I O N	Code of good practice followed (Y/N)	Y	Y	Y	Y	Y	Y	N	N	N	N	N	N
	Steps and procedures followed (Y/N)	Y	Y	Y	N	N	N	Y	Y	Y	N	N	N
	# PC members (0-2, 3-5, 6+)	0-2	3-5	6+	0-2	3-5	6+	0-2	3-5	6+	0-2	3-5	6+
A C T I O N	Mark as not payable	X			X			X	X	X	X	X	X
	Mark as payable		X	X		X	X						
	Pay _ standard amount					X	X						
	Pay standard amount		X										
	Pay double amount			X									

Figure 10.1 Validate case and determine payment amount

of these should you use? What about tests for invalid data? These issues are addressed by boundary value analysis.

Boundary Value Analysis

Boundary value analysis is a technique for targeting test data most likely to reveal bugs. The technique is based on the premise that the system is most error-prone at points of change.

Boundary value analysis can help you pinpoint test data for any requirements-based (black-box) test. If you are working from a decision table, then boundary value analysis can help you decide which data to use for the test(s) indicated by each column of the table. The technique covers both positive and negative testing:

- A *positive test* is one that tests the system's response to valid conditions (success scenarios).

- A *negative test* is one that tests the system's response to invalid conditions (errors).

The following is a summary of boundary value analysis rules:

1. If the condition states that the *number* of input (or output) values must lie within a specific range:

   ▪ Create two positive tests, one at either end of the range.

   ▪ Create two negative tests, one just beyond the valid range at the low end and one just beyond the high end.

   For example, for the system use case *Update case* that accepts 2–10 parties to a dispute, the positive tests would have the user enter exactly 2 and exactly 10 parties. Negative tests would try for 1 and 11 parties.

2. Similarly, if an input or output *value* must lie within a range of values and the whole range is treated the same way:

   ▪ Create two positive tests, one at either end of the range.

   ▪ Create two negative tests, one just beyond the valid range at the low end and one just beyond the high end.

   For example, if the *Ward Number* attribute of the *Peace Committee* class has a valid range of 1–100, create two positive tests: 1, 100. Also create two negative tests: 0, 101.

3. If an input or output value must lie within a range of values and different valid ranges are treated differently:

   ▪ Create a positive test for each end of each valid range.

   ▪ Create two negative tests, one just below the smallest acceptable value and one just above the highest.

   For example, the decision table for the system use case *Review case report* indicates that system response depends on *# Peace Committee Members*. The valid ranges are 0–2, 3–5, and 6–99. The positive test values are 0, 2, 3, 5, 6, and 100. The negative tests are –1 and 100.

4. If an input or output value must be one of a set of valid options and all options are treated the same way:

   ▪ Create one test for valid data using any value from the set.

   ▪ Create one invalid test, using any value not in the set.

   For example, the *reason code no gathering* attribute of the *Case* must match the code of one of the reason codes in the look-up table. Create one positive test where the code is found in the table, and one negative test where it is not.

5. If an input or output value must belong to a set of values and each one is treated differently:
   - Create one test for each valid option.
   - Create one invalid test using a value not in the set.

   For example, if the system treats criminal offenses differently than civil offenses, create a positive test for a case whose dispute code refers to a criminal dispute and another test where the code refers to a civil one. Also, create a negative test for where the dispute code is not found in the look-up table.

6. If the requirements state that a certain condition must be true:
   - Create one valid test where the condition is satisfied.
   - Create one invalid test where the condition is not satisfied.

   For example, the *testimony* attribute of the *Party to Dispute* must be non-null. Create a positive test where testimony is entered, and a negative test where it is not.

7. To limit the number of tests you have to run, you can combine as many valid tests as possible in a single run. However, you may not combine invalid tests.

8. Look out for any boundaries not covered in the above rules.

   For example, for any reports or screens, test one case where exactly one page or screen is filled and one test where the output goes over by one line.

   Wherever sorting occurs, test cases where everything is presorted; all values are the same; one value is the lowest possible, and one is the highest.

   For input values, try negative numbers and zero. Try entering no value at all.

Case Study J2: Select Test Data Using Boundary Value Analysis

You once again refer to the decision table for the system use case's review case report. Earlier, you noted that each column represents one or more test cases. Now you create precise test cases based on what you've learned about boundary value analysis, as shown in Figure 10.2. (For the purposes of this case study, I've set an upper limit of 99 on the number of *Peace Committee Members*.)

Case Study J2: Resulting Documentation

Boundary value analysis leads you to design the test cases in Table 10.2.

		1	2	3	4	5	6	7	8	9	10	11	12
C O N D I T I O N	Code of good practice followed (Y/N)	Y	Y	Y	Y	Y	Y	N	N	N	N	N	N
	Steps and procedures followed (Y/N)	Y	Y	Y	N	N	N	Y	Y	Y	N	N	N
	# PC members (0-2, 3-5, 6-99)	0–2	3–5	6–99	0–2	3–5	6–99	0–2	3–5	6–99	0–2	3–5	6–99
A C T I O N	Mark as not payable	X			X			X	X	X	X	X	X
	Mark as payable		X	X		X	X						
	Pay 1/2 standard amount					X	X						
	Pay standard amount		X										
	Pay double amount			X									

Figure 10.2 Selecting test data using boundary value analysis

Table 10.2 Test Cases Resulting from Boundary Value Analysis*

Test #	Decision Table Col #	Code Followed?	Steps?	# PC Members
1	1	Y	Y	0
2	2	Y	Y	3
3	3	Y	Y	6
4	4	Y	N	2
5	5	Y	N	3
6	6	Y	N	6
7	7	N	Y	2
8	8	N	Y	5
9	9	N	Y	6
10	10	N	N	2
11	11	N	N	3
12	12	N	N	99

Table 10.2 (continued)

Test #	Decision Table Col #	Code Followed?	Steps?	# PC Members
13		X	Y	2
14		–	Y	3
15		Y	–	5
16		N	X	2
17				1
18				X
19				100
20		N	Y	–

*Rows 13–20 are negative tests.

White-Box Testing

White-box testing is a testing methodology based on knowledge of the internal workings of the software.

Who Does White-Box Testing?

Developers perform these tests, since knowledge of programming code is required. But as a Business Analyst, you have a supporting role: You may be required to specify the *level* of white-box testing that the software must pass through before it is accepted. And after the tests are run, you might be called on to inspect evidence that the white-box tests have been carried out successfully. This proof sometimes comes in the form of a report produced by an automated testing product, confirming the level of white-box testing to which the software has been exposed. To support white-box testing, you need a basic understanding of what such testing can and cannot achieve and of the meaning of the white-box testing levels.

Limitations of White-Box Testing

To ensure that software is completely error-free, white-box testing would have to include enough tests to "exercise" the code thoroughly. This turns out to be impossible in practice. Why? At first glance, it might seem sufficient to execute a set of tests that causes every statement to be executed at least once. Unfortunately, this does not supply sufficient coverage, since some errors show up only when a program's execution follows a specific *path* through the code. To white-box test a program *fully*, then, you would need to try *all possible paths* of statement execution.

> Consider an operation containing 20 statements that are repeated up to 20 times. The body of the loop includes several nested IF-THEN-ELSE statements. It would take about 10^{14} tests to cover all of the possible sequences in which those statements could be executed.

Because the number of tests usually required for full coverage is so high, other approaches are used to winnow the set of tests to a manageable size.

White-Box Coverage Quality Levels

The following coverage levels are used to specify the degree of thoroughness of white-box testing, listed in order of increasing coverage. Depending on the level of risk, you may specify one of the following coverages:

- *Statement coverage*: Every coding statement is executed at least once. This coverage level is considered to be too low to be acceptable.

- *Decision coverage*: Every decision in the code has taken all possible outcomes at least once during the tests. Decision coverage is the minimum acceptable level of coverage. For example, if the source code contained the decision (AGE OVER 20 AND LICENCE IS UNDER SUSPENSION), this expression would have to evaluate to both "true" and "false" at least once during the tests.

- *Condition coverage*: Every simple condition takes all possible outcomes at least once. For example, in the preceding example, the decision is actually a complex condition made of two simple conditions: (AGE > 20) and (LICENSE IS UNDER SUSPENSION). For this level of coverage, the tests must include cases where the simple condition (AGE > 20) takes true and false outcomes and the condition (LICENSE IS UNDER SUSPENSION) takes true and false outcomes.

- *Multiple condition coverage*: Every combination of outcomes for simple conditions making up a complex condition is tested. For example, for the complex condition AGE > 20 AND LICENSE IS UNDER-SUSPENSION, you'd test:

  (AGE > 20) is true and (LICENSE IS UNDER SUSPENSION) is true.

  (AGE > 20) is true and (LICENSE IS UNDER SUSPENSION) is false (that is, the license is not under suspension).

  (AGE > 20) is false (i.e. AGE <= 20) and (LICENSE IS UNDER SUSPENSION) is true.

  (AGE > 20) is false and (LICENSE IS UNDER SUSPENSION) is false.

You might be wondering if decision tables have any part to play here. There is a role for decision tables—but not the in the context you learned to use them earlier in this chapter. The conditions and actions to the tables discussed earlier tables were based on the *requirements*. The coverage tests we're currently dealing with, however, involve condition expressions and actions written in the *source code*. (These condition expressions may sometimes have parallel conditions in the requirements—but they often do not.) Decision tables can also be used in a programming context to derive multiple condition coverage tests, using source-level conditions and actions. Use of decision tables in this context is beyond your role as BA because of the programming knowledge it requires.

Sequencing of White-Box Tests

When software is written, it is developed in modules, or units. In structured systems, the software unit is the *process*, known by various terms such as *subroutine, function,* or *subprogram*. In OO, the basic software unit is the class, which contains code for attributes and operations. In both structured and OO environments, a plan must be put together to sequence the testing of these units and their proper integration within the software. The process of planning and executing these piecemeal tests is called *unit testing*.

Unit Testing and the BA

While the developers usually carry out unit testing, the BA needs to be able to consult with the developers about the planning and scheduling of these tests. Since most systems in large organizations involved a hybrid of structured software (typically for back-end legacy systems) and OO (typically for Web-enabled front-end systems), as a BA, you'll need a basic understanding of unit testing in both environments.

Big Bang Approach to Unit Testing

There are a number of approaches for the sequencing of unit tests. In the *big bang* approach, each unit is first tested individually. Once this is complete, all units are integrated and tested in one "big bang" test.

In a structured system, these units are subroutines or functions. In an OO system, they are classes. In either environment, the developers often need to create "dummy" software to stand in for other units not being tested at that time. One of the disadvantages of the big bang approach is that, since units are first tested in complete isolation from the rest of the program, a large amount of this "dummy" software has to be written. Another disadvantage is that the final big bang test is the first opportunity to test whether the units have been integrated properly in the software. If an integration problem shows up at this time, it will be very hard to diagnose. For this reason, the big bang approach is not advised—but is still used because it is easy to manage.

Incremental Approaches to Unit Testing

A preferred approach is the *incremental* approach, where each unit is added to the system one by one. With each incremental test, the internal workings of a unit *and* its integration with the rest of the system are tested. Since not much is being added with each test, diagnosis is easier.

Top-Down Testing

In a structured environment, there are two types of incremental testing to choose from: *top-down* or *bottom-up*.

In top-down testing, the units are tested starting from the "mainline" program (the high-level module that coordinates the major functions) and advances toward the "low-level" units that carry out basic functions. The advantage of this sequence is that it mirrors the order in which software units are usually developed. The disadvantage is that since high-level subroutines are tested before the low-level routines they depend on, the tester must create "stubs"—"fake" units that take the place of the real low-level routines during testing.

Bottom-Up Testing

In bottom-up testing, the order is reversed: First the low-level routines are tested, followed by higher-level routines. The advantage of this approach is that it does not require the overhead of creating stubs. It does, however, require the creation of other stand-in software, called drivers, but these are usually easier to develop. The big disadvantage is that this sequence does not match the order in which the units are actually coded.

Incremental Testing in an OO Environment

In an OO environment, the units are not organized "top" to "bottom." Rather, objects are seen as being on the same level, collaborating with each other to carry out system use cases. It makes no sense, therefore, to speak of a "top-down" or "bottom-up" approach. Instead, the system use cases direct the sequencing of tests. When software is developed iteratively (as is commonly the case with OO systems), a set of system use cases is developed and released (internally or to the user). During each iteration, only the classes and operations required for the scheduled use cases are developed and tested. With each iteration, more classes and operations are developed and tested until the entire system has been covered.

System Tests

Once the black-box tests have been completed, another battery of tests is executed. These are called system tests. With the exception of usability testing (a type of system test), you will not typically perform these tests, but you may be involved in planning them and in verifying that the tests have been conducted, so you should be aware of the tests in this category.

Myers defines system testing as follows: "The purpose of *System testing* is showing that the product is inconsistent with its original objectives."

The idea behind system testing is that even if the code has been adequately tested for coverage (white-box testing) and has been shown to do everything expressed in the user requirements, it may still fail because it doesn't do these things well enough. It may not meet other objectives—such as those related to security, speed, and so on. Myers laid out a set of system tests designed to catch these kinds of failures.[4] These tests are still widely in use today. Following are some of the more popular of these tests.

Regression Testing

Regression testing validates whether features that were supposed to be unaffected by a new release still work as they should. The test helps avoid the "one step forward, two steps backward" problem: a programming modification designed to fix one problem inadvertently creating new ones. How much regression testing should you do? That depends on the level of risk. Often organizations create a problem review board to set standards for regression testing and to evaluate on a case-by-case basis the degree of regression testing required.

Volume Testing

Volume testing verifies whether the system can handle large volumes of data. Why is this necessary? Some systems break down only when volume is high, such as a system that uses disk space to store files temporarily during a sort. When the volume is high, the system crashes because there isn't enough room for these temporary files.

Also, some systems may become unbearably slow when volume is high. Often this is due to the fact that the data tables become so large that searches and look-ups take an inordinate amount of time.

Stress Testing

Stress testing subjects the system to heavy loads within a short period of time. What distinguishes this from volume testing is the time element. For example, an automated teller system is tested to see what happens when all machines are processing transactions at the same time, or a network server is tested to see what happens when a large number of users all log on at the same time.

Usability Testing

Usability testing looks for flaws in the human-factors engineering of the system. In other words, it attempts to determine whether the system is user-friendly. Isn't it enough that the system does what it's supposed to do? No. Users may reject it anyway due to frustration with the user interface.

---

[4]G. Myers, *The Art of Software Testing*, 1978, p, 106.

Questions investigated during usability testing include

- Is the user interface appropriate for the educational level of the users?
- Are system messages written in easy-to-understand language?
- Do all error messages give clear, corrective direction? The user must always be given a "way out."
- Are there any inconsistencies in the user interfaces of the system? Look for inconsistencies with respect to screen layout, response to mouse clicks, and so on.
- Does the system provide sufficient "redundancy checks" on key input? Important data should be entered twice, or in two complementary ways—for example, an social security number *and* a name for financial transactions.
- Are all system options and features actually useful to the user? Unused "extras" make the system harder to learn and clutter the interface.
- Does the system confirm actions when necessary? The system must confirm important actions, such as the receipt of a customer's on-line order.
- Does the flow dictated by the system support the natural flow of the business?

Security Testing

Security testing attempts to find "holes" in the system's security procedures. For example, the tests will attempt to "hack" through password protection or to introduce a virus to the system.

Performance Testing

Performance testing locates areas where the system does not meet its efficiency objectives. Performance tests include the measuring and evaluation of:

- *Response time:* The elapsed time it takes the system to respond to a user request.
- *CPU time:* The amount of processing time required.
- *Throughput:* The number of transactions processed per second.

Storage Testing

Storage testing checks for cases where storage objectives are not met. These objectives include requirements for random access memory (RAM) and disk requirements.

Configuration Testing

Configuration testing checks for failure of the system to perform under all of the combinations of hardware and software configurations allowed for in the objectives. For example, these tests look for problems occurring when a supported processor, operating system revision, printer driver, or printer model is used.

Compatibility/Conversion Testing

Often, the goal of an IT project is to replace some part of an existing system. The objective of *compatibility testing* is to verify whether the replacement software produces the same result as the original modules (with allowance for new or revised features) and is compatible with the existing system. *Conversion testing* verifies whether the procedures used to convert the old data into new formats work properly.

Reliability Testing

Reliability testing checks for failure to meet specific reliability objectives. For example, the objectives for one of my early programs—a food-testing program—stated that an automated count of bacteria grown on a grid be correct to a given accuracy. Reliability testing would verify whether this objective was met. Another metric that falls in this category is mean time to failure (MTTF).

Recovery Testing

Recovery testing checks for failure of the recovery procedures to perform as stated in the objectives. For example, an on-line financial update program keeps a log of all activity. If the master files are corrupted, the objectives state that a recovery procedure will be able to restore files to their state just before the crash by processing the day's transaction log against a backup of the previous day's files. A recovery test would look for failure of this procedure to recover the files.

Beyond the System Tests

The BA should plan for a final set of tests to take place after the system tests are complete. These are UAT, beta testing, parallel testing, and installation testing.

User Acceptance Testing (UAT)

Acceptance testing is the final testing of the system before the users sign off on it. This test is often performed by the users themselves, though, in some organizations, the BA performs the test, while the user looks on. There are two alternative approaches to UAT—a formal and informal approach.

In the formal approach, the developers and users sign a document beforehand that lays out the terms of the UAT. The document stipulates that if the users carry out the UAT under the terms described in the agreement and if the tests are successful, the users will accept the system. By having participants sign off on this document before the UAT, the BA sets the stage for a clean end to the project.

Proponents of the informal approach argue that the formal approach is inappropriate. In their view, users should have free reign to experiment with the system to make sure it can let them do their jobs, which might involve unexpected variations of usage.

For example, IBM's RUP methodology states, "In informal acceptance testing, the test procedures for performing the test are not as rigorously defined as for formal acceptance testing. The functions and business tasks to be explored are identified and documented, but there are no particular test cases to follow. The individual tester determines what to do. This approach to acceptance testing is not as controlled as formal testing and is more subjective than the formal one."

Beta Testing

Alpha testing is the testing of the system by the manufacturer; these are the kinds of tests you have been reading about until this point. *Beta testing* occurs after the alpha testing is complete. In beta testing, copies of the system are distributed to a wide group of users, selected to represent the various configurations, volume, stress, and functional needs of the target user population. The developers correct any errors uncovered by beta testing before releasing the production version. Beta testing is often used for systems that will have a wide distribution.

Parallel Testing

On some projects, the system undergoes *parallel testing* before final acceptance. With this approach, the new system is put into place and used while the old system is run concurrently. Both systems should provide equivalent outputs (except for any variations resulting from new enhancements and modifications). Parallel testing minimizes risk. If errors arise, the user can quickly revert to the old system until the problem is resolved.

Installation Testing

Installation testing is performed after the software is installed. Its purpose is to check for errors in the installation process itself. This test checks whether all files that should have been installed are, indeed, present, whether the content of the files is correct, and so on.

Step 2d: Specify Implementation Plan

The BRD must include an implementation plan so that steps required when releasing the system can be planned for in advance. The issues addressed typically include

Training:
- Who is to be trained?
- How will training be done?

- What resources (hardware, software, training rooms, trainers, administration, and so on) will be required?

Conversion:

- Identify existing data that will need to be converted (due to new file formats, new database management software, and so on).
- Plan promotion of programs (from the current version to the new one).
- Plan granting of privileges to the users.
- Schedule jobs (for batch systems):
- Advise operations which jobs to add to the production run: daily, weekly, monthly, quarterly, semi-annually, or annually.
- Ensure that the job is planned to be executed in the right sequence—that is, after certain jobs are run and before others.
- Advise operations of the reports to be printed and the distribution list for reports and files.

Rollout:

- Advise all affected users of the promotion date for the project.

End user procedures:

- Write up the procedures for the affected departments.
- Distribute an end user procedures document to affected departments.

Post Implementation Follow-Up

Follow up within a reasonable time frame after implementation to ensure that the project is running successfully and to verify that the project is achieving high-level goals. For example, check back six months after installation to see whether market share has indeed increased 6 percent as described in the BRD. Determine whether any further enhancements or changes are needed to ensure the success of the project. Also, the post-implementation follow-up offers a good opportunity to review lessons learned from the project.

Step 2e: Set Baseline for Development

Once the BRD is complete, save all analysis documentation so that team members will be able to refer back to it later. This copy becomes the "baseline"—or beginning point—for the next phase: the actual development of the software.

Chapter Summary

In this chapter, you learned how to design test cases that are most likely to uncover software bugs using the tools and principles of structured testing as applied to OO projects. Also, you learned about the features of an implementation plan and the need for a post-implementation follow-up.

Tools and concepts that you learned about in this chapter included the following:

1. Structured testing principles
    i. Structured walkthroughs for testing
    ii. White-box testing criteria (statement coverage, decision coverage, condition coverage, and multiple-condition coverage)
    iii. Black-box testing
    iv. Use-case scenario testing
    v. Decision tables
    vi. Unit testing
    vii. Black-box test
    viii. Boundary value analysis
    ix. System tests
    x. Regression testing
    xi. Volume testing
    xii. Stress testing
    xiii. Usability testing
    xiv. Security testing
    xv. Performance testing
    xvi. Storage testing
    xvii. Configuration testing
    xviii. Compatibility testing
    xix. Reliability testing
    xx. Recovery testing
    xxi. Implementation plan

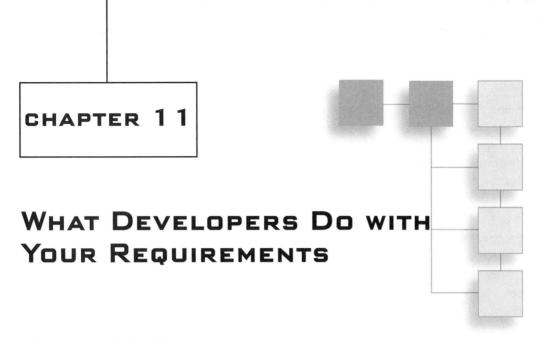

CHAPTER 11

WHAT DEVELOPERS DO WITH YOUR REQUIREMENTS

Chapter Objectives

As the project moves into the Execution phase, the developers (Systems Analyst, Systems Architect, Database Administrator, and so on) start the work of adapting your business model for technical use. This is the point at which your active participation stops—but you still need to be available to answer the questions that inevitably arise at this phase. To assist you in communicating with the developers, this chapter looks at some of the issues that occupy them as they turn your business model into a design specification.

Tools and concepts that you'll be introduced to in this chapter include the following:

1. OO analysis patterns
2. Visibility
3. Control classes
4. Boundary classes
5. Sequence diagrams
6. Communication diagrams
7. Timing diagrams
8. Deployment diagrams
9. Layered architecture
10. Interfaces
11. Implementing OOA using procedural languages
12. Implementing OOA using RDBMS

OO Patterns

Some problems are difficult to design a solution for, yet common to many systems. The idea of patterns is to provide a "best practices" solution for these common problems. A pattern consists of a problem description, one or more diagrams (class diagrams, sequence diagrams, and communication diagrams) that describe a design solution to the problem and, often, a segment of code that implements the design. It is typically the Systems Analyst who adapts the business model by incorporating these patterns.

Examples

- The business static model states that an object has many roles, and that some operations and attributes apply to all roles. The *Strategy* pattern offers a combination of aggregation and inheritance to standardize role handling.

- An object is composed of other objects that may be composed of other objects, and so on. Any composition level may be skipped. If one object at any level needs to be operated on, all the objects below it or above it will require a similar operation (for example, a recall of all components). The *Composite* pattern offers a combination of aggregation and inheritance to turn this complicated issue into a simple design solution.

Visibility

Visibility is a property that can be used to describe a class member.

> A *member* of a class is an attribute or operation.

Visibility determines whether other classes can refer to a class member, and whether other objects can "see" (and therefore use) this attribute or operation.

> What they say:
>
> *Visibility:* "An enumeration whose value (public, protected, or private) denotes how the model element to which it refers may be seen outside its enclosing namespace." (UML 2)
>
> What they mean:
>
> Visibility is a property of a model element such as a class member. Visibility may have only specific values (that is, it is an enumeration). These values—*public, private, protected* and *package*—describe whether the element can be seen outside of the context in which it is defined.

Example

The *CashAccount* class has an operation, *depositFunds()*, that other classes use. This operation entails adjusting the General Ledger, a process described in the internal operation *enterDepositIntoGeneralLedger()*. The Systems Analyst specifies the visibility of *depositFunds()* as *public*, meaning that operations in other classes can refer to it. The visibility of *enterDepositIntoGeneralLedger()*, on the other hand, is specified as *private*, meaning that only operations of the *CashAccount* class can refer it.

Visibility Options

- *Private*: Code for the class may refer to the member by name. Code in other classes may not. Specializations inherit the member but may not refer to it by name. The symbol for private is a minus sign("-"). For example, a specialized *ChequingAccount* class inherits a private attribute, *balance*, from a generalized *Account* class. Every *ChequingAccount* object will have a *balance* attribute but the attribute will be accessible only by operations defined for the *Account* class.

- *Protected*: The rules for a protected member are similar to those for a private member, except that that specializations may refer to the member by name. The symbol for protected is a pound sign ("#"). For example, a specialized *ChequingAccount* class inherits a protected attribute, *#accountNumber*, from a generalized *Account* class. Every *ChequingAccount* object will have an *AccountNumber* attribute and the attribute will be accessible to operations defined in the *ChequingAccount* class.

- *Public*: Any element may access the member. The symbol for public is a plus sign ("+").

- *Package*: The member is visible to all elements within the nearest enclosing package. Outside the nearest enclosing package, the member is not visible. The symbol for public is an ellipsis ("~").

Control Classes

In this book, we have only dealt with entity classes. Developers add other types of classes to the system. One of these is the *control class*. Ivar Jacobson introduced control classes to address one of the shortcomings of OO. He noted that while it is often easier to modify OO systems than the older "structured" systems, some changes are more difficult in OO. In particular, OO makes it harder to change the *sequencing* of the operations required by a system use case. The problem is that, in OO, these operations are scattered among the classes involved in the use case, instead of being listed in a single controlling program. To correct the problem, he suggested the addition of a control class to encapsulate, in one software unit, the sequencing logic of a use case. As a rule of thumb, one control class is introduced for each system use case.

Boundary Classes

Systems should be insulated as much as possible from changes in other systems. Otherwise, a change in one would create an unacceptable "ripple effect" on other systems. The OO approach is to define a boundary class for each external system. This creates a "bottle-neck" to the other system: The only way that the system under design is allowed to communicate with another is by sending a message to the boundary object. The advantage of this approach is that any changes or bugs affecting communication with the external system will be localized in the boundary class—and, therefore, easy to fix or modify. As a rule of thumb, one boundary class is allocated for each external system and one for each interaction between a human actor and a system use case, as depicted on the system use-case diagrams.

Sequence Diagrams

A *sequence diagram* describes the sequence of operations during one scenario of a system use case and determines which object carries out each operation.[1] The UML categorizes it as an *interaction diagram*—a diagram that highlights how objects interact with each other.

Some Business Analysts use sequence diagrams as an alternative to activity diagrams with partitions. Instead of drawing one complex activity diagram to cover all scenarios, the BA draws one simple sequence diagram for each scenario. Each diagram is simple, since it describes only one scenario. The disadvantage of sequence diagrams for this purpose is that they require the BA to work out not only which object *performs* each action but also *which object requests the action*. This is often difficult to determine in a business context. In addition, BAs tend to have more difficulty using this diagram than its counterpart, the activity diagram with partitions. For these reasons, sequence diagrams are not advised for BA use. On the other hand, sequence diagrams are an excellent way to design the distribution of operations among classes for programming purposes.

Example: A Sequence Diagram in UML

Figure 11.1 shows how a Systems Analyst might attempt to design the object interactions required for the steps within the *Disburse Payments* system use case required to create a payment to a *Peace Committee Member*. An excerpt from the use case follows:

System use case: *Disburse Payments*

   2 Flow of Events

     Basic flow:

       ...

---

[1]This is a feature it shares with activity diagrams with partitions.

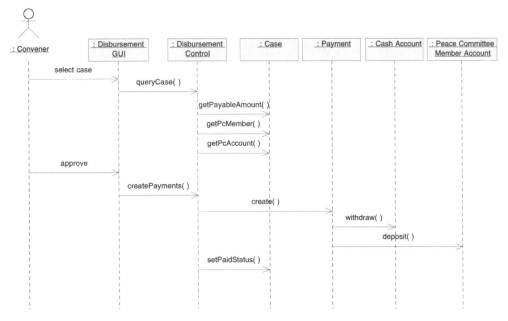

Figure 11.1 Designing object interactions with a sequence diagram

2.2 The user selects a case.

2.3 The system displays the amount payable for the case.

2.4 The system displays each *Peace Committee Member* assigned to the case.

2.5 The system displays the *Peace Committee Member Account* owned by each of the displayed *Peace Committee Members.*

...

2.7 The user approves the disbursement.

2.8 The system creates payments for the *Case.*

2.9 The system marks the *Case* as *Paid.*

Using a tool such as Rational Rose, the operations identified during the drawing of the sequence diagram can be automatically added to the classes involved, making the design process easier.

The diagram in Figure 11.1 indicates that

- The *Convener* selects a case on the *Disbursement GUI* (graphical user interface) screen.

- The *Disbursement GUI* sends the message *queryCase()* to the *Disbursement Control* object, requesting it to query payment-related details about the case.

- The *Disbursement Control* object services this request by passing a number of messages to the *Case* object: *getPaymentAmount()*, *getPcMember()*, and *getPcAccount()*. These are requests to retrieve payment and *Peace Committee Member* information relevant to the *Case*. (To keep the diagram simple, only one *Peace Committee Member Account* is shown, though more are involved.)

- The *Convener* approves the disbursement for the Case.

- The *GUI* responds to the approval by sending the message *createPayments()* to the *Disbursement Control* object.

- The *Disbursement Control* object responds by sending a *create()* message to each required *Payment* object. (The diagram only shows one of these.) Though not shown on this draft of the diagram, payment details such as the destination and amount of the payment are passed at this time as arguments.

- The *Payment* object sends a *withdraw()* message to *Cash* and a *deposit()* message to the *Peace Committee Member Account*.

- The *Disbursement Control* object finishes the process by sending the message *setPaidStatus()* to the *Case* object to indicate that payments have been made.

Later the Systems Analyst could add more steps to the diagram to indicate how payments are also made to the *Fund Accounts*.

Communication Diagrams

Like the sequence diagram, the communication diagram is categorized in the UML as an interaction diagram. Both diagrams are able to show the sequencing of operations for a scenario and indicate which object does which operation. However, each highlights a different aspect of the collaboration: The communication diagram highlights *structure*—the ways in which objects are linked to each other—while the sequence diagram highlights *timing*—the order in which messages are sent between objects.

In a communication diagram, objects are connected by solid lines (links). The messages are indicated as labeled arrows above the links. Each message is numbered to indicate sequencing. The communication diagram in Figure 11.2 illustrates the same scenario shown in the previous sequence diagram shown in Figure 11.1.

Other Diagrams

The UML contains other diagrams you might come across occasionally. Following is a brief introduction to two of these—the timing and deployment diagrams.

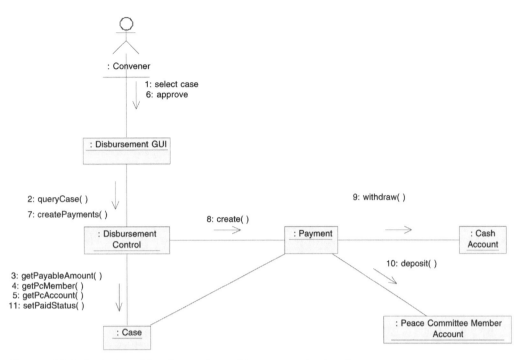

Figure 11.2 Designing object interactions with a communication diagram

Timing Diagrams

Timing diagram: "An interaction diagram that shows the change in state or condition of a lifeline (representing a Classifier Instance or Classifier Role) over linear time. The most common usage is to show the change in state of an object over time in response to accepted events or stimuli." (UML 2)

The timing diagram is a new UML 2 feature. It can be used to show the length of time that an object stays in each state. For example, suppose that rules dictated that a Peace Gathering had to spend 30 minutes in a fact-finding state, 60 minutes in deliberation, and 15 minutes in closing. A timing diagram might show all of this, as shown in Figure 11.3.

Deployment Diagrams

Deployment diagrams indicate how the software is to be installed across systems—for example, what will be installed on the server and what will be installed on the admin PCs.

Figure 11.3 A timing diagram

Layered Architecture

Layered architecture is an approach to splitting up software into packages. The term refers to breaking up a software application into distinct "layers" or "tiers."[2] These levels are arranged above one another, each serving distinct and separate tasks. Software in one tier may only access software in another tier, according to strict rules. In an OO system, the Systems Analysts create class packages for each tier and populate these with classes that implement the architecture. For example, they might add a class to handle the saving and retrieving of objects from the database.

There are a number of approaches to layered architecture:

- Two-tier
- Three-tier
- *N*-tier

Monolithic, Two-Tier, Three-Tier, and N-Tier Architecture

Any software application can be seen as consisting of three broad areas:

- *Data logic*: the software to manage the data.
- *Business (processing) logic*: the software that enacts the business rules.
- *Presentation (interface) logic*: the software that manages the presentation of the output (screens and such).

In *monolithic architecture*, these three areas are all bundled together in a single application. Monolithic architecture is often employed on mainframe systems.

The common approach for new systems is to separate the application into various layers, or tiers. In *two-tier architecture*, there are two layers: a server (a central computer system) and a client (one system at each desk). In the "thin client, fat server" variation on this

---

[2]The terms *layer* and *tier* are often used synonymously. The term *tier* emphasizes the "one-above-the-other" arrangement of the levels.

theme, the presentation logic and minimal business logic reside on the client system; the rest is on the server. In "fat client, thin server," the presentation logic and much of the business logic reside on the client.

In *three-tier architecture*, there are three layers, or subsystems: a client system, loaded with presentation logic; an application server[3] with business logic; and a data server with data logic.

Finally, in *n-tier architecture* any number *(n)* of levels is arranged, each serving distinct and separate tasks.

Interfaces

Interface: "A named set of operations that characterize the behavior of an element." (UML 2)

The developers may also add to the classes introduced by the BA by designing interfaces. An *interface*[4] acts like a generalized class except that it has no attributes and no process logic; only operation names and standard rules for invoking them are defined. Each class that obeys the interface must conform to the interface's rule regarding the operations. A class that obeys the interface is said to be a *type* of the interface.

There are a number of ways to indicate an interface in the UML. The simplest way is to use the simple box notation, with the stereotype *<<interface>>*. The types are connected to the interface with an arrow that looks like the generalization relationship, except that it is dashed, as shown in Figure 11.4.[5] The figure shows three different systems for checking

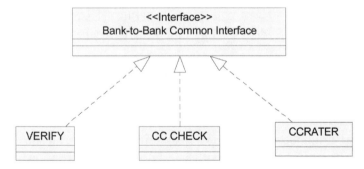

Figure 11.4 An interface

[3]Also called *middle tier*.

[4]This is not to be confused with classes that define user interfaces.

[5]Other notations are the lollipop and ball-and-socket notations.

a person's credit: *Verify*, *CC Check*, and *CCRater*. They must each have methods for performing the operations defined in the interface *Bank-to-Bank Common Interface*—but the methods may differ from system to system.

Mix-Ins

A *mix-in* is a generalized class used to add functionality to any class that inherits from it, such as the mix-in *Saveable to Disk*. Mix-ins are added to the model to avoid the problems usually associated with multiple inheritance.

Implementing OOA Using an OO Language

Once the Systems Analyst has added to and adapted the classes defined by the BA, the next step is to create code that conforms to the model. When the target programming language is OO-compliant (such as the .NET languages and C++), specifications for the classes and their relationships, attributes, and operations can all be converted to code in a straightforward manner. In fact, tools such as Rational Rose can do this automatically. Some tools, such as Rose, rely on the class diagrams for code generation. Others, such as Rational RealTime, rely on the state machine diagrams.

Implementing OOA Using Procedural Languages

The developers may use Object-Oriented Design (OOD) despite the fact that the target programming language is written in a non-OO, procedural language such as COBOL.[6] In fact, I worked in such an environment many years ago. The organization decided on this path because it wanted to take advantage of OO's reusability without having to convert to a new language. Non-OO languages can be used so that they emulate OO languages. The key is to use the available units—subroutines—and make them act like classes. In most cases, however, OOD is usually used only when the implementing language is object-oriented.

Implementing an RDBMS Database from an OOA Model

You've learned that the class diagrams provide guidance in the design of the database. OO database management systems that support OO ideas such as inheritance do exist, but currently, they are rarely used. Most organizations use another technology called Relational Database Management Systems (RDBMS). Examples of RDBMS technology are DB2, SQL, and Access. RDBMS does not directly support OO features such as inheritance and class operations. Nevertheless, with a little effort, you can implement the class diagrams of OO using RDBMS, and in fact this is commonly done. To do this, each entity class is imple-

---

[6]OO COBOL exists but is not widely used.

mented as a table (file) in the RDBMS database. The attributes are implemented as fields. Extra attributes (called *foreign keys*) are added, when necessary, in order to link records to each other. While RDBMS databases do not directly support inheritance and aggregation, they can be adapted to behave as though they do. For example, each generalized and specialized class is implemented as a table. Each specialized object appears twice: once as a record in the generalized file, and once in the specialized file. The records share the same unique identifier (primary key).

Chapter Summary

In this chapter, you were introduced to advanced OO topics.

Tools and concepts in this chapter included the following:

1. OO analysis patterns
2. Visibility
3. Control classes
4. Boundary classes
5. Sequence diagrams
6. Communication diagrams
7. Timing diagrams
8. Deployment diagrams
9. Layered architecture
10. Interfaces
11. Mix-ins
12. Implementing OOA using OO and procedural languages
13. Implementing OOA using RDBMS

JOB AIDS

These appendices contain information to keep by your side while performing business analysis tasks.

APPENDIX A

THE B.O.O.M. PROCESS

Adapt the following process to your project management methodology. Artifacts created or revised by each activity are shown in brackets.

1: Initiation

The purpose of Initiation is to get a rough cut at the business case for a proposed IT project.

1a) Model business use cases

      i) Identify business use cases (business use-case diagram)

      ii) Scope business use cases (activity diagram)

1b) Model system use cases

      i) Identify actors (role map)

      ii) Identify system use-case packages (system use-case diagram)

      iii) Identify system use cases (system use-case diagram)

1c) Begin static model (class diagrams for key business classes)

1d) Set baseline for analysis (Business Requirements Document/Initiation)

2: Analysis

The purpose of this phase is to elicit the detailed requirements from stakeholders, analyze them and document them for verification by stakeholders and for use by the developers.

2a) Dynamic analysis

      i) Describe system use cases (use-case description)

      ii) Describe state behavior (state machine diagram)

            1. Identify states of critical objects

            2. Identify state transitions

            3. Identify state activities

            4. Identify superstates

            5. Identify concurrent states

2b) Static analysis (class and object diagrams): Perform in parallel with 2a

      i) Identify entity classes

      ii) Model generalizations

      iii) Model transient roles

      iv) Model whole/part relationships

      v) Analyze associations

      vi) Analyze multiplicity

      vii) Link system use cases to the static model

      viii) Add attributes

      ix) Add look-up tables

      x) Distribute operations

      xi) Revise class structure

2c) Specify testing (test plan/decision tables)

      i) Specify white-box testing quality level

      ii) Specify black-box test cases

      iii) Specify system tests

2d) Specify implementation plan (implementation plan)

2e) Set baseline for development (BRD/analysis)

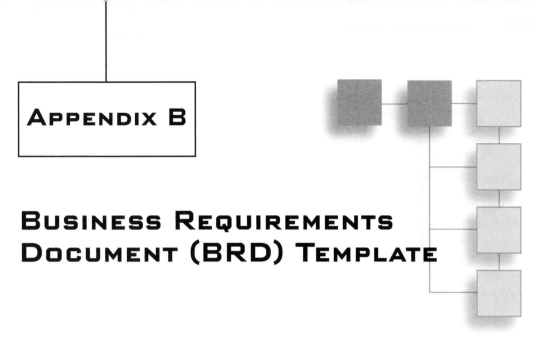

APPENDIX B

BUSINESS REQUIREMENTS DOCUMENT (BRD) TEMPLATE

The rest of this page is left intentionally blank. The template follows on the next page.

Business Requirements Document (BRD)

Project No. _____

Production Priority _____

Target date: _____

Approved by:

_____   _____

Name of user, department   Date

_____   _____

Name of user, department   Date

Prepared by: _____

Date: _____

Filename: _____

Version no.: _____

Table of Contents

- Version Control
  - ▲ Revision History
  - ▲ RACI Chart
- Executive Summary
  - ▲ Overview
  - ▲ Background
  - ▲ Objectives
  - ▲ Requirements
  - ▲ Proposed Strategy
  - ▲ Next Steps
- Scope
  - ▲ Included in Scope
  - ▲ Excluded from Scope
  - ▲ Constraints
  - ▲ Impact of Proposed Changes
- Risk Analysis
  - ▲ Technological Risks
  - ▲ Skills Risks
  - ▲ Political Risks
  - ▲ Business Risks
  - ▲ Requirements Risks
  - ▲ Other
- Business Case
  - ▲ Cost/Benefit Analysis, ROI, etc.
- Timetable
- Business Use Cases
  - ▲ Business Use-Case Diagrams
  - ▲ Business Use-Case Descriptions (text and/or activity diagram)
- Actors
  - ▲ Workers
  - ▲ Business Actors
  - ▲ Other Systems
  - ▲ Role Map

- User Requirements
  - ▲ System Use-Case Diagrams
  - ▲ System Use-Case Descriptions
- State Machine Diagrams
- Nonfunctional Requirements
  - ▲ Performance Requirements
    - ◆ Stress Requirements
    - ◆ Response-Time Requirements
    - ◆ Throughput Requirements
  - ▲ Usability Requirements
  - ▲ Security Requirements
  - ▲ Volume and Storage Requirements
  - ▲ Configuration Requirements
  - ▲ Compatibility Requirements
  - ▲ Reliability Requirements
  - ▲ Backup/Recovery Requirements
  - ▲ Training Requirements
- Business Rules
- State Requirements
  - ▲ Testing State
  - ▲ Disabled State
- Static Model
  - ▲ Class Diagrams: Entity Classes
  - ▲ Entity Class Documentation
- Test Plan
- Implementation Plan
  - ▲ Training
  - ▲ Conversion
  - ▲ Scheduling of Jobs
  - ▲ Rollout
- End User Procedures
- Post Implementation Follow-Up
- Other Issues
- Sign-Off

Version Control

Revision History

Version #	Date	Authorization	Responsibility (Author)	Description

RACI Chart for This Document

RACI stands for Responsible, Accountable, Consulted, and Informed. These are the main codes that appear in a RACI chart, used here to describe the roles played by team members and stakeholders in the production of the BRD. The following table describes the full list of codes used in the table:

*	Authorize	Has ultimate signing authority for any changes to the document.
R	Responsible	Responsible for creating this document.
A	Accountable	Accountable for accuracy of this document (for example, the project manager).
S	Supports	Provides supporting services in the production of this document.
C	Consulted	Provides input (such as an interviewee).
I	Informed	Must be informed of any changes.

Name	Position	*	R	A	S	C	I

Executive Summary

(This is a one-page summary of the document, divided into the following subsections.)

Overview

(This one-paragraph introduction explains the nature of the project.)

Background

(This subsection provides details leading up to the project that explain why the project is being considered. Discuss the following where appropriate: marketplace drivers, business drivers, and technology drivers.)

Objectives

(This subsection details the business objectives addressed by the project.)

Requirements

(This is a *brief* summary of the requirements addressed in this document.)

Proposed Strategy

(This subsection recommends a strategy for proceeding based on alternatives.)

Next Steps

Action: (Describe the specific action to be taken.)

Responsibility

(State who is responsible for taking this action.)

Expected Date

(State when the action is expected to be taken.)

Scope

Included in Scope

(This is a brief description of business areas covered by the project.)

Excluded from Scope

(This subsection briefly describes business areas *not* covered by the project.)

Constraints

(These are predefined requirements and conditions.)

Impact of Proposed Changes

Business Use Case	New?	Desired Functionality	Current Functionality (If a Change)	Stakeholders/ Systems	Priority

Risk Analysis

(A risk is something that could impact the success or failure of a project. Good project management involves a constant reassessment of risk.)

For each risk, document:

- Likelihood
- Cost
- Strategy: Strategies include:
    - *Avoid*: Do something to eliminate the risk.
    - *Mitigate*: Do something to reduce damage if risk materializes.
    - *Transfer*: Pass the risk up or out to another entity.
    - *Accept*: Do nothing about the risk. Accept the consequences.

Technological Risks

(This subsection specifies new technology issues that could affect the project.)

Skills Risks

(This subsection specifies the risk of not getting staff with the required expertise for the project.)

Political Risks

(This subsection identifies political forces that could derail or affect the project.)

Business Risks

(This subsection describes the business implications if the project is canceled.)

Requirements Risks

(This subsection describes the risk of erroneous requirements. List areas whose requirements are most likely to be incorrectly captured.)

Other Risks

Business Case

(Describe the business rationale for this project. This section may contain estimates on cost/benefit, return on investment (ROI), payback [length of time for the project to pay for itself], market share benefits, and so on. Quantify each cost or benefit so that business objectives may be measured after implementation.)

Timetable

Business Use Cases

(Complete this section if the project involves changes to the workflow of end-to-end business processes. Document each end-to-end business process affected by the project as a business use case. If necessary, describe existing workflow for the business use case as well as the new, proposed workflow.)

Business Use-Case Diagrams

(Business use-case diagrams describe stakeholder involvement in each business use case.)

Business Use-Case Descriptions

(Describe the workflow of each business use case with text and/or an activity diagram. If you are documenting with text, use an informal style or the use-case template described in the "User Requirements" section below.)

Actors

Workers

(List and describe stakeholders who act within the business in carrying out business use cases.)

Department/ Position	General Impact of Project

Business Actors

(List and describe external parties, such as customers and partners, who interact with the business.)

Actor	General Impact of Project

Other Systems

(List computer systems potentially impacted by this project. Include any system that will be linked to the proposed system.)

System	General Impact of Project

Role Map

(The role map describes the roles played by actors [users and external systems] that interact with the IT system.)

User Requirements

(Describe requirements for automated processes from a user perspective.)

System Use-Case Diagrams

(System use-case diagrams describe which users use which features and the dependencies between use cases.)

System Use-Case Descriptions

(During Initiation, only short descriptions of the use cases are provided. During Analysis, the following template is filled out for each medium to high-risk use case. Low-risk use cases may be described informally. This template may also be used to document the business use cases included earlier in the BRD.)

Use-Case Description Template

1. *Use case*: (The use-case name as it appears on system use-case diagrams.)
   Perspective: Business use case/system use case
   Type: Base use case/extension/generalized/specialized

   1.1 Brief Description
        (Briefly describe the use case in approximately one paragraph.)

   1.2 Business Goals and Benefits
        (Briefly describe the business rationale for the use case.)

   1.3 Actors

        1.3.1 Primary Actors
               (Identify the users or systems that initiate the use case.)

        1.3.2 Secondary Actors
               (List the users or systems that receive messages from the use case.
               Include users who receive reports or on-line messages.)

        1.3.3 Off-Stage Stakeholders
               (Identify non-participating stakeholders who have interests in this
               use case.)

   1.4 Rules of Precedence

        1.4.1 Triggers
               (Describe the event or condition that "kick-starts" the use case:
               such as *User calls Call Center*; *Inventory low*. If the trigger is time-
               driven, describe the temporal condition, such as *end-of-month*.)

        1.4.2 Preconditions
               (List conditions that must be true before the use case begins. If a
               condition *forces* the use case to occur whenever it becomes true, do
               not list it here; list it as a trigger.)

   1.5 Postconditions

        1.5.1 Postconditions on Success
               (Describe the status of the system after the use case ends success-
               fully. Any condition listed here is guaranteed to be true on success-
               ful completion.)

        1.5.2 Postconditions on Failure
               (Describe the status of the system after the use case ends in failure.
               Any condition listed here is guaranteed to be true when the use case
               fails as described in the exception flows.)

   1.6 Extension Points
        (Name and describe points at which extension use cases may extend this use
        case.)
        Example of extension point declaration:

        1.6.1 Preferred Customer: 2.5-2.9

1.7 Priority

1.8 Status
Your status report might resemble the following example:
Use-case brief complete: 2005/06/01
Basic flow + risky alternatives complete: 2005/06/15
All flows complete: 2005/07/15
Coded: 2005/07/20
Tested: 2005/08/10
Internally released: 2005/09/15
Deployed: 2005/09/30

1.9 Expected Implementation Date

1.10 Actual Implementation Date

1.11 Context Diagram
(Include a system use-case diagram showing this use case, all its relationships [includes, extends, and generalizes] with other use cases and its associations with actors.)

2. Flow of Events

Basic Flow

2.1 (Insert basic flow steps.)

Alternate Flows

2.Xa (Insert the alternate flow name.)
(The alternate flow name should describe the condition that triggers the alter-
nate flow. "2.X" is step number in basic flow where interruption occurs.
Describe the steps in paragraph or point form.)

Exception Flows

2.Xa (Insert the exception flow name.)
(The flow name should describe the condition that triggers the exception
flow. An exception flow is one that causes the use case to end in failure and
for which "postconditions on failure" apply. "2.X" is the step number in the
basic flow where interruption occurs. Describe the steps in paragraph or
point form.)

3. Special Requirements
(List any special requirements or constraints that apply specifically to this use case.)

3.1 Nonfunctional Requirements
(List requirements not visible to the user during the use case—security, performance, reliability, and so on.)

3.2 Constraints
(List technological, architectural, and other constraints on the use case.)

4. Activity Diagram
(If it is helpful, include an activity diagram showing workflow for this system use case, or for select parts of the use case.)

5. User Interface
(Initially, include description/storyboard/prototype only to help the reader visualize the interface, not to constrain the design. Later, provide links to screen design artifacts.)

6. Class Diagram
(Include a class diagram depicting business classes, relationships, and multiplicities of all objects participating in this use case.)

7. Assumptions
(List any assumptions you made when writing the use case. Verify all assumptions with stakeholders before sign-off.)

8. Information Items
(Include a link or reference to documentation describing rules for data items that relate to this use case. Documentation of this sort is often found in a data dictionary. The purpose of this section and the following sections is to keep the details out of the use case proper, so that you do not need to amend it every time you change a rule.)

9. Prompts and Messages
(Any prompts and messages that appear in the use case proper should be identified by name only, as in *Invalid Card Message*. The *Prompts and Messages* section should contain the actual text of the messages or direct the reader to the documentation that contains text.)

10. Business Rules
(The "Business Rules" section of the use-case documentation should provide links or references to the specific business rules that are active during the use case. An example of a business rule for an airline package is "Airplane weight must never exceed the maximum allowed for its aircraft type." Organizations often keep such rules in an automated business rules engine or manually in a binder.)

11. External Interfaces
(List interfaces to external systems.)

12. Related Artifacts
(The purpose of this section is to provide a point of reference for other details that relate to this use case, but would distract from the overall flow. Include references to artifacts such as decision tables, complex algorithms, and so on.)

State Machine Diagrams

(Insert state machine diagrams describing the events that trigger changes of state of significant business objects.)

Nonfunctional Requirements

(Describe across-the-board requirements not covered in the use-case documentation. Details follow.)

Performance Requirements

(Describe requirements relating to the system's speed.)

Stress Requirements

(This subsection of performance requirements describes the degree of simultaneous activity that the system must be able to support. For example, "The system must be able to support 2,000 users accessing financial records simultaneously.)

Response-Time Requirements

(This subsection of performance requirements describes the maximum allowable wait time from the moment the user submits a request until the system comes back with a response.)

Throughput Requirements

(This subsection of performance requirements describes the number of transactions per unit of time that the system must be able to process.)

Usability Requirements

(Describe quantitatively the level of usability required. For example, "A novice operator, given two hours of training, must be able to complete the following functions without assistance…." Also, refer to any usability standards and guidelines that must be adhered to.)

Security Requirements

(Describe security requirements relating to virus protection, firewalls, the functions and data accessible by each user group, and so on.)

Volume and Storage Requirements

(Describe the maximum volume [for example, the number of accounts] that the system must be able to support, as well as random access memory [RAM] and disk restrictions.)

Configuration Requirements

(Describe the hardware and operating systems that must be supported.)

Compatibility Requirements

(Describe compatibility requirements with respect to the existing system and external systems with which the system under design must interact.)

Reliability Requirements

(Describe the level of fault-tolerance required by the system.)

Backup/Recovery Requirements

(Describe the backup and recovery facilities required.)

Training Requirements

(Describe the level of training required and clearly state which organizations will be required to develop and deliver training programs.)

Business Rules

(List business rules that must be complied with throughout the system. For example, an inventory system might have a rule that whenever inventory falls below a trigger level that an automatic order is placed with the supplier. If an external rules engine is being used, this section should refer the reader to the location of these rules.)

State Requirements

(Describe how the system's behavior changes when in different states. Describe the features that will be available and those that will be disabled in each state.)

Testing State

(Describe what the user may and may not do while the system is in the test state.)

Disabled State

(Describe what is to happen as the system goes down. Clearly define what the user will and will not be able to do.)

Static Model

(During Initiation, only strategic classes are modeled.)

Class Diagrams: Entity Classes

(Insert class diagrams representing classes of business objects and relationships among the classes. This section centralizes rules that govern business objects, such as the numerical relationships between objects, the operations associated with each class, and so on.)

Entity Class Documentation

(Insert documentation to support each of the classes that appear in the class diagrams. Not every class needs to be fully documented. First do a risk analysis to determine where full documentation would most benefit the project.)

Class Name

Alias: (List any other names by which the class is known within the business domain.)

Description:

Example: (Provide an example of an object of this class.)

Attributes: (These may be documented in a table, as follows.)

Attribute	Derived?	Derivation	Type	Format	Length	Range	Dependency

(When your requirements are complete up to this point and approved by the appropriate people, submit them to developers. You can then work on the test plan, implementation plan, and end user procedures.)

Test Plan[1]

(To standardize the testing, you should develop a test plan document for analysts to follow when constructing projects test plans. Although every project is different, the following may be used as a guideline. Each project should consider the following stages during testing):

1. Submit the requirements to the technical team. The technical team completes development. Concurrently, the BA builds numbered test scenarios for requirements-based testing. Consider using decision tables to identify scenarios and boundary value analysis to select test data. The technical team conducts white-box testing, to verify whether programs, fields, and calculations function as specified. The BA or technical team specifies the required quality level for white-box testing, such as multiple-condition coverage.

2. Perform requirements-based testing. The BA or dedicated QA (Quality Assurance) staff administers or supervises tests to prove or disprove compliance with requirements. Ensure that all formulae are calculated properly. Describe principles and techniques to be used in black-box testing, such as structured testing guidelines and boundary value analysis.

3. Conduct system testing. Ensure that the integrity of the system and data remain intact. For example:
   - *Regression test*: Retest all features (using a regression test bed).
   - *Stress test*: Test multiple users at the same time.
   - *Integration tests*: Make sure that the changes do not negatively affect the overall workflow across IT and manual systems.
   - *Volume test*: Test the system with high volume.

4. Perform user acceptance testing. Involve the end users at this stage. Choose key users to review the changes in the test environment. Use the testing software as a final check.

Implementation Plan

Training

(Specify who is responsible for training.)

(Specify who is to be trained.)

(Specify how training will be done.)

---

[1]These requirements are often described in a separate test plan. If they are not addressed elsewhere, describe them here in the BRD.

Conversion

(Specify existing data that must be converted. Promote programs to new release. Grant privileges to the users.)

Scheduling of Jobs

(Advise Information Systems [IS] operations which jobs to add to the production run. Specify the frequency of the run: daily, weekly, monthly, quarterly, semi-annually, or annually. Ensure that the job is placed in the correct sequence. Advise IS operations of the reports to be printed and the distribution list for reports and files.)

Rollout

(Advise all affected users when the project is promoted.)

End User Procedures

(Write up the procedures for the affected departments. Distribute this document to them in addition to providing any hands-on training.)

Post Implementation Follow-Up

(Follow up within a reasonable time frame after implementation to ensure that the project is running successfully. Determine whether any further enhancements or changes are needed to ensure success of the project.)

Other Issues

Sign-Off

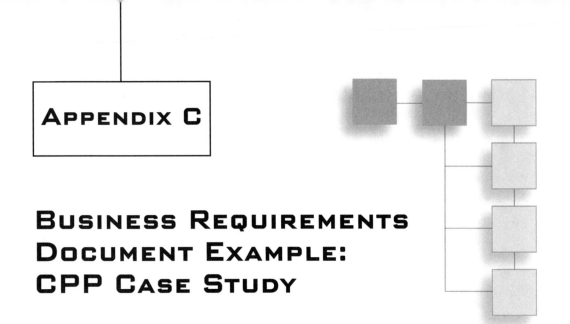

APPENDIX C

BUSINESS REQUIREMENTS DOCUMENT EXAMPLE: CPP CASE STUDY

Business Requirements Document (BRD)

Project No. _____

Production Priority: _____

Target date: _____

Approved by:

_____   _____

Name of user, department   Date

Prepared by: _____

Date: _____

Filename: _____

Version no.: _____

Table of Contents

- Version Control
  - ▲ Revision History
  - ▲ RACI Chart
- Executive Summary
  - ▲ Overview
  - ▲ Background
  - ▲ Objectives
  - ▲ Requirements
  - ▲ Proposed Strategy
  - ▲ Next Steps
- Scope
  - ▲ Included in Scope
  - ▲ Excluded from Scope
  - ▲ Constraints
  - ▲ Impact of Proposed Changes
- Risk Analysis
  - ▲ Technological Risks
  - ▲ Skills Risks
  - ▲ Political Risks
  - ▲ Business Risks
  - ▲ Requirements Risks
  - ▲ Other
- Business Case
  - ▲ Cost/Benefit Analysis, ROI, Etc.
- Timetable
- Business Use Cases
  - ▲ Business Use-Case Diagrams
  - ▲ Business Use-Case Descriptions (text and/or activity diagram)
- Actors
  - ▲ Workers
  - ▲ Business Actors
  - ▲ Other Systems
  - ▲ Role Map

- User Requirements
  - System Use-Case Diagrams
  - System Use-Case Descriptions
- State Machine Diagrams
- Non-functional Requirements
  - Performance Requirements
    - Stress Requirements
    - Response-Time Requirements
    - Throughput Requirements
  - Usability Requirements
  - Security Requirements
  - Volume and Storage Requirements
  - Configuration Requirements
  - Compatibility Requirements
  - Reliability Requirements
  - Backup/Recovery Requirements
  - Training Requirements
- Business Rules
- State Requirements
  - Testing State
  - Disabled State
- Static Model
  - Class Diagrams: Entity Classes
  - Entity Class Documentation
- Test Plan
- Implementation Plan
  - Training
  - Conversion
  - Scheduling of Jobs
  - Rollout
- End User Procedures
- Post Implementation Follow-Up
- Other Issues
- Sign-off

Version Control

Revision History

Version #	Date	Authorization	Responsibility (Author)	Description
0.1	06/05		Mbuyi Pensacola	Initial draft
1.0	07/05	J. Carter	Mbuyi Pensacola	Final version/ Initiation
2.0	08/05	J. Carter	Mbuyi Pensacola	Final version/ Analysis

RACI Chart for This Document

*	**Authorize**	This individual has ultimate signing authority for any changes to the document.	
R	Responsible	Responsible for creating this document.	
A	Accountable	Accountable for accuracy of this document (e.g., Project Manager).	
S	Supports	Provides supporting services in the production of this document.	
C	Consulted	Provides input (interviewee, etc.).	
I	Informed	Must be informed of any changes.	

Name	Position	*	R	A	S	C	I
C. Ringshee	Director, CPP	×					
J. Carter	Manager, Operations			×			
Mbuyi Pensacola			×				

Executive Summary

Overview

This project is for a software system to govern the tracking and reporting of cases by the Community Peace Program (CPP).

Background

The project is being developed for the Community Peace Program (CPP), a South African non-profit organization that provides infrastructure for community-based justice systems based on the model of restorative justice.[1] The main objective of the CPP is to provide an effective alternative to the court system. Its advantages are improved cost-effectiveness and a decreased recurrence rate, since problems are treated at their source. All parties to a dispute must consent to having the case diverted to the CPP. The advantage to the *perpetrator* is the avoidance of incarceration and other severe punishment; for the *complainant*, the advantages lie in the possibility for a true resolution to the problem and a decreased likelihood that the problem will recur. The advantages to the *justice system* are

- A reduction in case volume due to the offloading of cases to the CPP and a decrease in recurrence rates.
- A decrease in the cost of processing a case.

The system is being deployed in the townships of South Africa under the auspices of the CPP and with the support of the Justice Department. Similar approaches are being used throughout the world, for example, the "Forum," in use by Canada's Royal Canadian Mounted Police (RCMP).

The CPP operates by working with local communities to set up Peace Committees. Most of these are currently in townships on the Cape Town peninsula. Each Peace Committee is composed of "peacemakers"—members of the community who are trained in conflict-resolution procedures based on principles of restorative justice. The complainants and accused must all agree to adhere to the procedure, or the case is passed on to the state justice system.

Due to increasing demand for its services in conflict resolution, the CPP is undergoing a rapid expansion. Current manual practices will not be able to keep up with the expected rise in case volume.

Objectives

The most urgent need is for timely statistics regarding cases handled by the CPP. Because of the anticipated increase in caseload, these statistics will be difficult to derive using the current, manual systems. Timely statistics will be essential in justifying the project to its funders. Also, the tracking of funds disbursement and monitoring of cases will become increasingly difficult as the program expands.

[1]The principles of restorative justice were developed by Terry O'Connel.

Requirements

The project will leave current manual systems in place for the initial recording of case information up to and including the conduct of a Peace Gathering and the completion of subsequent monitoring. Workflow after that point will be within the scope of the project; i.e., recording of case data, validation of CPP procedures, disbursement of payments, and the generation of statistical reports.

Proposed Strategy

An iterative SDLC will be employed as follows: The Business Analyst(s) will analyze all use cases at the start for the project (Analysis phase); the design and coding will proceed iteratively. In the first iteration, general administration and case tracking will be developed. In the second iteration, payments will be disbursed and reports generated.

Next Steps

Action: Select software developer

Responsibility: J. Carter

Expected Date: One month after acceptance of this document

Scope

Included in Scope

The system will provide statistical reports for use by funders. Also, it will provide limited tracking of individual cases, to the degree required for statistics and, wherever possible, in a manner that will facilitate expansion of the system to include complete case monitoring. The project includes manual and automated processes. The system will encompass those activities that occur after a case has been resolved. These are primarily: the recording of case data, disbursement of payments, and the generation of reports. CPP members will be the only direct users of this system.

Excluded from Scope

The system becomes aware of a case only when it has been resolved. All activities prior to this point are not included in this project; i.e., it excludes the tracking of cases from the time of reporting, convening of Peace Gathering, and monitoring of cases. The activities will continue to be performed manually, although the manual forms will be changed to comply with new system requirements.

Constraints

1. Eighty percent match (minimum) between CPP's needs and OTS (off-the-shelf) product(s).

2. One integrated solution is preferred. No more than two OTS products should be needed.
3. M. Williams will be main liaison for the project.
4. Final approval for a system is estimated to take six weeks to two months.

Impact of Proposed Changes

Business Use Case	New?	Desired Functionality	Current Functionality (If a Change)	Stakeholders/ Systems	Priority
Manage administration	Yes	General administrative functions, e.g., creation/updating of Peace Committees, members, etc.	Manual systems only in place	CPP General Administration	High
Manage case	Yes	Manage a case: identify new cases, update case information, etc.	Manual systems only in place	Peace Committee, Facilitator, Monitor, Convener	High
Administer payments	Yes	Make payments to individuals who assisted in a case and to various funds.	Manual systems only in place	Convener, Peace Committee Member, AP System	Medium
Generate reports	Yes	Report on cases by region and by period; compile stats on caseload, # cases per type of conflict, etc.	Manual systems only in place	Any worker (members of the CPP), government body (any governmental organizational receiving reports), funder	High

Risk Analysis

Strategies for dealing with risk include

- *Avoid*: Do something to eliminate the risk.
- *Mitigate*: Do something to reduce damage if risk materializes.
- *Transfer*: Pass the risk up or out to another entity.
- *Accept*: Do nothing about the risk. Accept the consequences.

Technological Risks

Risk: Difficulty linking database management system (DBMS) to programming language. Programmers have had experience using proposed DBMS but not with accessing it from proposed programming language.

Likelihood: Medium.

Cost: Project delays.

Strategy: Mitigate. Build early proof-of-concept in order to iron out problems early.

Skills Risks

TBD

Political Risks

Risk: Source of funding discontinued. Funding for this project is provided by a foreign government and is granted only on an annual basis after yearly inspections of the organization and based on the government's policy toward foreign aid.

Likelihood: Low.

Cost: Cancellation of the project.

Strategy:

- *Avoid*: Through regular project reports to funders and lobbying of government ministers.
- *Mitigate*: Search out "plan B" funders: University of Cape Town School of Governance.

Business Risks

Risk: IT project cancelled.

Likelihood: Medium.

Cost: Increase in administration costs to handle growing volume. Inability to produce timely progress reports may lead to loss of funder.

Strategy: Mitigate: Plan early release of highest-priority system use cases.

Requirements Risks

Risk: Payment disbursement rules improperly documented. Rules regarding payments made due to a case are volatile and complex and, therefore, may not be accurately described to programmers.

Likelihood: High.

Cost: Faulty payments, software modifications.

Strategy: Plan Structured Walkthroughs with stakeholders. Review again before coding begins.

Other Risks

TBD

Business Case

Initial investment = 2 person-years @ US$50,000/yr = $100,000. Hardware: Use existing PCs at office location

Annual cost: 1 new half-time position, IT maintenance staff = US$25,000/yr

Annual benefits: Reduce administration staff by 2 due to automatic generation of reports to funders and increased efficiency of case tracking = US$60,000/yr

ROI (Return On Investment) = ([Annual benefit] – [Annual cost])/[Initial investment] = (60,000 – 25,000)/ 100,000 = 35%

Payback period = [Initial investment]/ ([Annual benefit] – [Annual cost]) = 100,000/(60,000-25,000) = 2.9 or approximately 3 years

These numbers are expected to improve over the years as the project expands, since the efficiencies of the IT system relative to a manual system are more pronounced the greater the volume of the cases.

Timetable

Analysis: Complete 08/2005

Execution: TBD

Testing: TBD

Close-Out: TBD

Business Use Cases

Business Use-Case Diagrams

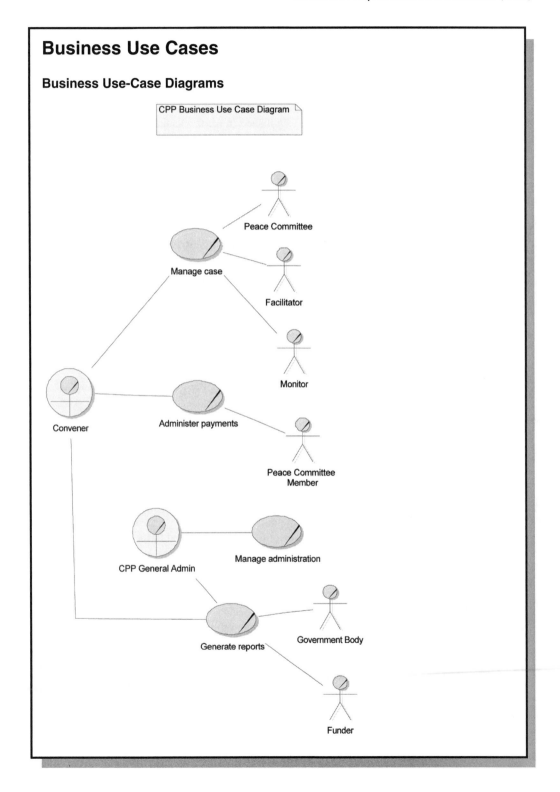

CPP Business Use Case Diagram

Business Use-Case Descriptions

Business Use Case: Manage Case (Dispute)

(Semi-formal style)

Precondition: A Peace Committee has been established in the township.

Postconditions on success: A case report has been prepared.

Flow:

1. The Peace Committee in the area initiates a Peace Gathering.
2. The Peace Committee prepares an individual interview report for each party to the dispute.
3. Once all reports have been taken, the Facilitator summarizes the reports to the Peace Gathering.
4. The Facilitator verifies the facts in the reports with those present.
5. The Facilitator solicits suggestions from the gathering.
6. The Facilitator solicits a consensus for a plan of action.
7. If the gathering has decided to refer the case to the police, the Facilitator escorts the parties to the police station, after which the Convener prepares a case report as per Step 10.
8. If, on the other hand, a consensus has been reached, the Facilitator appoints a Monitor.
9. The Monitor performs ongoing monitoring of the case to ensure its terms are being met.
10. When the deadline for monitoring has been reached, the ongoing monitoring immediately ends. At this time, if the conditions of the case have been met, the Convener prepares a case report. If the conditions have not been met, then the process begins again (return to Step 1).
    10.1 The conditions described in point 10 do not apply to cases referred to police. That is, once the parties have been escorted to the police, a case report is always prepared.

Business Use Case: Administer Payments

(Semi-formal style)

Precondition: A case report has been prepared and submitted.

Postconditions on success: Payments have been made to funds and to accounts of the Peace Committee members involved in the case.

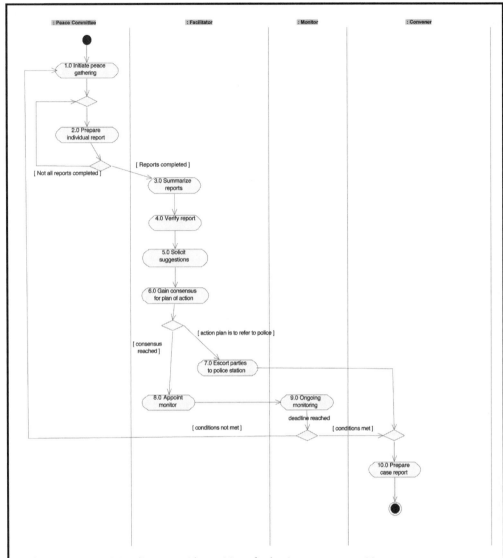

Figure C.1 Activity diagram with partitions for business use case: *Manage case*

Flow:

1. The Convener reviews the case report to determine whether rules and procedures have been followed.
2. If rules and procedures have been followed:
   a. The Convener marks the case as payable.
   b. The Convener then disburses payments to the various funds and to the accounts of Peace Committee members who worked on the case.
   c. The existing Accounts Payable system actually applies the payments. (Constraint: The AP system must continue to be used for this purpose when the project is implemented.)
3. If the rules and procedures have not been followed, the Convener marks the case as non-payable.

Actors

Workers

(List and describe stakeholders who act within the business in carrying out business use cases.)

Department/Position	General Impact of Project
Convener	(Member of the CPP.) Will use IT to updates cases and administer payments.
CPP General Admin	(Member of the CPP.) Will use IT to perform administrative functions, such as updating Peace Committees and members in the system.

Business Actors

(List and describe external parties, such as customers and partners, who interact with the business.)

Actor	General Impact of Project
Facilitator	A member of the community trained to facilitate Peace Gatherings. Current manual processes will remain with slight changes to forms as required for reporting purposes.
Monitor	A member of the community assigned to monitor parties' compliance with plan of action agreed to during Peace Gathering. Current manual process will remain in place.

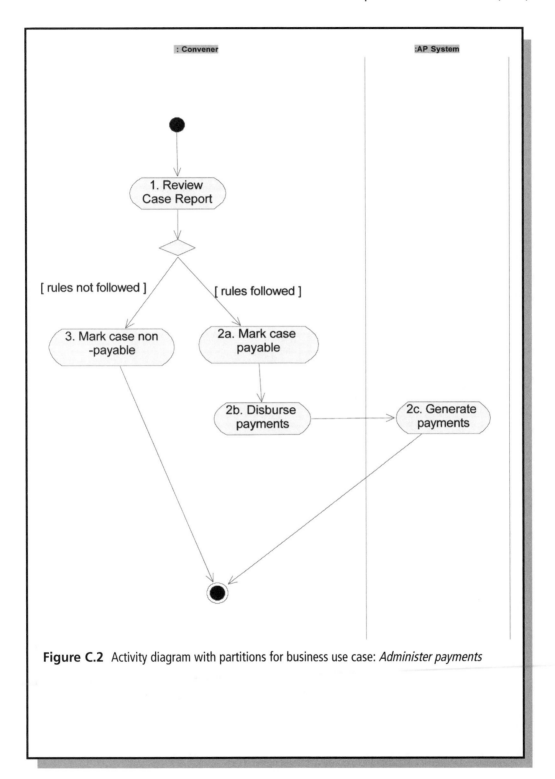

Figure C.2 Activity diagram with partitions for business use case: *Administer payments*

Peace Committee	An organization set up within a community and consisting of local members of the community, trained by the CPP to assist in dispute resolution. Current manual process will remain in place. Will need to report to head office about any changes to the organization, membership, etc.
Peace Committee Member	A member of a Peace Committee. A local, trained by the CPP to assist in dispute resolution. Will receive notification of payment for services by the IT system.
Government Body	Represents any government organization that receives reports from the new system.
Funder	Source of CPP funding. Will receive analytical reports from IT system.

Other Systems

| *System* | *General Impact of Project* |
| AP System | Existing system for tracking Accounts Payable. This system must remain in place. |

Role Map

(The role map describes the roles played by actors—users and external systems—that interact with the IT system.)

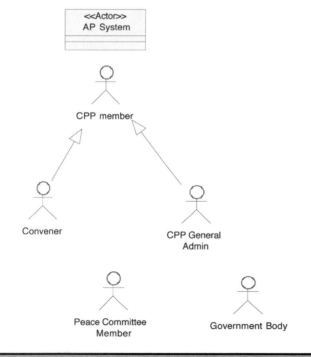

User Requirements

System Use-Case Diagrams

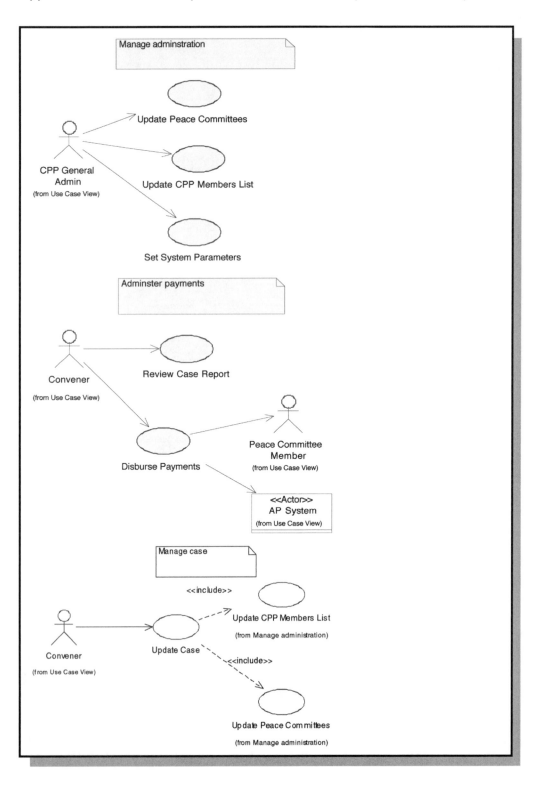

System Use-Case Descriptions

Package: Manage administration

(Following is an example of a brief description used for a low-risk use case.)

System Use Case: Update Peace Committees.

Description: Add/change/delete Peace Committees; update Peace Committee membership.

Package: Administer payments

(Following is an example of a formal use-case description.)

1. *Use case*: Review case report

   Perspective: System use case

   Type: Base use case

   1.1 Brief Description
        Review a case report in order to determine whether it is payable based on adherence to rules and procedures. Mark case as payable/non-payable.

   1.2 Business Goals and Benefits
        IT tracking of payments will allow for generation of up-to-date reports to funders upon request, required for continuance of funding for the organization.

   1.3 Actors

        1.3.1 Primary Actors
               Convener

        1.3.2 Secondary Actors

        1.3.3 Off-Stage Stakeholders
               Funders

   1.4 Rules of Precedence

        1.4.1 Triggers
               Convener calls up *Review* option.

        1.4.2 Preconditions
               Case has transitioned from *Monitored* state and monitoring conditions have been met, or case has transitioned from the *Referred to Police* state. Case must not have already been reviewed.

   1.5 Postconditions

        1.5.1 Postconditions on Success
               Case is marked as reviewed and prevented from being reviewed again.

        1.5.2 Postconditions on Failure

   1.6 Extension Points

   1.7 Priority: High

1.8 Status
Use-case brief complete: 2005/06/01
Basic flow + risky alternatives complete: 2005/06/15
All flows complete: 2005/07/15

1.9 Expected Implementation Date: TBD

1.10 Actual Implementation Date: TBD

1.11 Context Diagram

Review Case Report

Convener

2. Flow of Events

Basic Flow:

2.1 The system displays a list of resolved cases that have not been reviewed.

2.2 The user selects a case.

2.3 The system validates that the case is payable. (12.1)

2.4 The system determines the payment amount. (12.1)

2.5 The system marks the case as payable.

2.6 The system records the payment amount.

2.7 The system checks the Cash fund records to ensure adequate funds exist.

.1 No funds shall be removed from cash fund or disbursed at this time.

2.8 The system records the fact that the case has been reviewed.

Alternate Flows:

2.3a Non-payable case:

.1 The system marks the case as non-payable.

.2 The user confirms the non-payable status of the case.

.3 Continue at Step 2.8.

2.3a.2a User overrides non-payable status:

.1 The user indicates that the case is to be payable and enters a reason for the override.

2.7a Cash funds low but sufficient:

.1 The system marks the case as payable

.2 The system displays the *low funds warning*. (9.1)

Exception Flows:

3. Special Requirements

    3.1 Non-functional requirements

        3.1.1 Security: Case details must only be accessible by CPP members.

    3.2 Constraints

        (List technological, architectural, and other constraints on the use case.)

4. Activity Diagram

    N/A

5. User Interface

    TBD

6. Class Diagram

7. Assumptions

8. Information Items

9. Prompts and Messages

    9.1 See external design specifications/messages: *low funds warning*

10. Business Rules

    Rule 103: (Cash fund low trigger point)

11. External Interfaces

12. Related Artifacts

    12.1 Decision Table A: Review Case Report (see Figure C.3)

System use case: *Disburse payments*

1. *Use case*: Disburse payments

    Perspective: System use case

    Type: Base use case

    1.1 Brief Description

        Create record of payments made for the case to Peace Committee Members and Fund Accounts.

    1.2 Business Goals and Benefits

        IT tracking of payments will allow for generation of up-to-date reports to funders upon request, required for continuance of funding for the organization.

		1	2	3	4	5	6	7	8	9	10	11	12
C O N D I T I O N	Code of good practice followed (Y/N)	Y	Y	Y	Y	Y	Y	N	N	N	N	N	N
	Steps and procedures followed (Y/N)	Y	Y	Y	N	N	N	Y	Y	Y	N	N	N
	# PC members (<3,3-5, 6+)	<3	3-5	6+	<3	3-5	6+	<3	3-5	6+	<3	3-5	6+
A C T I O N	Mark as not payable	X			X			X	X	X	X	X	X
	Mark as payable		X	X		X	X						
	Pay 1/2 standard amount					X	X						
	Pay standard amount		X										
	Pay double amount			X									

Figure C.3 Decision Table A: Review case report

1.3 Actors

    1.3.1 Primary Actors:
        Convener

    1.3.2 Secondary Actors:
        Peace Committee Member, AP System

    1.3.3 Off-Stage Stakeholders:
        Funders.

1.4 Rules of Precedence

    1.4.1 Triggers
        The user calls up the Disburse Payments option.

    1.4.2 Preconditions
        The case is in the payable state and a payment amount for the case has been determined.

1.5 Postconditions

    1.5.1 Postconditions on Success

        1.5.1.1   Payments are made into the accounts of all Peace Committee Members involved in the Case and into the Fund Accounts.

        1.5.1.2   The case is in the Paid state.

1.6 Extension Points

1.7 Priority: High

1.8 Status
Basic flow + risky alternatives complete: 2005/06/20
All flows complete: 2005/07/27

1.9 Expected Implementation Date: TBD

1.10 Actual Implementation Date: TBD

1.11 Context Diagram

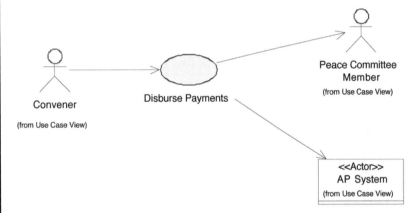

2. Flow of Events

Basic flow:

    2.1 The system displays a list of payable cases.

    2.2 The user selects a case.

    2.3 The system displays the amount payable for the case.

    2.4 The system displays each Peace Committee Member assigned to the case.

    2.5 The system displays the Peace Committee Member Account owned by each of the displayed Peace Committee Members.

2.6   The system displays the payment amounts to be disbursed to each Peace Committee Member Account and invested into each fund.

    2.6.1   Payments are made to Peace Committee Member Accounts according to a standard rate, set by the CPP Director.

    2.6.2   The remaining amount payable for the case is disbursed evenly amongst the Fund Accounts.

2.7   The user approves the disbursement.

2.8   The system creates payments for the Case.

    2.8.1   Each payment invests a specified amount from the Cash Account into one of the Fund Accounts or deposits an amount into one Peace Committee Member Account.

    2.8.2   The system sends a notice letter to a Peace Committee Member whenever a deposit is made to the member's account.

2.9   The system marks the Case as Paid.

Alternate flows:

2.3a   User changes disbursement amounts:

    .1   The user overrides the disbursement amounts.

    .2   The system confirms that the total payable for the case has not changed.

2.3a.2a   Total payable has changed:

    .1   The system displays a message indicating the amount of the discrepancy.

    .2   Continue at step 2.3a.1.

2.8a   Payment causes a withdrawal from cash that pushes balance below a specified trigger point:

    .1   The system sends a notice to Admin requesting new cash funds.

6. Class Diagram
   (Include Class Diagram depicting business classes, relationships, and multiplicities of all objects participating in this use case.)

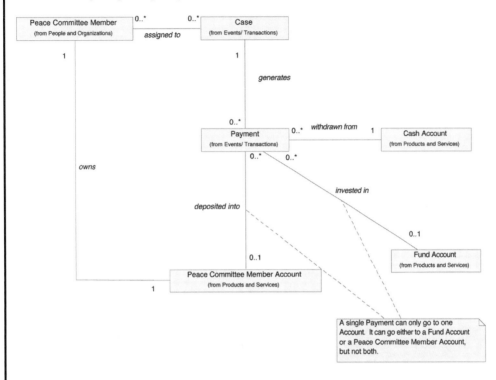

7. Assumptions
8. Information Items
9. Prompts and Messages
10. Business Rules
11. External Interfaces
12. Related Artifacts

State-Machine Diagrams

State Machine Diagram: Case

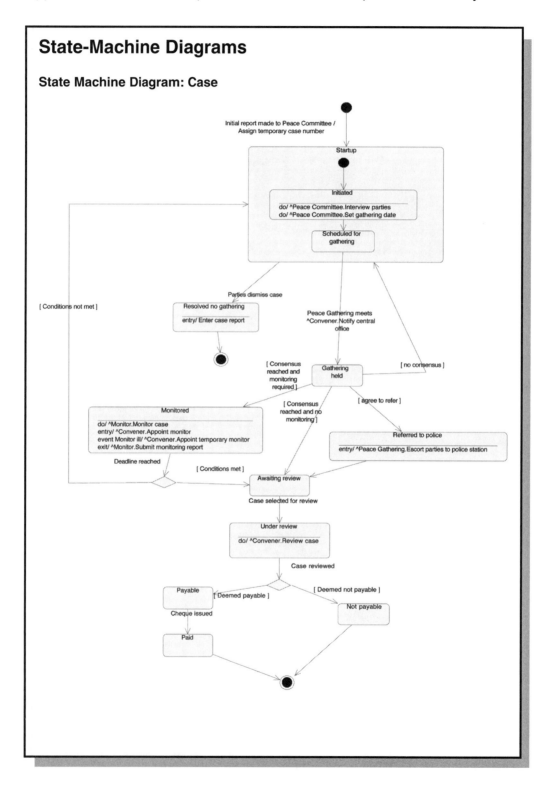

Nonfunctional Requirements

(Describe across-the-board requirements not covered in the use-case documentation. Details follow.)

Performance Requirements

Stress Requirements

The system must be able to support 10 users accessing case records simultaneously.

Response-time Requirements

Three seconds.

Throughput Requirements

(Describe the number of transactions per unit time that the system must be able to process.)

Usability Requirements

System must conform to usability guidelines V2.1.

Security Requirements

Case details must only be accessible to CPP officials.

Volume and Storage Requirements

First iteration of the System must support a volume of 60 Peace Committees and a total caseload of 25000 cases/year.

Configuration Requirements

(Describe the hardware and operating systems that must be supported.)

PC-compatible. Microsoft XP Professional.

Compatibility Requirements

(Describe compatibility requirements with respect to the existing system and external systems that the system under design must interact with.)

System must interface with existing AP System.

Reliability Requirements

(Describe the level of fault-tolerance required by the system.)

Total daily downtime must not exceed 1 hour during normal business hours (9:00 A.M. – 5:00 P.M.).

Backup/Recovery Requirements

Daily backup of data files onto DVD. Weekly backup of entire system.

Training Requirements

Software development company to be responsible for end user training.

Business Rules

See business rules engine. *BR09-35.*

State Requirements

(Describe how the system's behavior changes when in different states. Describe the features that will be available and those that will be disabled in each state.)

Testing State

(Describe what the user may and may not do while the system is in the test state.)

Disabled State

(Describe what is to happen as the system goes down [that is, how it "dies gracefully"]. Clearly define what the user will and will not be able to do.)

Static Model

Main Entity Class Diagram

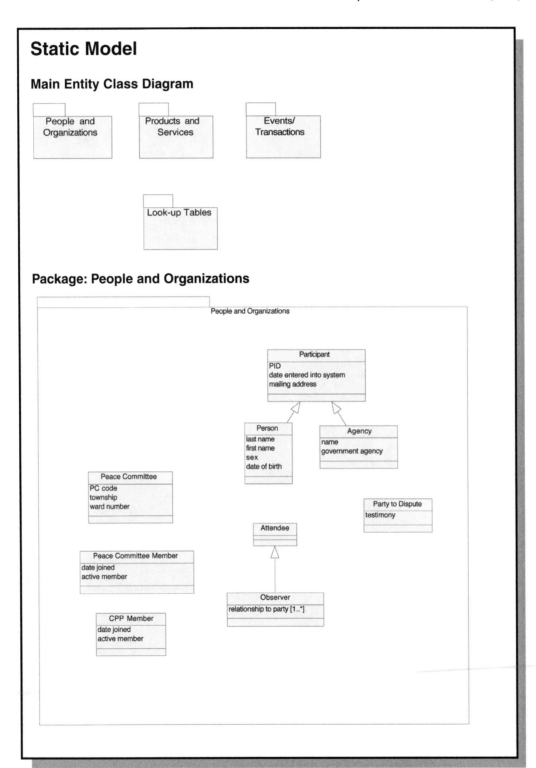

People and Organizations

Products and Services

Events/ Transactions

Look-up Tables

Package: People and Organizations

People and Organizations

Participant
PID
date entered into system
mailing address

Person
last name
first name
sex
date of birth

Agency
name
government agency

Peace Committee
PC code
township
ward number

Party to Dispute
testimony

Attendee

Peace Committee Member
date joined
active member

Observer
relationship to party [1..*]

CPP Member
date joined
active member

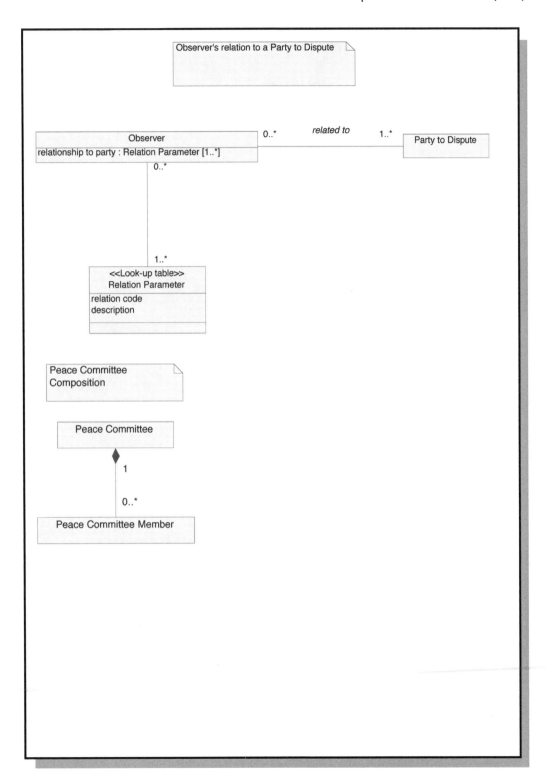

Package: Products and Services

Package: Events/Transactions

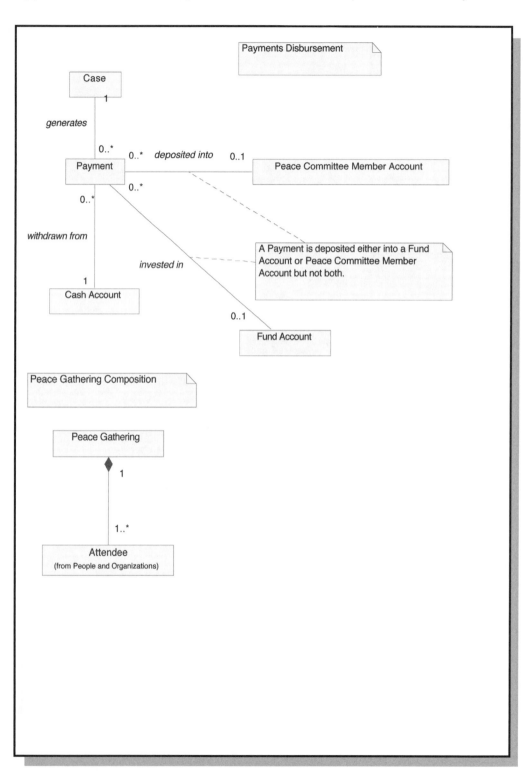

Package: Look-Up Tables

Look-up tables

| <<Look-up table>>
Reason No Gathering Parameter |
| reason code no gathering
description |
| |

| <<Look-up table>>
Dispute Parameter |
| dispute type
description
criminal offense |
| |

| <<Look-up table>>
Relation Parameter |
| relation code
description |
| |

Entity-Class Documentation

(Insert documentation to support each of the classes that appear in the class diagrams. Not every class needs to be fully documented. First do a risk analysis to determine where full documentation would most benefit the project.)

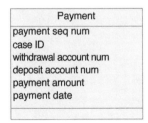

Figure C.4 Example of entity-class documentation: *Payment*

Class name: Payment

Alias: Payout

Description: One of many possible payments made per case. Each payment is deposited into a single account, such as a Peace Committee Member Account.

Example: Payment #111000 for Case #134567 to the Microenterprise Fund.

Attributes: See Table C.1.

Table C.1

Attribute	Der- ived?	Deri- vation	Type	Format	Length	Range	Dependency
payment seq num			Char	999999	6	000001– 999999	
case ID							
withdrawal account num							
deposit account num							Must not be same as with-drawal account num.
payment amount			Num	999,999.99		0–999,999.99	
payment date			Date	yy/mm/dd		On or before system date	

(Note: *Case ID* and *withdrawal account* num are described in the Case and Internal Account classes respectively.)

Test Plan[2]

(To standardize the testing, you should develop a test plan document for analysts to follow when constructing projects test plans. Although every project is different, the following may be used as a guideline. Each project should consider the following stages during testing):

1. Submit the requirements to the technical team.
2. The technical team completes development. Concurrently, the BA builds numbered test scenarios for requirements-based testing. Use decision tables to identify scenarios and boundary value analysis to select test data. The technical team conducts white-box testing to verify whether programs, fields, and calculations function as specified. The BA or technical team specifies the required quality level for white-box testing, such as multiple-condition coverage.
3. Perform requirements-based testing. The BA or dedicated QA (Quality Assurance) staff administers or supervises tests to prove or disprove compliance with requirements. Ensure that all formulae are calculated properly. Describe principles and techniques to be used in black-box testing, such as structured testing guidelines and boundary value analysis.
4. Conduct system testing. Ensure that the integrity of the system and data remain intact. For example,
   - *Regression test*: Retest all features (using a regression test bed).
   - *Stress test*: Test multiple users at the same time.
   - *Integration tests*: Make sure that the changes do not negatively affect the overall workflow across IT and manual systems.
   - *Volume test*: Test the system with high volume.
5. Perform user acceptance testing. Involve the end users at this stage. Choose key users to review the changes in the test environment. Use the testing software as a final check.

Implementation Plan

Training

- IT firm is responsible for training.
- *Training audience*: Conveners, General administrators, Director.
- *Forum*: Four 1-day sessions on-site.

---

[2]These requirements are often described in a separate test plan. If they are not addressed elsewhere, describe them here in the BRD.

Conversion

- Convert existing manual case records to electronic records.
- Scheduled completion date: 07/15/2006
- Grant privileges to the users.
- Scheduled date: 07/20/2006

Scheduling of Jobs

Government reports to be run on demand and at end of month.

Funder reports to be run on demand and at end of year.

Rollout

Advise all affected users when the project is promoted.

End User Procedures

(Write up the procedures for the affected departments. Distribute this document to them in addition to providing any hands-on training.)

Post Implementation Follow-Up

(Follow up within a reasonable time frame after implementation to ensure that the project is running successfully. Determine whether any further enhancements or changes are needed to ensure success of the project.)

Other Issues

Sign-Off

APPENDIX D

DECISION TABLE TEMPLATE

		1	2	3	4	5	6	7	8	9	10	11	12
C O N D I T I O N													
A C T I O N													

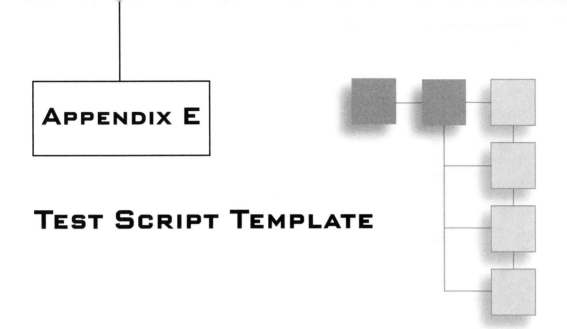

APPENDIX E

TEST SCRIPT TEMPLATE

Test #: _____   Project #: _____

System: _____   Test environment: _____

Test type (e.g., regression/requirements-based, etc.): _____

Test objective: _____

System use case: _____   Flow: _____

Priority: _____

Next step in case of failure: _____

Planned start date: _____   Planned end date: _____

Actual start date: _____   Actual end date: _____

times to repeat: _____

Preconditions (must be true before test begins): _____

Req #	Action/Data	Expected Result/Response	Actual Result	Pass/ Fail

Tester ID: _____

Pass/Fail: _____   Severity of failure: _____

Solution: _____

Comments: _____

Sign-Off: _____

(Req # is short for requirement number and corresponds to the number used to identify the requirement in the BRD. Many organizations number their requirements so that they can be traced forward to test cases and other project artifacts. The numbering may be manual or automatically generated with the use of requirements-tracking software.)

APPENDIX F

GLOSSARY OF SYMBOLS

Business Use-Case Diagram

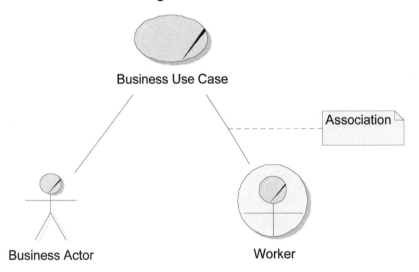

Business Use Case

Association

Business Actor

Worker

System Use-Case Diagram

Generalized Actor

Specialized Actor

Use Case

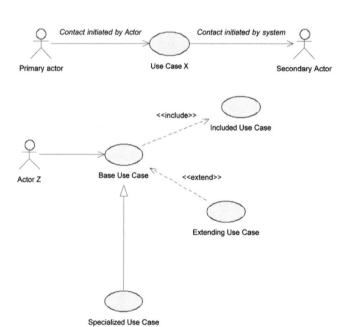

Contact initiated by Actor

Contact initiated by system

Primary actor

Use Case X

Secondary Actor

<<include>>

Included Use Case

Actor Z

Base Use Case

<<extend>>

Extending Use Case

Specialized Use Case

Initiating Actor

Use-Case
Package

Non-initiating
actor

Package Diagram

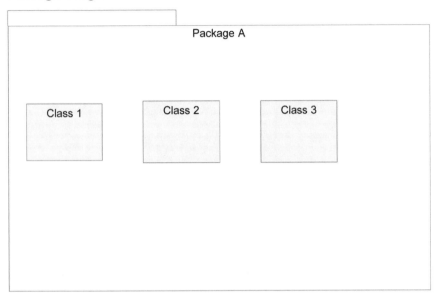

Class Diagram

Allowable multiplicities[1]:

1	One and only one
0..1	Zero or one
0..*	Zero or more
1..*	One or more
n	*n* and only *n*. For example, 5
n..m	*n* through *m*. For example, 5..10

[1]Discontinuous multiplicities such as 5, 8 were dropped from the standard in UML 2.

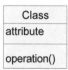

Class
attribute
operation()

Object Diagram

Composite Structure Diagram

Timing Diagram

Activity Diagram

State Diagram

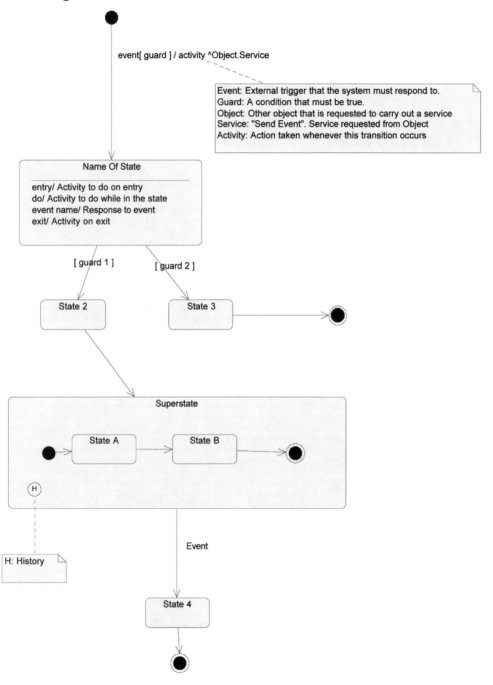

(Note: Superstate is an alternate term for composite state.)

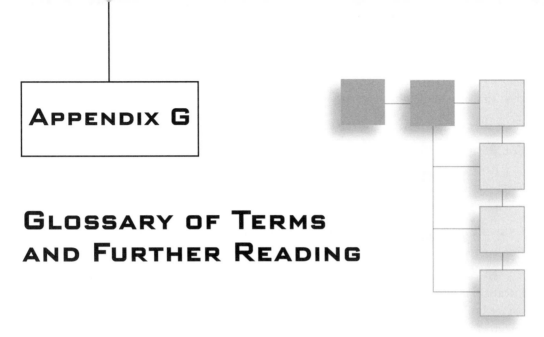

APPENDIX G

GLOSSARY OF TERMS AND FURTHER READING

Activity: (UML term) A task or process.

Activity diagram: (UML term) A diagram that describes the sequencing of business activities. An *activity diagram with partitions* also describes which object is responsible for each activity.

Actor: (UML term) A type of user or an external system that interacts with a *use case*. For example, the *Customer* actor initiates the use case *Deposit Funds*.

Aggregation: (UML term) The relationship that exists between a whole and its parts. For example, the relationship between a *Line-Of-Products* and *Product* is an aggregation.

Association: (UML term) A relationship defined at the class level that describes a link that the business maintains between objects belonging to classes at either end of the association. Objects may be linked because information about one is tied to data about the other, for example, information about an *Invoice* object is *associated* with data about a *Customer* object. Other reasons for an association between objects include: One object collaborates with another to complete a task (for example, an *ATM* object collaborates with an *Account* object during cash withdrawal); one object acts on the other object (for example, a Manager *manages* an Employee).

Attribute: (UML term) An attribute is defined at the class level to identify a property that the system tracks for all the objects of that class. Similar to the term "field." (*Field* is used within the context of database design.) For example, an attribute of *Car* is *year of manufacture.*

Black-box test: (Structured Testing term) A test that can be designed without knowledge of the inner workings of the system. (See *requirements-based testing.*)

Business model: An abstract representation of a business system.

363

Class: (UML term) A category that a group of objects may belong to. Objects in the same class share the same *attributes* and *operations*.

Class diagram: (UML term) Describes how classes are related to other classes.

Composition: (UML term) The term used to describe the association between a whole and its parts in cases where the whole completely owns the part and where destruction of the whole causes destruction of the part. For example, an *Invoice* is composed of *Line Items*; when the Invoice is destroyed, so are the *Line Items*.

Dynamic model: The part of the model that describes behavior—what the system does and how it does it. Diagrams included as part of the dynamic model include *use-case diagram*, *activity diagram*, and *state machine diagram*.

Encapsulation: (OO term) A principle that states that the description of a class encompasses both its operations (actions) and attributes (data) and that no object may refer directly to another's attributes or rely on a knowledge of how its operations are carried out. Encapsulation requires that objects only interact by passing messages, that is, by asking other objects to perform operations.

Entity class: (UML term) A subject that the business tracks. For example, *Customer*, *Invoice*.

ERD: (Data Modeling term) *ERD* stands for Entity Relationship Diagram. An ERD describes the relationships between subjects tracked by the business—for example, the relationship between *Customers* and their *Accounts*. ERDs were developed prior to OO. The UML *Class Diagram* encompasses everything that can be depicted in an ERD.

Extends: (UML term) One use case can be described as *extending* a base use case if it adds to or alters the behavior of the base at specified extension points and under a specified condition. For example, the use case *Apply for preferred mortgage* extends the base use case *Apply for mortgage*.

Fork: (UML term) A bar on an activity diagram that indicates a point after which parallel activities are executed. Parallel activities may begin in any order after the fork.

Generalized class: (UML term) A class that describes features common to a group of classes. For example, *Account* is a Generalized class that describes features that the specialized classes *Chequing Account*, *Power Account*, and *Savings Account* all have in common. (Also called Generalization class, Superclass, Parent class, Base class.) Specialized classes inherit the attributes, operations, and relationships of the generalized class.

Guard: (UML term) A condition that must be true before something may occur. For example, a *deposit transaction* may only be processed if the guard *Funds available in account* is *true*. Guards may appear on *activity diagrams* and *state machine diagrams*.

Includes: (UML term) When a number of use cases share some common requirements, the commonalities may be factored out into an inclusion use case. Each of the original use cases is said to *include* this new use case. For example, each of the two use cases *Withdraw cash* and *Pay Bills* includes the use case *Check available funds*.

Inheritance: (UML term) A relationship that models partial similarities between elements. In the context of classes, inheritance is used when a number of classes share some but not all features. The shared features are described in a Generalized class. Each variation is described as a Specialized class. A Specialized class inherits all the operations, attributes, and relationships of the Generalized class. For example, *Chequing Account* inherits the attributes, etc., of *Account*.

Instance: (UML term) An object is an *instance* of (specific case of) a class. For example, the customer "Jane Dell Ray" is an object—an instance of the class *Customer*.

Join: (UML term) A bar on an activity diagram marking the end of parallel acidities. All parallel activities flowing into it must end before flow can proceed beyond the join.

Merge: (UML term) A diamond on an activity diagram marking the point where divergent paths off of a previous decision converge back to a common flow.

Method: The procedure used to carry out an operation.

Multiplicity: (UML term) Defines the number of objects that may be associated with each other. In Structured Analysis, the equivalent term is *Cardinality*. For example, a *Mortgage* is signed by at least one and at most three *Parties*.

Object: (UML term) A thing that is a part of the system. In Business Analysis, something is considered an object if it is responsible for carrying out business activities or if the business needs to track information about it. An object is an *instance* of (specific case of) a class. For example, the customer "Jane Dell Ray" is an object—an instance of the class *Customer*.

Object-Oriented: (UML term) An approach to analysis, design, and coding based upon decomposing a system into basic units, called *objects*, each of which represents information and operations related to one aspect of the system. A system described as *Object-Oriented* must also support other concepts such as classes and inheritance.

OMG: Object Management Group. Sets OO standards.

OO: See *Object-Oriented*.

Operation: (UML term) A function that an object may carry out or that is carried out on the object. For example, *Apply price increase* is an operation of *Product*. Alternative terms: *Service, Message*.

Package: (UML term) A container used to organize model elements into groups. Packages may be nested within other packages. Alternative term: *Subsystem.*

Package diagram: (UML term) A diagram that depicts how model elements are organized into packages and the dependencies among them, including package imports and package extensions.

Polymorphism: (UML term) May take many forms. The term is applied to objects and operations. With respect to operations, it means that the same operation may be carried out in different ways (that is, using different methods) by different classes. For example, *Chequing Account* and *Savings Account* each have their own polymorphic version of the operation *Determine service charge.*

Requirements-based testing: (Structured Testing term) Testing techniques that determine the degree to which a system complies with the requirements set out in the Business Requirements Document (BRD). The test cases are designed based on knowledge of the requirements, but not on the inner workings of the system. Equivalent term: *Black-box testing.*

Sequence diagram: (UML term) A diagram that depicts how operations are sequenced and which objects carry them out.

Specialized class: (UML term) If a group of classes share some but not all features, then the commonalities are described in a Generalized class and the peculiarities of the subtypes are described in Specialized classes. A Specialized class acquires all the relationships, attributes, and operations of the Generalized class. A Specialized class should be used only for full-time subtypes. (Part-time subtypes are described as Transient Roles.) For example, a *Chequing Account* is a Specialization of *Account.* Alternative terms: *Specialized Class, Subclass, Child Class, Derived Class.*

State machine diagram: (UML term) A diagram that depicts the different states of an object and the rules that govern how it passes from state to state. For example, a State machine diagram for *Insurance Claim* describes how the Claim's state passes from *Initiated* to *Adjusted* to *Paid.*

Static model: The portion of a business model that describes structural aspects of a system, in particular business classes and their relationships.

Structured Analysis: Structured Analysis is a set of techniques for analyzing a system by organizing processes hierarchically—from general to specific. Predates OO Analysis.

Subclass: (OO term) See *Specialized class.*

Superclass: (OO term) See *Generalized class.*

Transient role: (B.O.O.M. term) A role that may change during an object's lifetime. (If the role is not likely to change, describe it instead as a Specialized class.) For example, *PTA Board Member* is a transient role played by a *Parent* in a school.

UML: Unified Modeling Language. A widely accepted standard for OO adopted by the Object Management Group (OMG).

Use case: (UML term) An end-to-end interaction between an actor and a system that achieves a useful result for the actor.

Use-case diagram: (UML term) A diagram that depicts the main services that the system performs and the actors that interact with the system during each use case.

Further Reading

Booch, Grady. *The Unified Modeling Language User Guide.* Addison-Wesley Professional: 2005.

Cockburn, Alistair. *Writing Effective Use Cases.* Pearson Education Canada: 2000.

Eriksson, Hans-Erik and Magnus Penker. *Business Modeling with UML: Business Patterns and Business Objects.* Wiley: 1999.

Eriksson, Hans-Erik, Magnus Penker, Brian Lyons, and David Fado. *UML 2 Toolkit.* Wiley: 2003.

Fowler, Martin and Kendall Scott. *UML Distilled: A Brief Guide to the Standard Object Modeling Language.* 3rd Edition; Paperback. Addison-Wesley Professional: 2003.

Gamma, Erich, Richard Helm, and Ralph Johnson. *Design Patterns: Elements of Reusable Object-Oriented Software.* Pearson Education Canada: 1994.

Hoffer. Jeffrey A. *Modern Systems Analysis and Design.* Pearson Education Canada: 2004.

Jacobson, Ivar. *The Unified Software Development Process.* Pearson Education Canada: 1999.

Larman, Craig. *Applying UML and Patterns: An Introduction to Object-Oriented Analysis and Design and Iterative Development.* Prentice Hall PTR: 2004.

Leffingwell, Dean and Don Widrig. *Managing Software Requirements: A Unified Approach.* Pearson Education Canada (Addison-Wesley): 1999.

Marshal, Chris. *Enterprise Modeling with UML: Designing Successful Software through Business Analysis.* Paperback edition. Pearson Education Canada: 1999.

Robertson, Suzanne and James Robertson. *Mastering the Requirements Process.* Pearson Education Canada: 1999.

Rumbaugh, James, Ivar Jacobson, and Grady Booch. *The Unified Modeling Language Reference Manual.* 2nd Edition. Addison-Wesley Professional: 2004.

Schneider, Geri and Jason P. Winters. *Applying Use Cases: A Practical Guide.* Paperback edition. Addison Wesley Longman: 2001.

Wiegers, Karl. *Software Requirements.* Paperback edition. Microsoft Press: 2003.

Related Sites

(Please be advised that Web site URLs are always subject to change.)

www.ideaswork.org

Home page for "Ideaswork"—the organization behind the South African restorative justice project that is the basis of the CPP case study.

www.omg.org

Home page for the OMG—the organization that sets standards for OO.

www.uwsg.iu.edu/usail/network/nfs/network_layers.html

ISO/OSI Network Model, Trustees of Indiana University.

www.15seconds.com/issue/011023.htm

The article is called "Application Architecture: An N-Tier Approach—Part 1" by Robert Chartier, INT Media Group, Inc.

www-128.ibm.com/developerworks/rational/rationaledge

For business use-case modeling, see "Effective Business Modeling with UML: Describing Business Use Cases and Realizations," Pan-Wei Ng, the Rational Edge at www.therationaledge.com/content/nov_02/t_businessModelingUML_pn.jsp.

INDEX

C